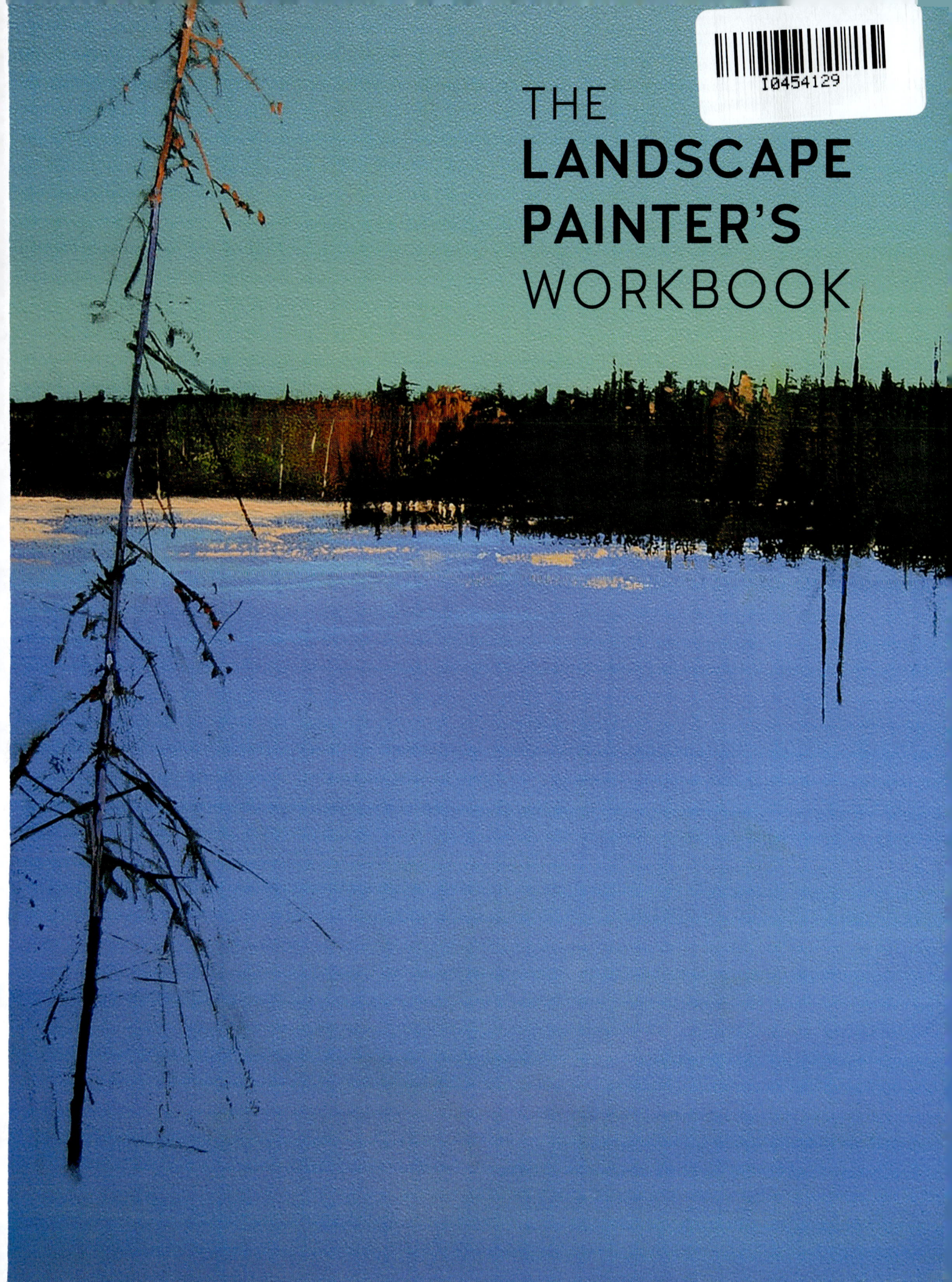

THE
LANDSCAPE
PAINTER'S
WORKBOOK

Mitchell Albala, *The Lighthouse Keeper's House*, oil on canvas, 38" × 32" | 96.5 × 81 cm

THE
LANDSCAPE PAINTER'S WORKBOOK

ESSENTIAL STUDIES IN SHAPE, COMPOSITION, AND COLOR

MITCHELL ALBALA

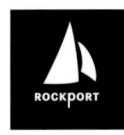

Quarto.com

© 2021 Quarto Publishing Group USA Inc.
Text and images © 2021 Michell Albala

First published in 2021 by Rockport Publishers, an imprint of The Quarto Group,
100 Cummings Center, Suite 265-D, Beverly, MA 01915, USA.
T (978) 282-9590 F (978) 283-2742

EEA Representation, WTS Tax d.o.o.,
Žanova ulica 3, 4000 Kranj, Slovenia.
www.wts-tax.si

Rockport Publishers titles are also available at discount for retail, wholesale, promotional, and bulk purchase. For details, contact the Special Sales Manager by email at specialsales@quarto.com or by mail at The Quarto Group, Attn: Special Sales Manager, 100 Cummings Center, Suite 265-D, Beverly, MA 01915, USA.

13

ISBN: 978-0-76037-135-0

Digital edition published in 2021
eISBN: 978-0-76037-136-7

Library of Congress Cataloging-in-Publication Data available

Page Layout: Megan Jones Design

Cover: Sue Charles, *Smoldering*, Oil on panel, 12" × 12" | 30.5 × 30.5 cm
Page 1: David Lidbetter, Detail, *Five More Minutes* , Oil on panel, 12" × 16" | 30.5 × 40.5 cm
Page 5: Mitchell Albala, *Study, Copper Morning*, Watercolor, 3½" × 3½" | 9 × 9 cm

Printed in Guangdong, China TT012026

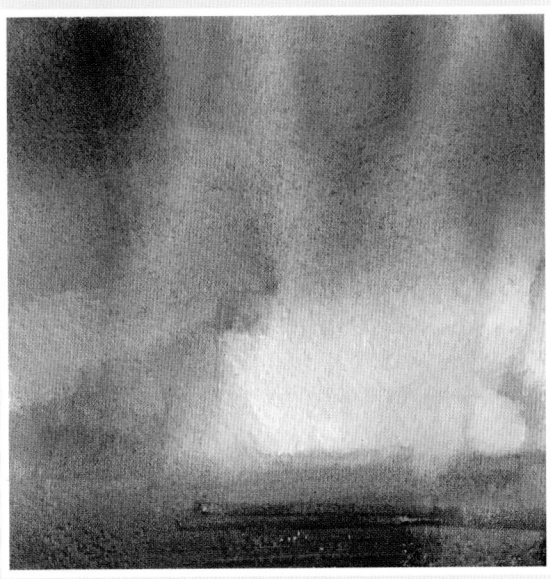

For every painter who has ever to tried to translate light into
paint, and to my students, whose tenacity and openness to
new ideas make me a better instructor and a better painter.

CONTENTS

Introduction 8

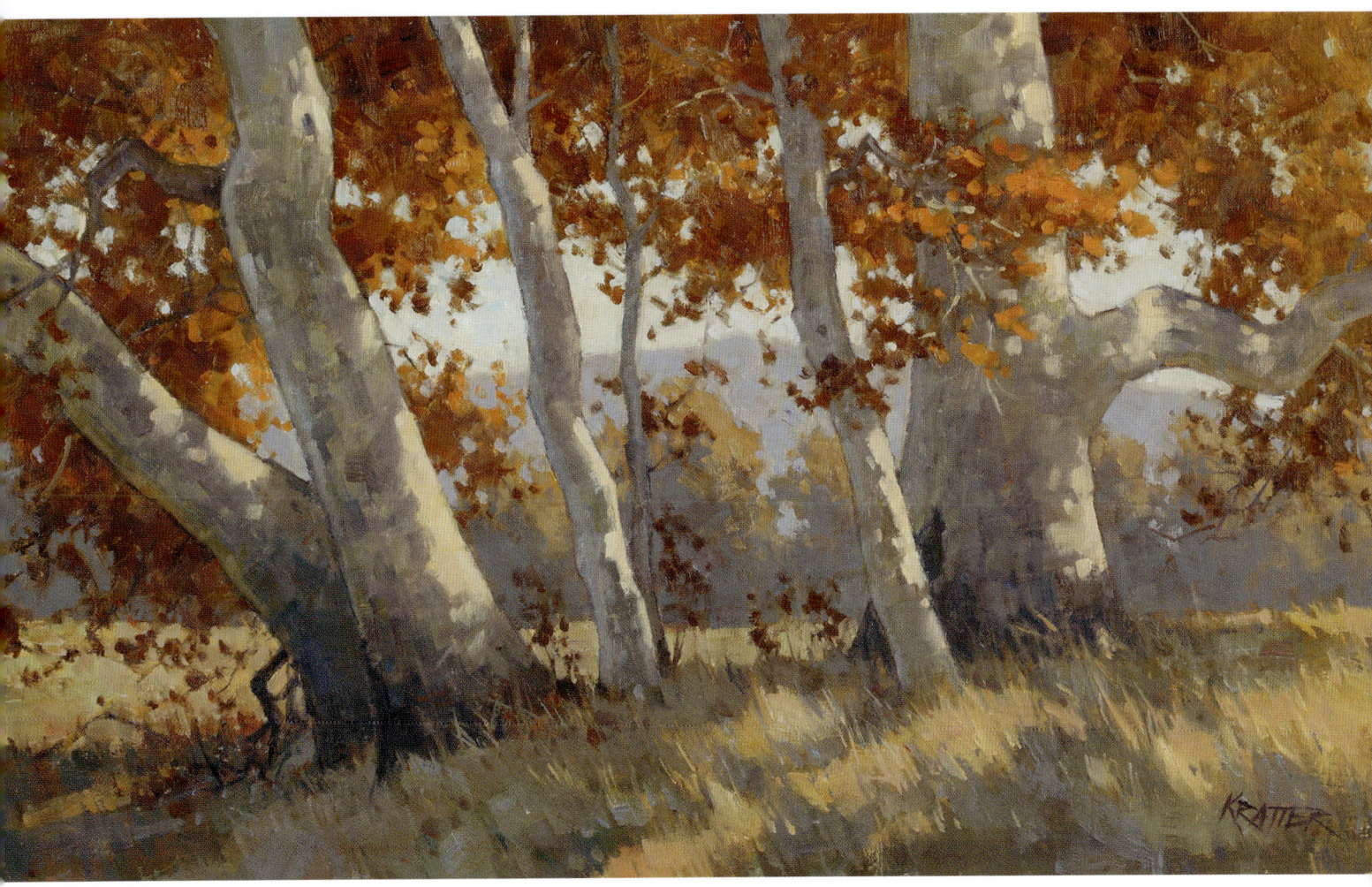

Paul Kratter, *From Under the Sycamores*, oil on panel, 12" × 20" | 30.5 × 51 cm

INTRODUCTION

If you're reading this book, it is likely that you found your way here because of my first book, *Landscape Painting: Essential Concepts and Techniques for Plein Air and Studio Practice*. That book has been the best-selling book on landscape painting in the United States for over ten years. Readers often write to me, telling me how helpful they found it.

The obvious question, then, is why another book on landscape painting? Quite simply, there was more to say and more to show. In the years between the publication of my first book and *The Landscape Painter's Workbook*, I grew both as an artist and as an instructor. I developed new material and new exercises for my workshops, which were working very well for my students. These needed to be shared.

WHAT'S NEW IN *THE LANDSCAPE PAINTER'S WORKBOOK*?

The Landscape Painter's Workbook differs from my first book in three significant ways. First, it covers entirely new topics that were not included in the first book, such as "complete" color strategies, color grouping, the harmony of neutrals, picture formats, notan, and movement.

Second, it includes over ten useful exercises. Over the years, I realized that watching demonstrations or following them in a book, although inspiring, was not as helpful as exercises that showed painters how to do it *themselves*—and do it in a way that was *achievable*. If you do these exercises, I believe you will make faster progress and have more "ah-ha!" moments than if you only read about them or look at the illustrations.

Third, *Workbook* is intended for painters working in any media, not just oil. The lessons and exercises on shape, composition, and color are universal and so are applicable to all landscape painters. *Workbook* features more than forty-five contemporary painters—over eighty paintings in all—working in oil, acrylic, pastel, and watercolor. Regardless of what medium or style you prefer, you'll find meaningful lessons in this book.

A QUESTION-ORIENTED APPROACH

In my workshops, I always tell students that the difference between painters who make progress and those who don't isn't necessarily talent. It's whether or not they have trained themselves to ask the right questions. Solutions to painting problems are much more difficult to come by if we don't know what questions to ask. For example, when I present new ideas about composition, no one ever has a problem seeing what I am referring to—once it's pointed out to them. In large part, what this book does is teach painters what to look for in their subjects and what questions to ask about shape interpretation, composition, and color. Each chapter also concludes with a Q&A section that summarizes the key questions for that topic.

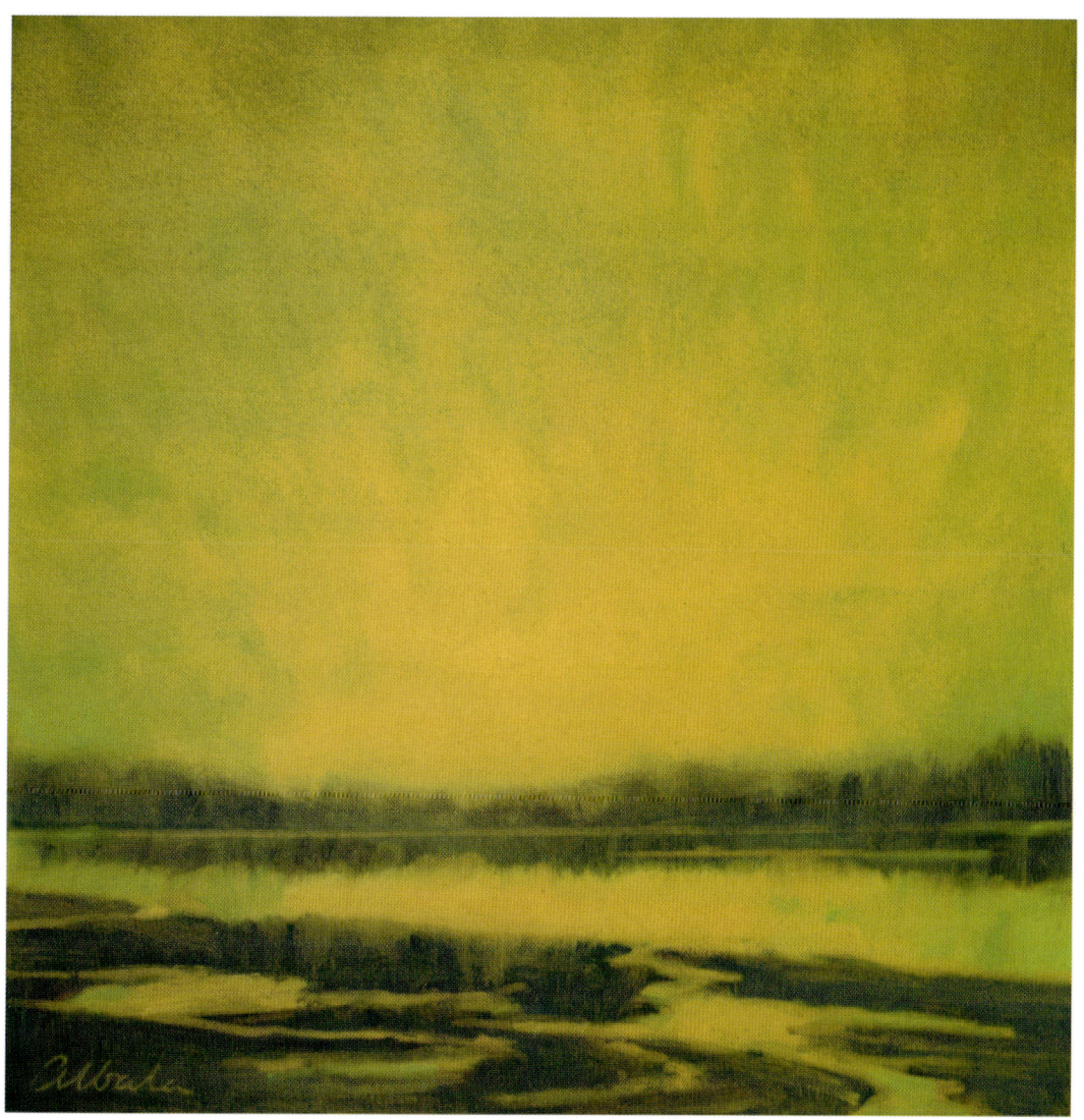

Mitchell Albala, *Study, Grasser's Lagoon in Gold*, oil on gold gesso ground, 8" × 8" | 20.5 × 20.5 cm

We all want to be motivated and inspired. These feelings are the fuel that keeps our creative engines humming. But to make real progress on our creative path, to improve our skill level, we also need practices and principles that are understandable and can be readily applied. That's why I have written this book and why I have made each lesson and exercise as practical and realizable as possible.

I have adopted the practices I promote, and as a result, I'm a better problem solver and a better painter. It really works! I have asked the same questions you are asking now, about shape, composition, and color. This book contains the answers I've found. It is my sincere hope that if you apply these lessons and do the exercises, achieving your goals in painting will become easier, faster, and more enjoyable.

MITCHELL ALBALA

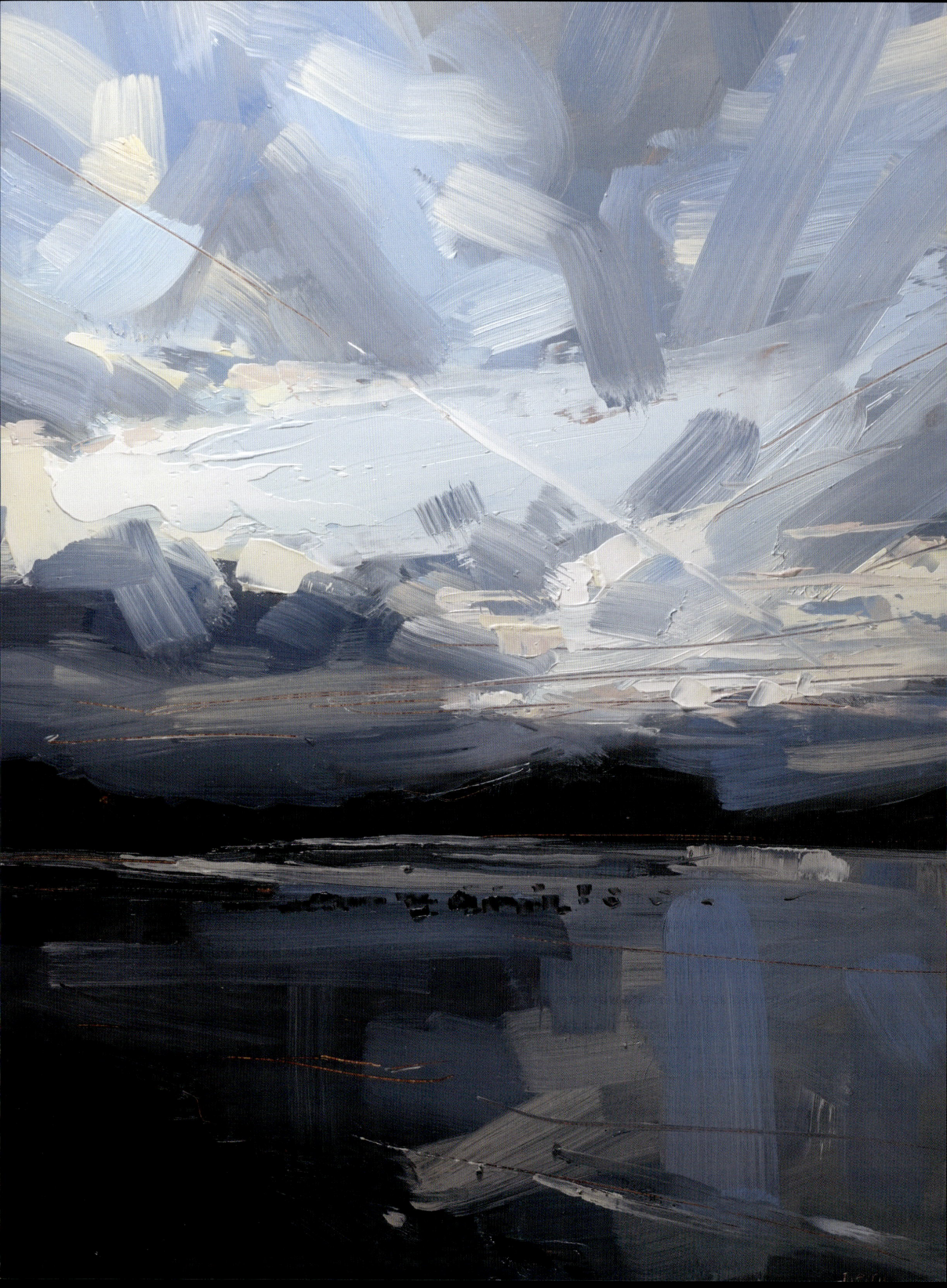

1

SHAPE
INTERPRETATION

One of the recurring themes throughout this book is that landscape painting is an art of interpretation. Our goal is not to reproduce what we see exactly as we see it. Rather, all we observe—every color, shape, and detail—is filtered through an interpretive lens. The painting we produce may resemble a landscape, but is now a *painting*, a unique interpretation of the world in its own visual language. This process of translation is never more demanding than when trying to interpret the landscape at its most fundamental level: shape.

Nature is terribly complex. It has innumerable shapes, from the minute to the monumental, and in its raw, unedited state, can seem quite overwhelming. The key to translating all this into a painting is not to capture every bit of it but to reduce it into a simpler set of shapes and masses. This is the landscape painter's first and most important task. Remarkably, this reductionist approach doesn't detract from the overall impression—it enhances the painting, making it more comprehensible to the viewer.

◄ Hester Berry, *Bosley Mere*
Oil on board, 12" × 8½" | 30.5 × 21.5 cm

A landscape painter's first and most important task is to reduce nature's vastness and complexity into clearer, more visually concise shapes. Each of Berry's expressive brushstrokes is a distinct shape, defined from adjacent strokes through value and color differences.

A REDUCTIONIST APPROACH TO SHAPE

When we observe the natural world, in all its depth and breadth, we are able to apprehend its many values and colors, and all its parts and pieces, with no thought at all. Trying to *paint* that subject, however, requires us to look through a different visual lens. To convert such an overwhelming amount of information into the language of painting, we must begin to see the subject in simpler terms.

Every painting, even a complicated one, has a foundation that is built upon simplified shapes. Yet, this isn't necessarily what we see first. We are distracted by a sea of details, colors, and narrative content. To simplify, we have to see through all the layers of complexity and busyness. We have to interpret and extrapolate.

Our goal isn't to include everything we see, but to know what to leave out. One of the most satisfying "ah-ha!" moments a painter can experience is when they discover that a simplified picture structure captures the essence of a subject more effectively than small parts and details.

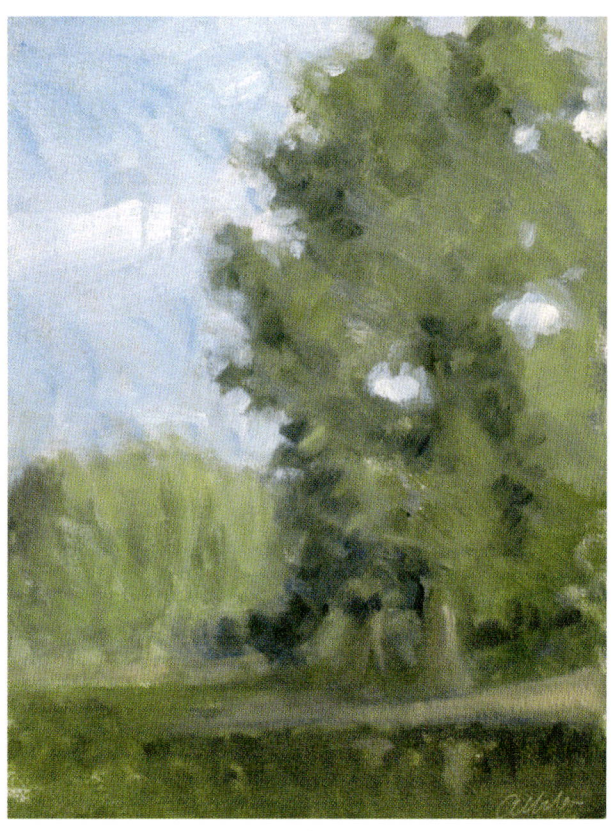

A LESSON IN REDUCTIONISM
Mitchell Albala, *First Easel*
Oil on paper, 12" × 9" | 30.5 × 23 cm

One of my formative lessons in painting took place many years ago in New York City's Central Park. I had just bought my first French easel. On my first day, after an hour or so, I had lost my way and disappointment was setting in. The shapes were spotty and the tree unconvincing. With a few furious strokes of the rag, I wiped out the painting. To my surprise, the hazy image that remained was a great improvement. My overworked and spotty tree had been consolidated into a more simplified mass. The frustrated wipes of my rag turned out to be the best strokes in my painting.

REDUCTIONISM

Reductionism is an approach used in many disciplines, from biology to philosophy. In a reductionist approach, one attempts to explain complex ideas by reducing them to more fundamental ones. This is precisely what landscape painters do when they try to reduce the landscape's myriad forms into more simplified shapes and patterns.

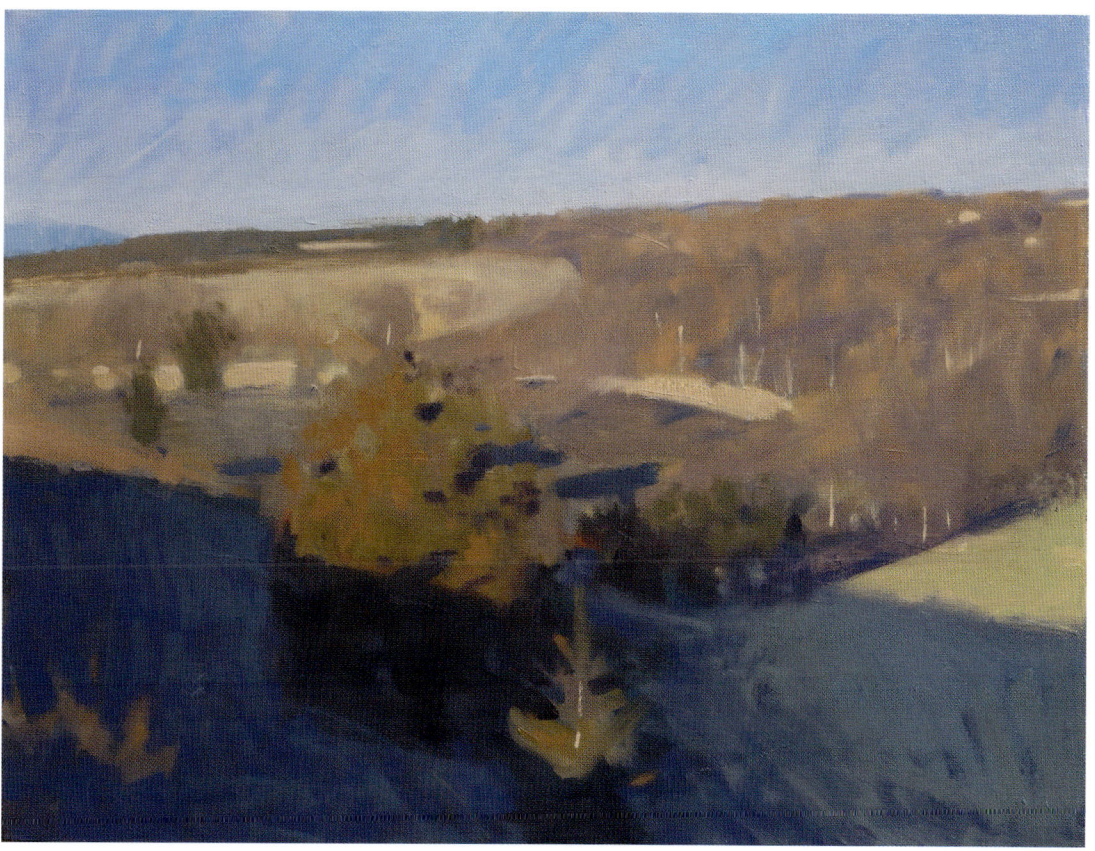

Frank Hobbs, *Augusta County, VA, Near Staunton, Winter*
Oil on canvas, 18" × 24" | 46 × 61 cm

Through a simplified approach, the whole truly becomes greater than the sum of its parts.
Hobbs' *Augusta County* is composed of just a few major shapes: the sky, the background hill,
and the foreground tree and shadow. Smaller elements, like the trees in the background and the
grasses in the foreground, are only hinted at. "We know that a tree is composed of millions of
tiny leaves and branches," Hobbs writes. "This knowledge alone nearly overwhelms us. Luckily,
the eye is more intelligent than the mind, and in the end, it's the eye that enables the painter to
sift out the essential masses of nature into something that actually makes sense on the canvas."
(Also see Hobbs' simplified shape painting on page 36).

PLAYING WELL TOGETHER: SIMPLIFIED SHAPES AND DETAIL

When those new to landscape painting hear how much simplification is stressed, they are quick to ask,
"What about the details?" Details play an important role in landscape painting. They have great descriptive potential and often hold information that is essential to the visual story. Leading with simplified
shapes does not mean the exclusion of detail, however. Detail and simplified shapes can and do play
well together—as long as they are created in the correct order and properly balanced. (See "Balancing
Simplified Shapes and Detail with the 80/20 Rule" on page 25.)

THE BENEFITS OF SIMPLIFICATION

If you've taken workshops or read other books on landscape painting, you have certainly heard the common refrain: *Simplify, simplify, simplify!* Why is a reductionist approach to shape so important?

- **Simplification Is Practical.** The natural world presents so much information, across such a wide field, that to create a clear and visually concise picture of nature, we have no choice but to simplify. Simplification is a visual imperative.
- **Simplification Is Our Starting Point.** A painting develops in stages from the *general* to the *specific*. We always begin a painting with simplified foundational shapes; smaller elements or details are integrated into the foundational shapes later.
- **Simplification Is Beautiful.** A subject that undergoes the translation from complex to simple is elegant, a demonstration of the visual poetry of a landscape painting.

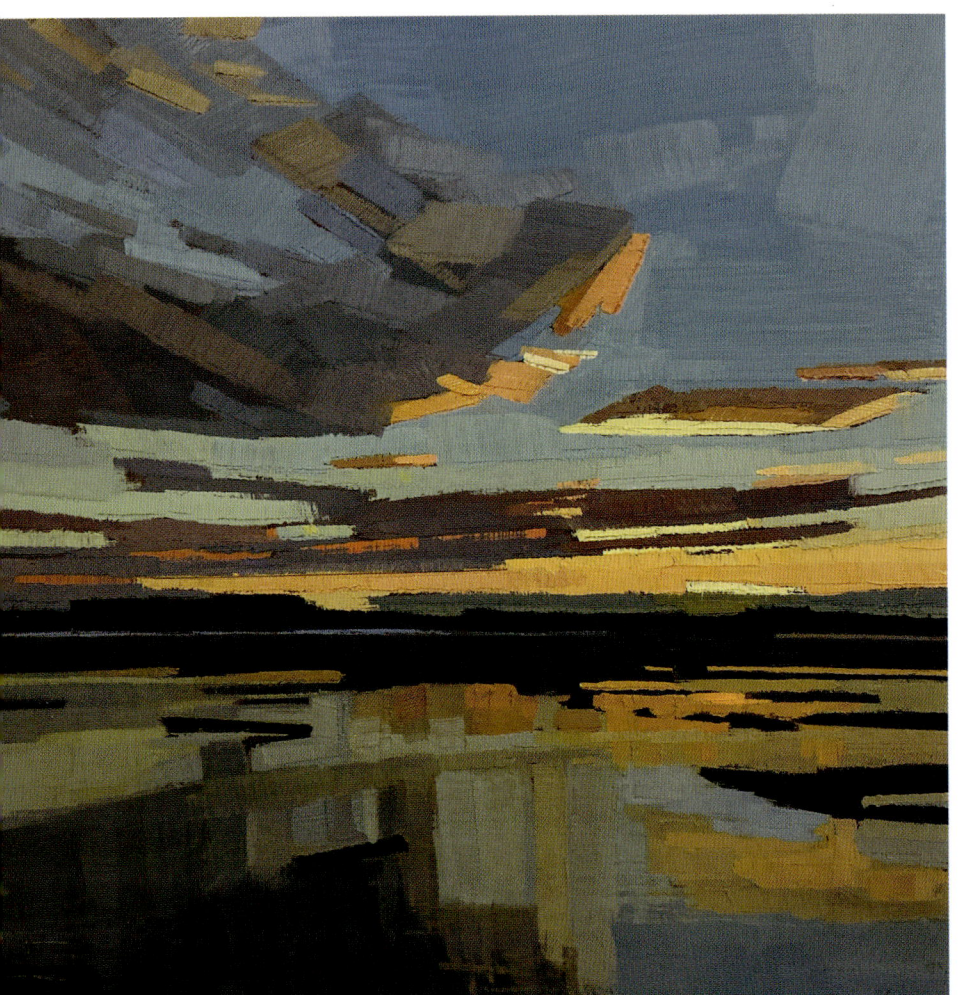

Sue Charles, *Smoldering*
Oil on panel, 12" × 12" | 30.5 × 30.5 cm

Sue Charles is a true shape master. Each of her shapes defines structure and form—even forms as seemingly amorphous and unstructured as clouds. Each shape is defined by a single stroke, and each stroke is a distinct color and value. Charles was inspired by her early experiences as a stained glass artist. "At the core of my work is a love of pattern and the way everything in nature fits together perfectly like a puzzle," she explains. "Each stroke is a carefully considered shape of a specific color, placed in relationship to the whole design." *Smoldering* can be appreciated on the level of a cloudscape and as a visual shape poem.

SIMPLIFICATION IS PRACTICAL

The natural world and our paintings of that world are made up of the same fundamental building blocks—shapes. Yet the shapes that end up in our final painting don't necessarily correspond to everything we see in the subject. Even the most highly detailed paintings don't replicate the scene exactly, shape for shape. Our goal is not to transcribe every shape we see. There are too many of them. We must be selective. We combine smaller shapes into larger ones. We decide which shapes are essential to the composition and which ones are superfluous.

We place greater emphasis on some shapes, while downplaying others or even eliminating them altogether, until we can convey the essence of the subject in the most visually concise way possible.

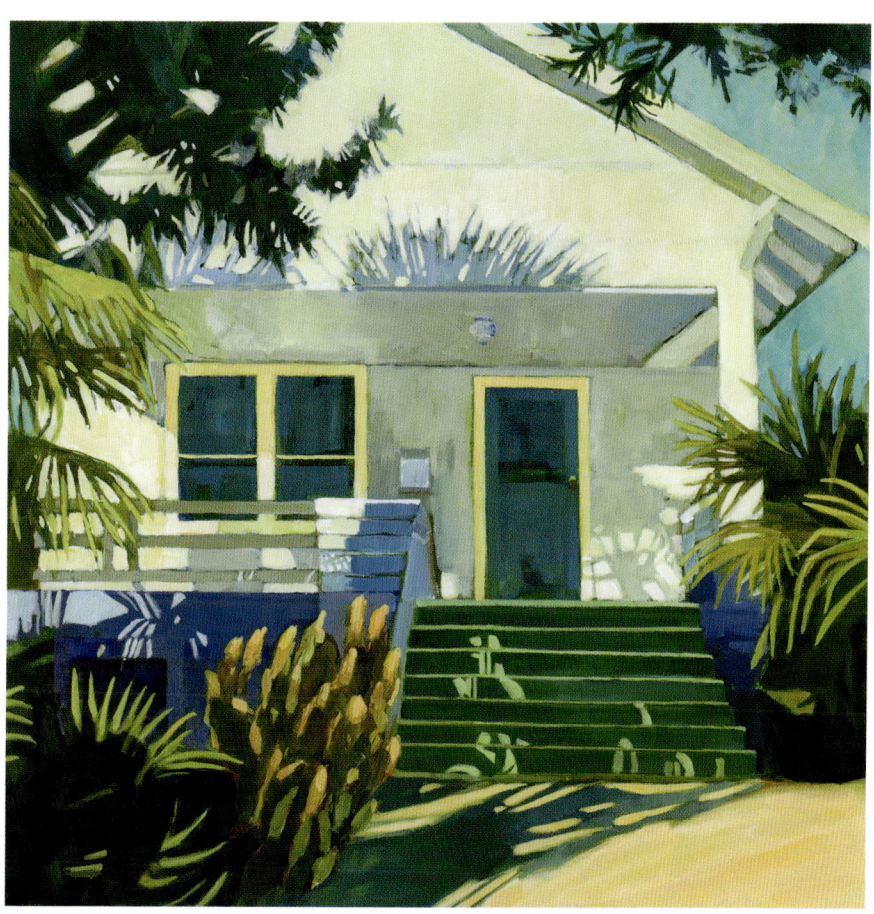

Lisa Snow Lady, *Palm Garden*
Acrylic on canvas, 30" × 30" | 76 × 76 cm

Snow Lady's style is one that translates natural forms into flat, crisply defined shapes, almost like cut paper. *Palm Garden* includes landscape elements of all types—earth, sky, ground, vegetation, and man-made—yet all are reduced to decisive shapes that snugly fit together. "I believe a good painting starts with a strong composition and strong shapes," says Snow Lady. "If I am going to invest a lot of time in the work, the design has to hold my interest throughout."

SIMPLIFICATION IS OUR STARTING POINT

The stages of a painting have a logical flow that moves from the *general* (basic foundational shapes) to the *specific* (additional details, values, and colors). Just as a builder first lays the foundation of a house, so does a painter begin with a foundation that establishes the basic structure and composition of a painting. We never begin a painting with details, even if the painting will ultimately include many.

A painting always begins with basic, foundational shapes—which are always simple. Small parts, details, and colors are attached to those basic shapes later.

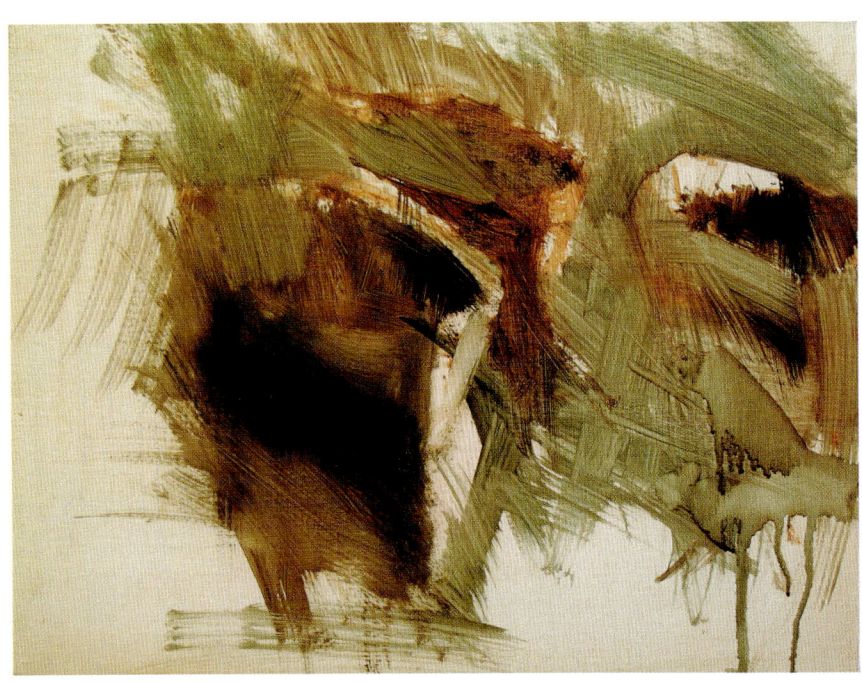

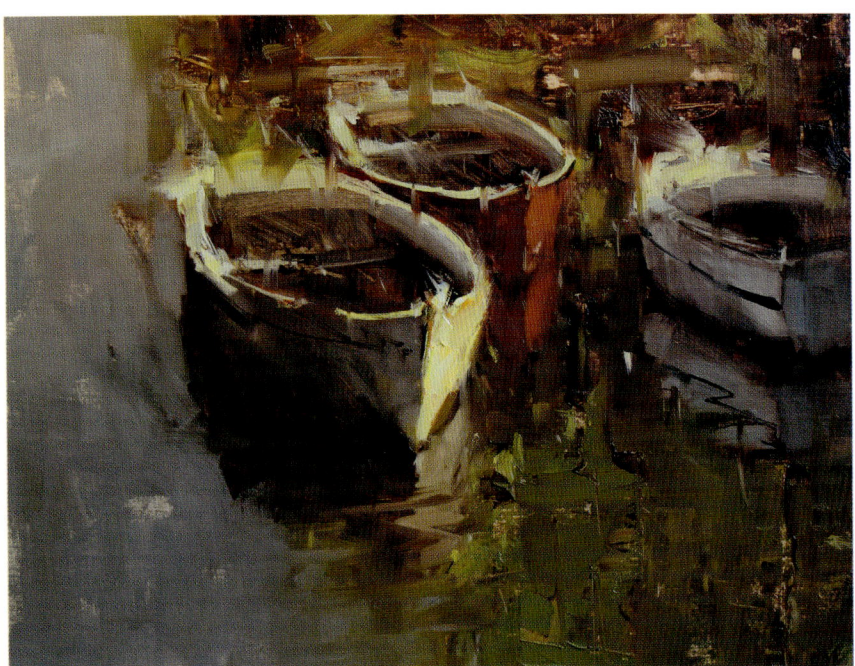

Tibor Nagy, *The Lazy Afternoon*
Oil on linen, 12" × 16" | 30.5 × 40.5 cm

When you watch experienced painters work, you see them establish the simplest and most basic shapes first. Sometimes, this is done monochromatically, with only one pigment tone; sometimes, it's done with a combination of values and colors, as we see in Nagy's first stage. His block-in captures the general placement of shapes and is heading toward defining the broad areas of value. Only later does he build in detail and smaller strokes. "At the start, the most important thing for me is the position of the main shapes," says Nagy. "In the later stages, I try not to lose this foundation, as it forms the basis of the whole painting."

SIMPLIFICATION IS BEAUTIFUL

A poet expresses an idea or emotion in a metered string of carefully chosen words, which is far more eloquent than the same idea expressed in a long, wordy paragraph. Similarly, when the painter converts nature's "wordy" excesses into more visually concise and meaningful shapes, it is nothing less than visual poetry. Indeed, what makes a painting special—what makes it a *painting*—is the visual poetry of the shape interpretation.

When simplified shapes become the primary impression, viewers are often touched in a place that is beyond words and thought.

A painting simplified in this way doesn't tell the whole story. An observer must fill in the gaps in their mind's eye, which evokes a different kind of response than a painting that tells the viewer everything. Viewer participation is required.

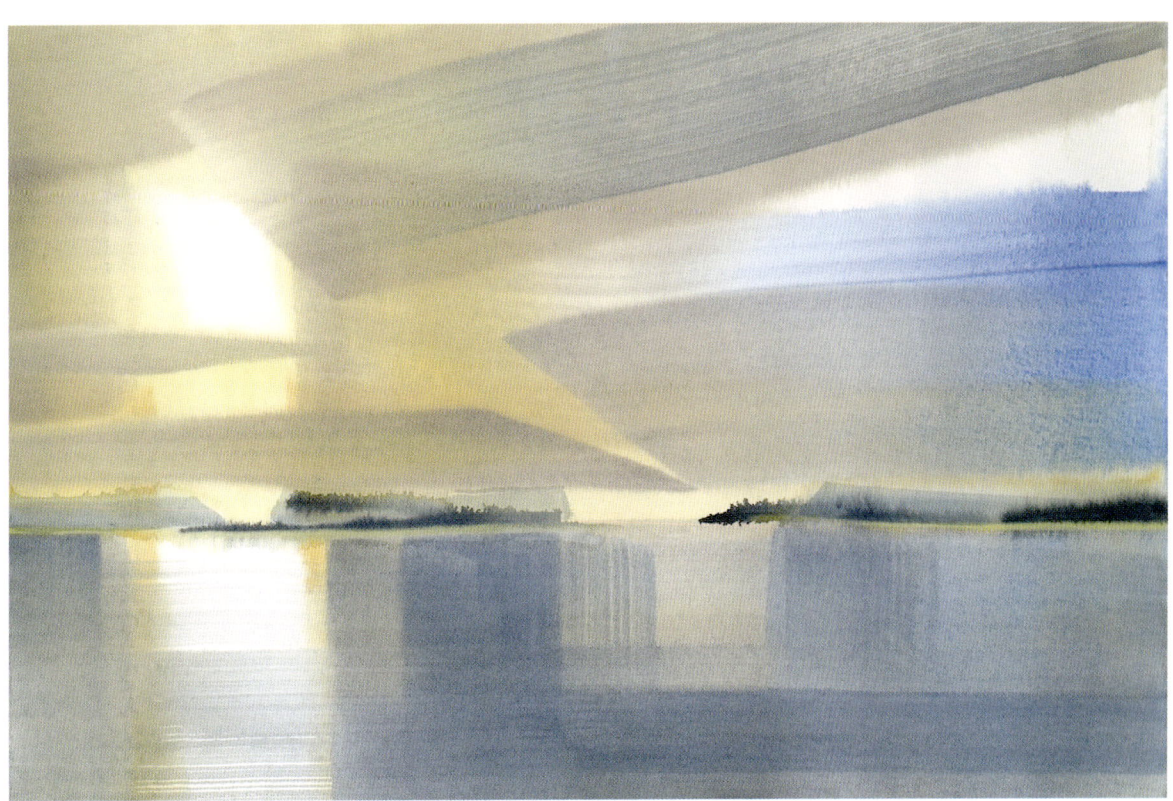

Tom Hoffmann, *Long Day*
Watercolor, 15" × 22" | 38 × 56 cm

Simplification not only liberates us from nature's excesses, it lends greater poetry to the painting itself. "Simplification involves letting go of everything that doesn't matter, of discovering what is enough for the viewer to connect the dots," says Hoffmann. "The artist begins with zero, then adds as little as possible, and stops while the illusion still feels incomplete." When a painting is this simplified, one is able to apprehend the primary shapes in an instant—in one visual sweep—without needing to assemble the small parts and pieces in the mind's eye. Such an immediate, holistic impression elicits a different emotional response than a painting that leads with narrative and detail.

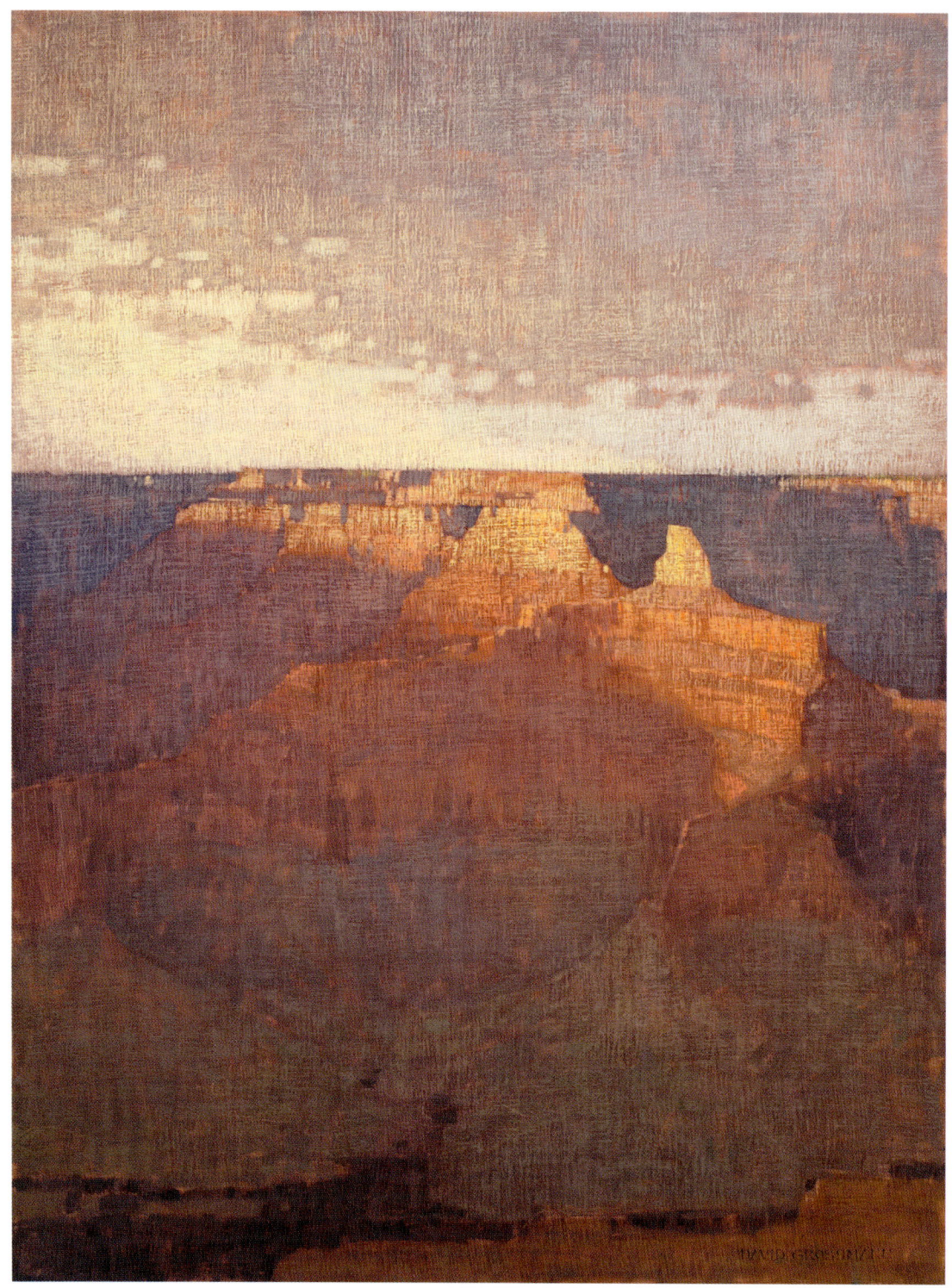

David Grossmann, *Sunset Light Over the Grand Canyon*
Oil on linen panel, 40" × 30" | 101.5 × 76 cm

The landscape painter aspires to communicate to the viewer their emotional response to a subject. One powerful way to do this is through simplification. In *Sunset Light*, all details, such as the subtle textures on the canyon walls, are subordinated in favor of a few large shapes. When interpreted this way, the viewer's experience of the canyon at sunset is sublime.

THE ROLE OF VALUE IN SHAPE INTERPRETATION

Every painting workshop and every art book discusses values—and for good reason. The differences between values are largely responsible for our ability to achieve separation between shapes. Wherever there is a difference in value, we are at an edge, at the border between two shapes or planes.

Value is the single most important key to seeing and interpreting shapes.

The range between light and dark values is also responsible for conveying a believable sense of light, depth, volume, and atmosphere.

CONSIDER: Value can exist independent of color (as in a drawing), but color can never exist independent of value because value is one of the three basic attributes of color. Every color is also a particular value.

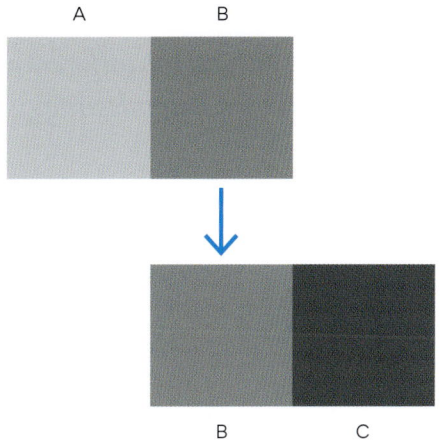

THE RELATIVITY OF VALUE

Value describes the relative lightness or darkness of a color. Is an area "light" (closer to white) or is it "dark" (closer to black)? Or somewhere in between? A value is never light or dark on its own; it is only lighter *than* or darker *than* something else. We assess each value by comparing it to an adjacent value. In these swatches, value B is darker than A. But when B is placed in a different context, alongside C, it appears lighter. And of course, all four are darker than the white of the page.

THE POWER OF SQUINTING

The best method for reducing myriad values into simplified patterns is built right into our own heads—*squinting*. Thousands of shapes and values demand our attention. How do we know which ones are most important and which ones can be left out? When we squint, midvalues tend to group with either the light or dark ends of the value range, producing a simplified, high-contrast view of the subject. Basic light and dark patterns are revealed. Small value differences evaporate.

CONSIDER: Are the small details that dissolve when we squint really a necessary part of the foundational structure of our picture?

LIMITED VALUES AND SHAPE DEFINITION

Defining shapes through value differences is not as easy as it might seem. This is in large part because there are so many values to contend with. There may be as many as 25, 50, or 100 values in any given subject—far too many to effectively discriminate. Painters get around this problem by restricting themselves to working with a much narrower range of values than they actually see, with as few as 5 values.

When we limit our values, the differences between those values becomes more apparent, which in turn helps distinguish one shape from another.

LIMITED VALUES: SAYING MORE WITH LESS

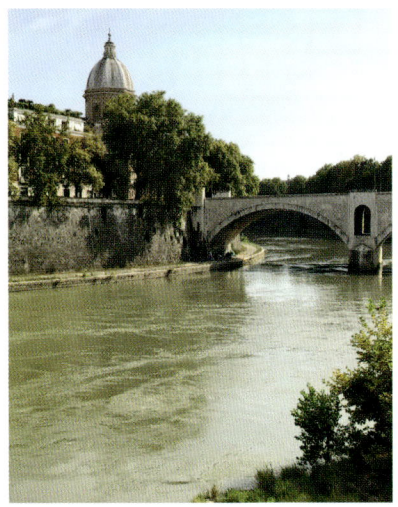

ORIGINAL: FULL VALUE

The original scene has a full range of values, from very light in the sky and water to very dark in the shadows of the trees to intermediate tones in the middle ground. Can the character of the subject be conveyed with fewer values?

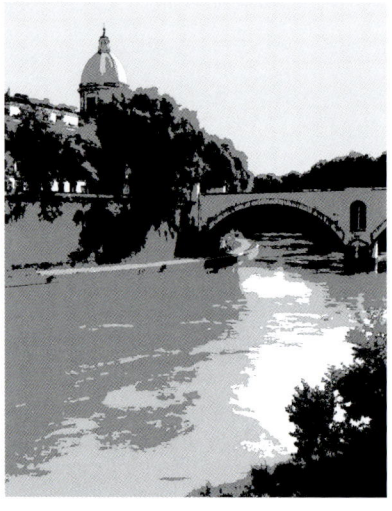

5 VALUES

When the scene is converted to 5 values, it's remarkable how much structure, light, and depth can still be conveyed. This is because the essence of a subject lies not in capturing every detail but in its foundational shapes, which are each a specific value.

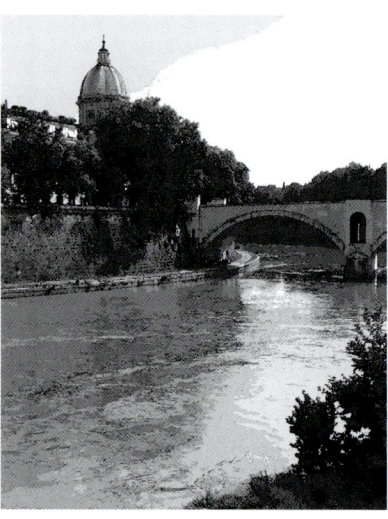

10 VALUES

When the subject is converted to 10 values, there is greater nuance of value and articulation of detail, but in terms of composition, it is not appreciably stronger than the 5-value study. In most instances, more than 9 or 10 values does little to enhance the fidelity that can be achieved with fewer values.

VALUE SCALES AND ENDPOINTS

To better help identify values, painters often refer to a value scale. Scales can have different numbers of steps: usually 5, 7, or 10. Each scale has white on one end and black on the other, with evenly stepped gradations in between. The 5- and 7-step scales are limited value scales. The 10-step scale is not as limited; it offers a wider range of values, but not so many that one can't discriminate between them.

CONSIDER: A value scale is only a guide, not a hard and fast value-matching system. Ultimately, you have to judge a value in the context of the painting where you can compare it alongside other values.

CONSIDER: Scales can also be divided into segments of light, middle, and dark. This serves as a reminder of the values typically associated with areas of light and shadow. Painters often place a printed version of the scale on their palette so they can better evaluate the values of their color mixtures.

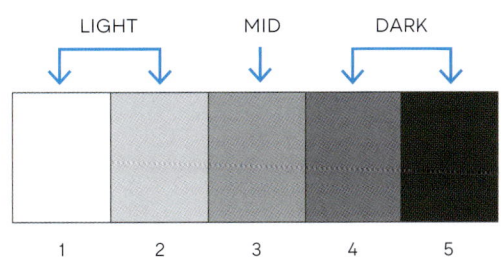

THE 5-STEP SCALE

The fewer values used, the more differentiated each value will be from the other. This makes the 5-step scale useful for those first learning to identify values. It is ideal for subjects that have a range of values from full light (white) to full dark (black). However, it doesn't work as well for subjects with values only in the midrange. Without using the white and black, you would only have three middle values to work with, which is usually not enough for a complete value study.

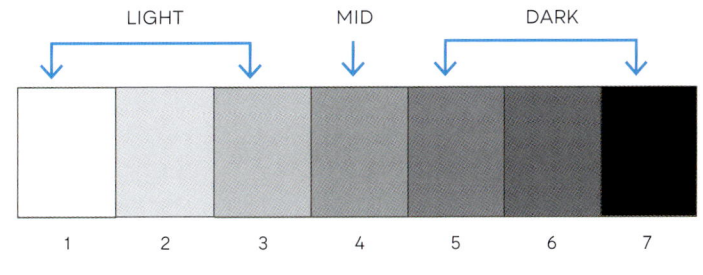

THE 7-STEP SCALE

The 7-step scale is a bit more flexible than the 5-step. It has few enough steps to make managing values easier, yet enough to adequately render any subject. In subjects with a full range of values, from white to black, you have all seven values to work with. If the subject has a more compressed value range, and you eliminated the white and black endpoints, you would still have a full five values (2 to 6) to work with.

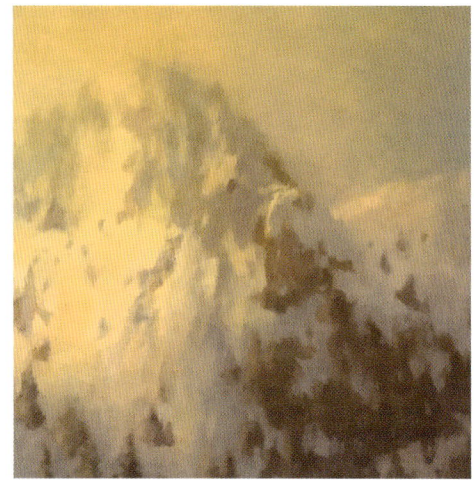

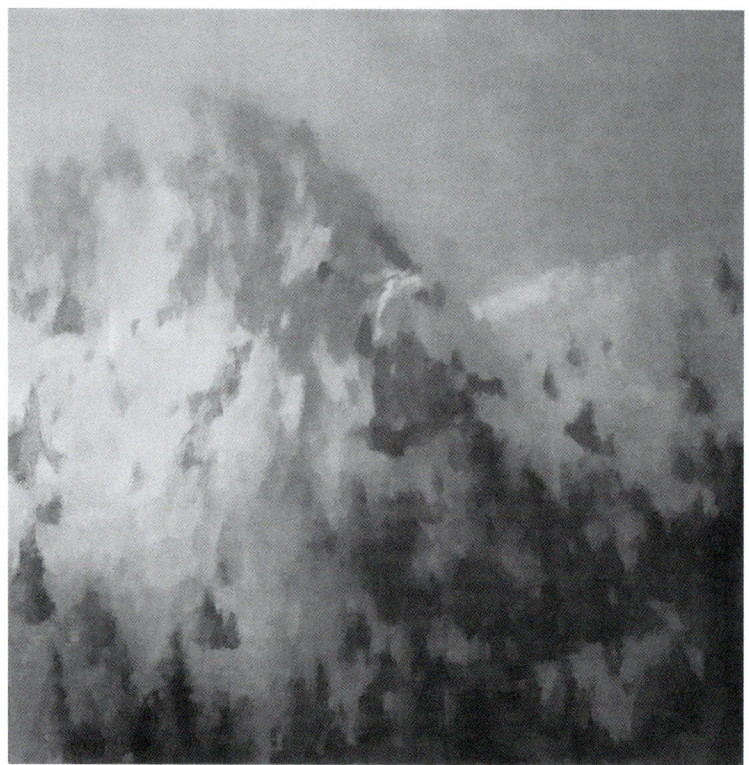

Mitchell Albala, *Ascension, Winter*
Oil on panel, 18" × 18" | 46 × 46 cm

Ascension has a compressed tonal range. None of its values correspond to full light (white) or full dark (black). The lightest values in the painting, in the upper left, are about a 3 on the 10-step scale. The darkest passages in the lower right are equivalent to an 8. A compressed value range is key to conveying atmospheric effects like fog, humidity, and atmospheric perspective.

WORKING WITH A COMPRESSED VALUE RANGE

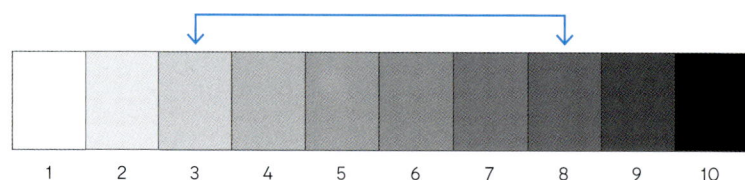

1 2 3 4 5 6 7 8 9 10

TARGET YOUR ENDPOINTS

Every value scale has full light (white) and full dark (black) as its endpoints. This doesn't mean that the values in *every* painting must use a full range of values. Many paintings, like *Ascension, Winter* (top left), don't have any values that correspond to white or black. It has a compressed value range.

CONSIDER: When assessing the range of values in a subject, always ask yourself, *What is the lightest light and the darkest dark?* Do they correspond to white and black? They often don't. Where do those lights and darks fall on the scale? These will determine the endpoints of your value range. All other values will fall somewhere in between.

WORKING WITH VALUE ZONES

Earlier in this chapter, we saw how every painting begins with a simplified foundation. ("Simplification Is Our Starting Point" on page 16.) Of course, as we develop a painting, we will want to add additional values, colors, and details. How can we do this without losing the basic foundation we established at the start? By working within *value zones*.

The broad shapes and planes in landscape form value zones. We can maintain the foundational value structure of our painting by making sure that any modulations of value we make within a zone never vary so much as to break with the overall continuity of that zone.

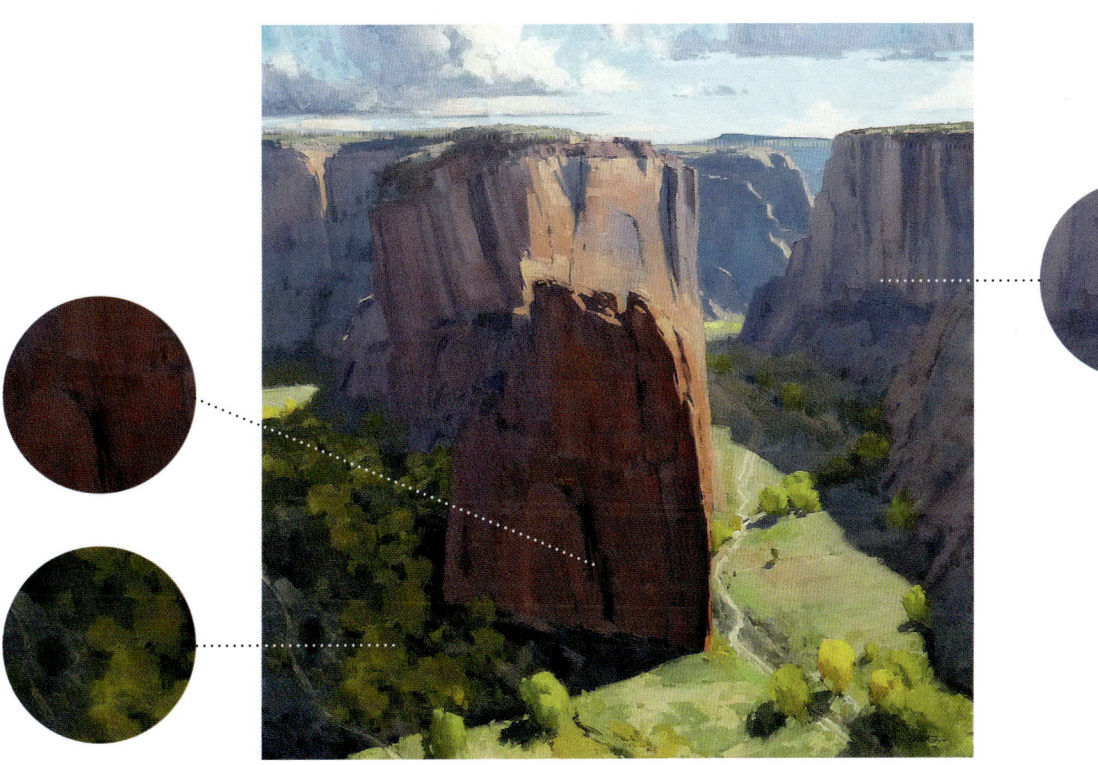

VALUE ZONES IN NATURE

Bill Cramer, *Canyon Fortress*
Oil on canvas, 36" × 36" | 91.5 × 91.5 cm

Value zones are formed by shapes and planes of consistent value. Three of the zones in *Canyon Fortress* are called out in the circles. The sunny ground plane in the lower right and the sky also form zones. Cramer maintains tight control by allowing only small modulations of value within each zone. This is the key to maintaining the cohesiveness of a zone.

VALUE ZONES IN THE URBAN SETTING

Chien Chung Wei, *Shantou in the Rain*
Watercolor, 29½" × 22" | 75 × 56 cm

The urban landscape is the most complex and drawing-intensive subject a painter can work with. With so many planes and lines and details, the only way a painter can keep their structure and values organized is to work within clearly defined zones. Within each of the zones indicated, there are only small variations of tone and color. If these variations become too great, they will stand out too much and disrupt the overall continuity of the zone.

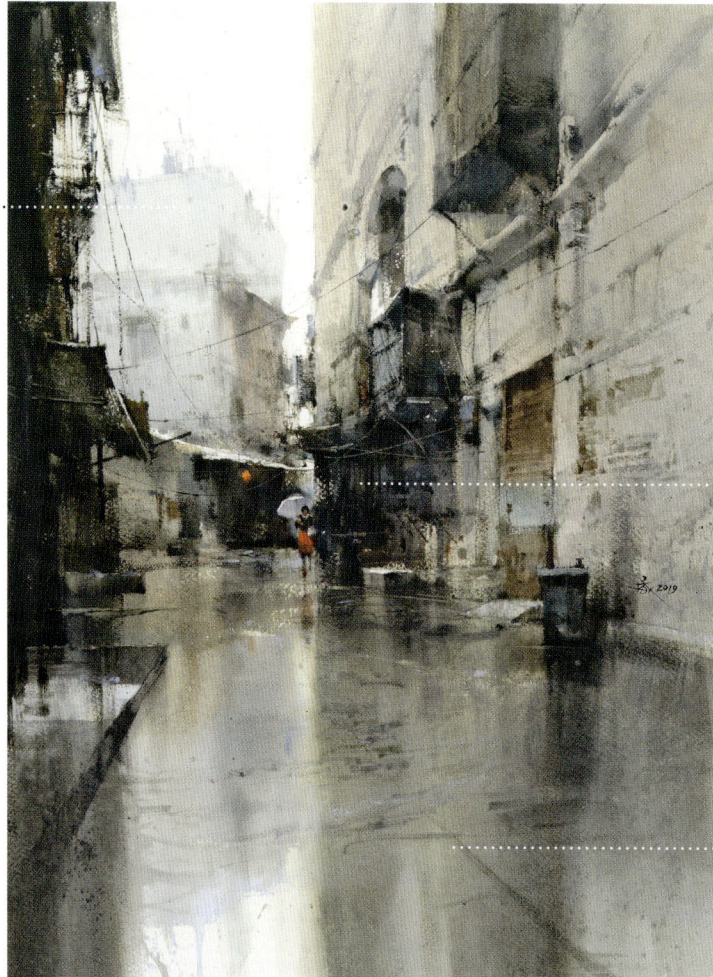

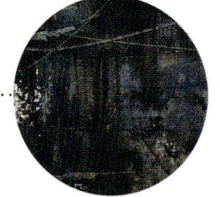

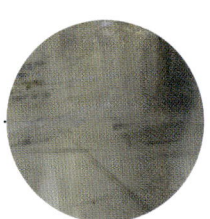

BALANCING SIMPLIFIED SHAPES AND DETAIL WITH THE 80/20 RULE

When first learning to translate nature's forms into painting, it's easy to go overboard with detail. It takes a lot of experience before one realizes "simplified shapes capture the essence of a subject more effectively than small parts and details."

Yet, those small parts and details do matter. They hold information that may be essential to the visual story. They also provide a compelling visual counterpoint to the larger elements within the subject. How do we know how much detail is too much or how much is too little? The answer can be found by considering the *balance* between the larger foundational shapes and the

details. As a general rule of thumb, the main masses should occupy around 80 percent of our visual focus and the details around 20 percent.

The 80/20 rule reminds us that large foundational shapes and details exist within a visual hierarchy. Viewers should identify with the large shapes and masses first and the details second.

If we experience the opposite, if we notice details *first*, then the viewer will have a different kind of perceptual experience. As important as details may be, they must always remain subordinate to the dominant masses.

80/20—GIVE OR TAKE

Of course, 80/20 is an approximation. Depending on the subject and one's interest in detail, this balance may vary. It might be 90/10 or 75/25. What matters is that we notice the larger shapes first. The 80/20 rule is simply a way to check that we are leading with the large foundational shapes.

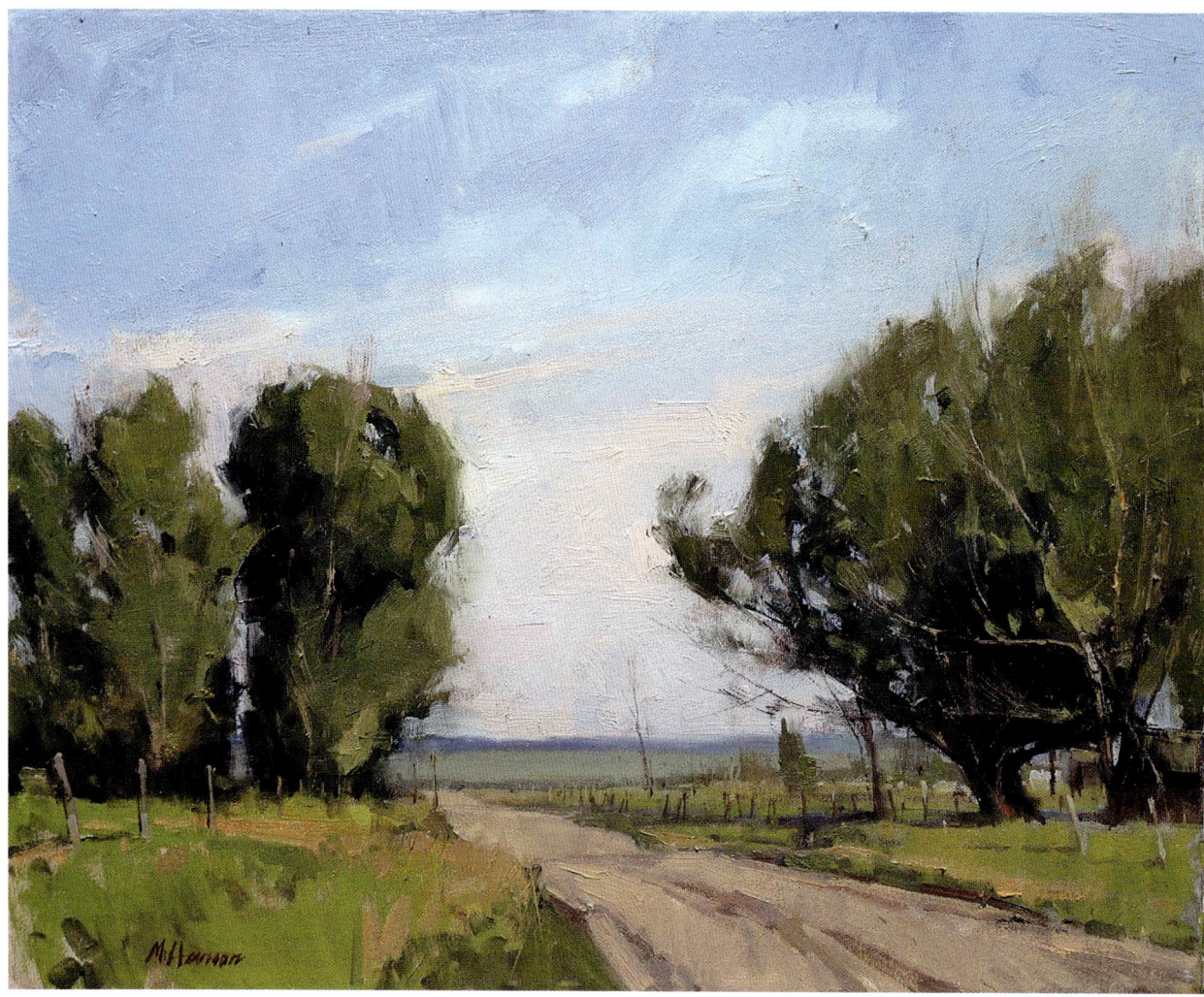

80/20 IN THE NATURAL WORLD

Marc Hanson, *Mormon Row*
Oil on board, 16" × 20" | 40.5 × 51 cm

Trees are among nature's most detailed forms. This makes them an excellent subject for the 80/20 rule. A tree has many leaves, fine branches, and small perforations (sky holes). They are essential parts of the tree, but do we need to paint every one of them to convey its essential character? No. In *Mormon Row*, around 85 percent of our attention is directed toward the basic three-dimensional masses of the trees and only 15 percent to the leaves, branches, and sky holes. It is surprising how little detail it actually takes to portray a particular tree.

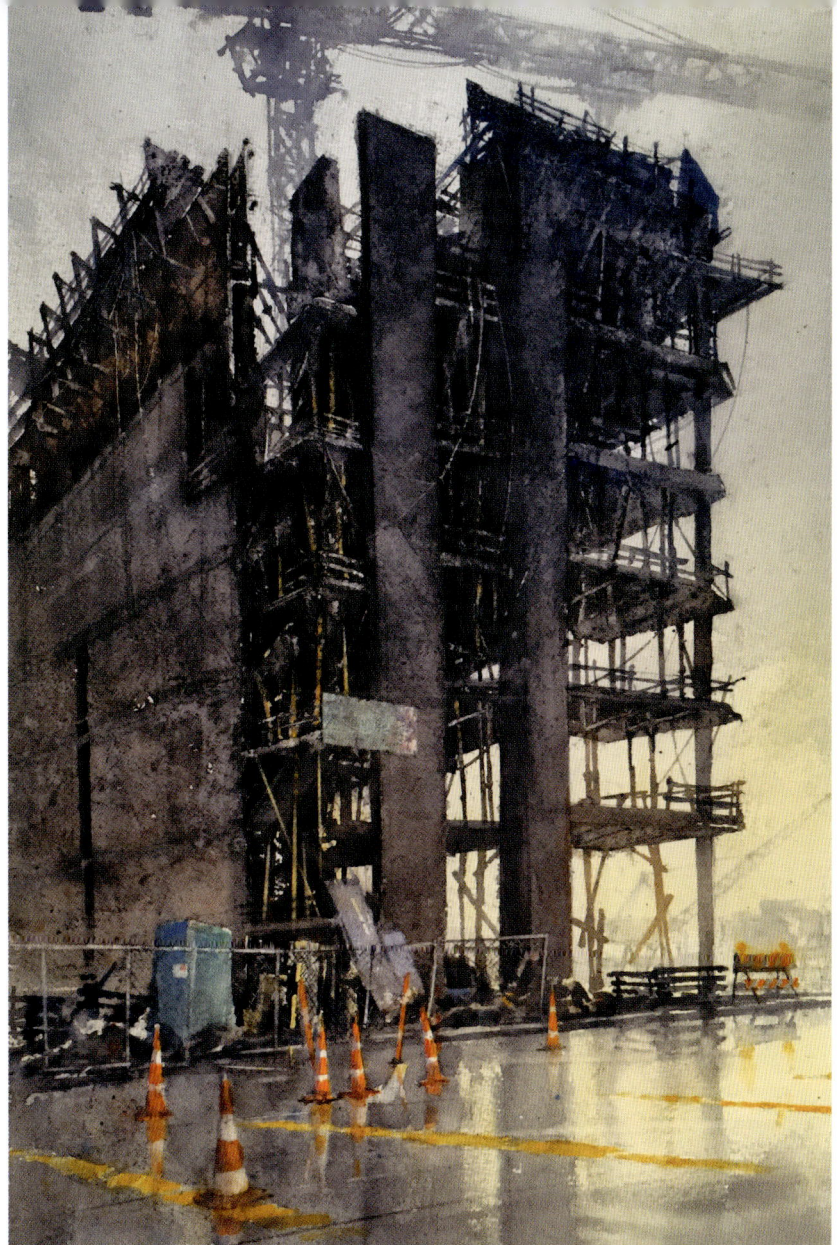

80/20 IN THE URBAN LANDSCAPE

William Hook, *Going Up,* **2020**
Watercolor, 21" × 14" |
53.5 × 35.5 cm
Sketch, 4" | 10 cm wide

By any measure, *Going Up* is a detailed painting. As important as those details are to an urban landscape, Hook's dominant foci are the large dark and light masses. Details can be embedded into every square inch of a painting as long as they remain subordinate to the dominant masses.

Hook's thumbnail study for *Going Up* shows his interest in prioritizing the main masses. "I am very interested in the shape of the light and dark masses in my paintings," Hook says. "I often make a small study to remind me of that pattern as I develop the image."

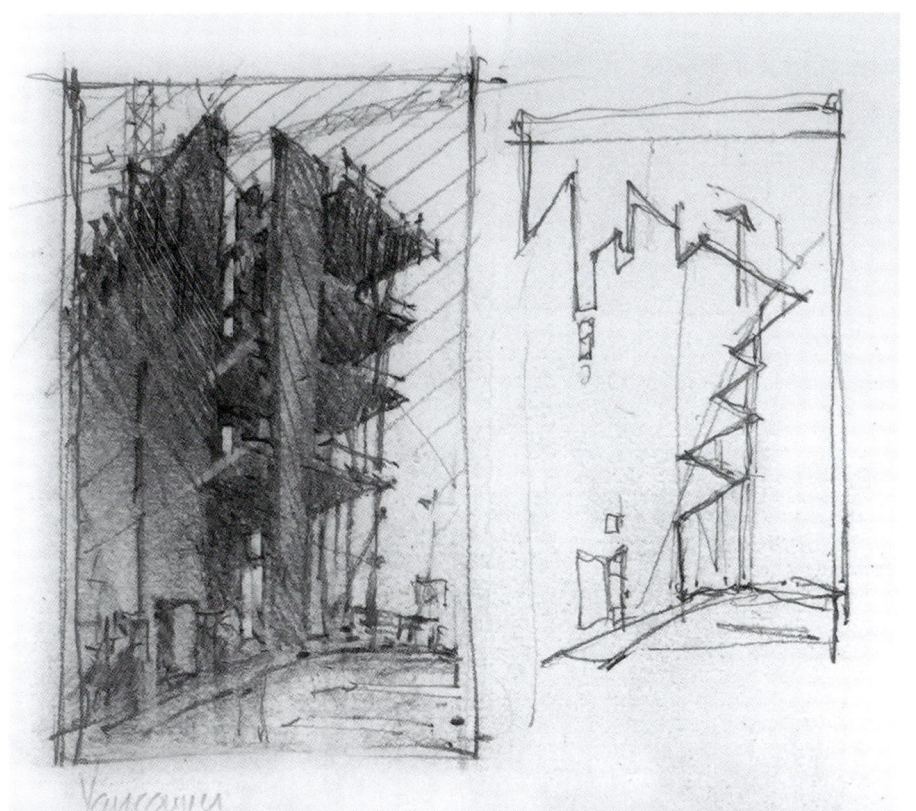

REVIEW QUESTIONS:
SHAPE INTERPRETATION

SIMPLIFICATION

Are you beginning the painting with large foundational shapes?

Or are you starting with small shapes and details that distract from the picture's foundational structure? Regardless of how much detail you will ultimately include, always begin with a foundation of simplified light and dark masses.

Are you squinting to help yourself see basic light and dark patterns?

Details and small value differences evaporate when you squint, revealing the basic light and dark structure of the composition. This basic structure is your starting point.

Are more shapes needed or fewer?

Which shapes are essential to the visual story and which ones are superfluous? Will the picture suffer if you eliminate a particular shape or if you combine several shapes into one?

How are you managing detail?

Detail is an important part of a landscape painting, but too much can be overwhelming to you, who has to paint it all, *and* to the viewer. Use the 80/20 rule to strike the right balance between foundational shapes and details (page 25). Use value zones to contain detail (page 23).

VALUES AND DIFFERENTIATION

Are the shapes in your subject well-differentiated?

Whether working from life or from a photo, are there passages where it is hard to tell where one shape begins and another ends? The separation of shapes must be emphasized. Value and color differences are the primary means of doing so.

Are you using limited values?

Limited values are a reliable means of differentiating shapes. The more you stick to a limited value plan, the more clearly defined the shapes will be.

Have you targeted the endpoints of your value range?

Not every subject has values that stretch from full light (white) to full dark (black). What is the lightest light and the darkest dark in the painting? Find those on your value scale. These are the endpoints that you will work between.

Are you working with value zones to help maintain control of your values?

Broad shapes and planes in landscape form value zones. You can better control your values by making sure that any shifts of value you make within a zone never vary so much as to break with the overall continuity of that zone.

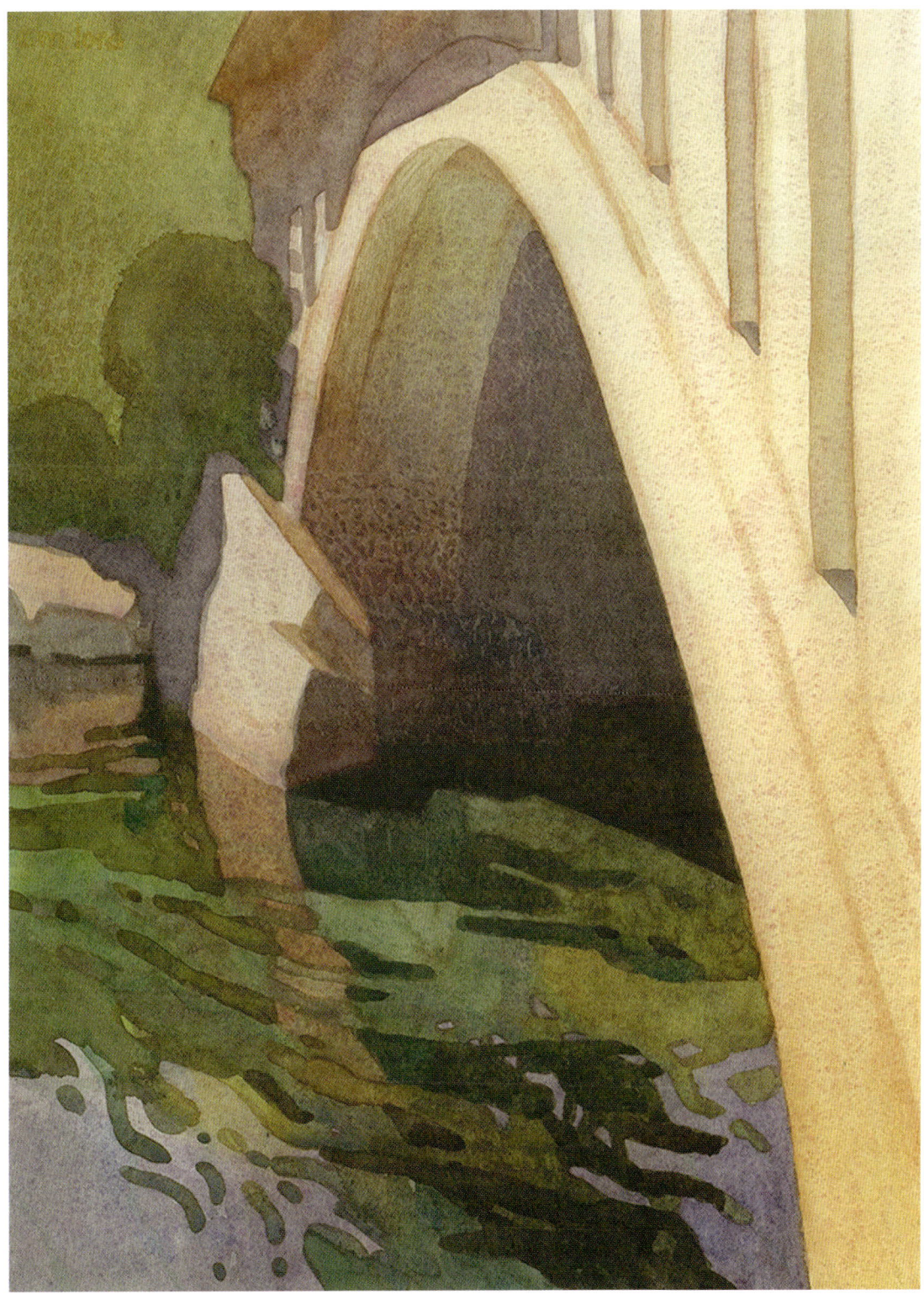

Carolyn Lord, *Bridge Over Calm Water, American River*
Watercolor on paper, 15" × 11" | 38 × 28 cm

Lord's rigorous approach to shape definition not only gives the subject its structure and form, but also lends a distinctive style to her work.

EXERCISE: **SIMPLIFY AND DIFFERENTIATE WITH LIMITED VALUES**

OVERVIEW: In this exercise, you will do a painting in black and white, using just five values. This is the most powerful of all the shape exercises because it exposes you to three essential keys of shape interpretation. First, you'll learn to control value mixtures by mixing five evenly stepped values. Second, working with limited values will force you to differentiate shapes and to simplify. And finally, the exercise reinforces your awareness of value zones because each discrete shape in the painting corresponds to a zone.

MEDIA: This exercise can be done in any medium, but it works best with acrylics, even if you're not an acrylic painter. It's easier to alter shapes and values with acrylics because they dry fast and lend themselves to quick revisions.

MATERIALS: Photo reference | Acrylic paint | Brushes | Paper palette (white) | Palette knife | Painting surface (paper, canvas, or panel)

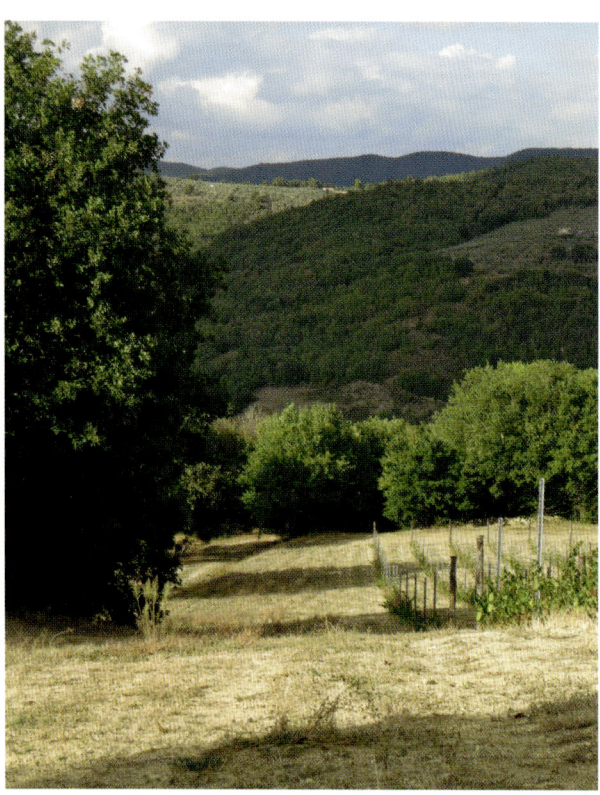 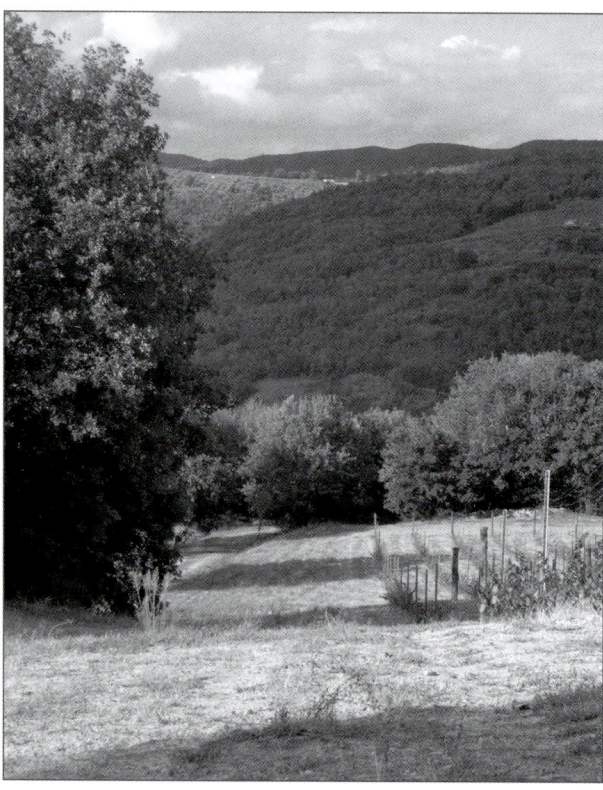

STEP 1: PHOTO SELECTION

Select a photo and print it out in both black and white and color. Make sure it has well-differentiated shapes and clear patterns of light and shadow.

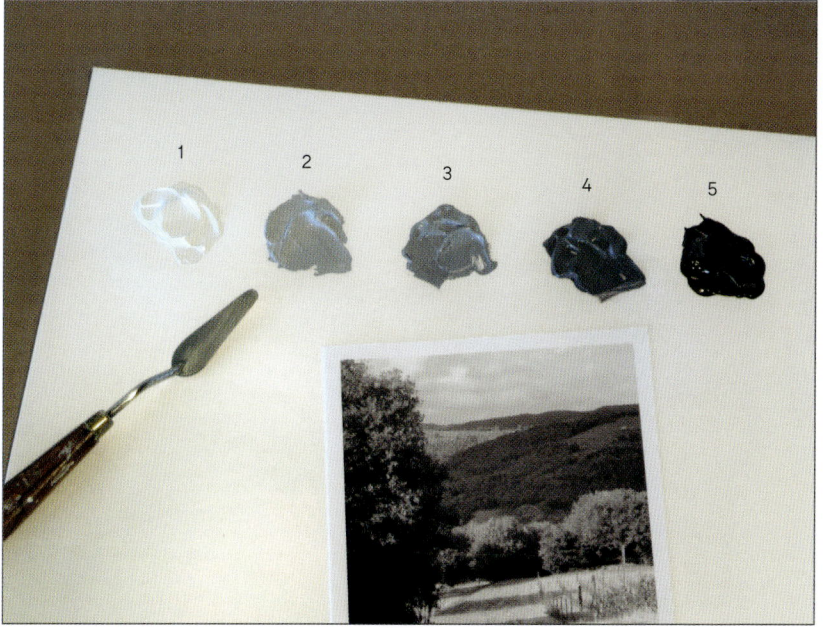

TIP

Don't begin your mixtures with black and then try to lighten with white. That will require a *tremendous* amount of white. Instead, start with white and *gradually* add black. Mix big enough piles to last the whole painting.

STEP 2: MIX VALUES

The white and black values can be used straight from the tube. But you will have to mix the three intermediary values (2, 3, and 4). If you haven't mixed values like this before, you'll find that it's not as easy as it looks. It takes fine control to get all five values evenly stepped without any two being too close to each other. If, say, values 4 and 5 are too close, you effectively lose one of your values. Even steps assures that each value is well-differentiated from the other.

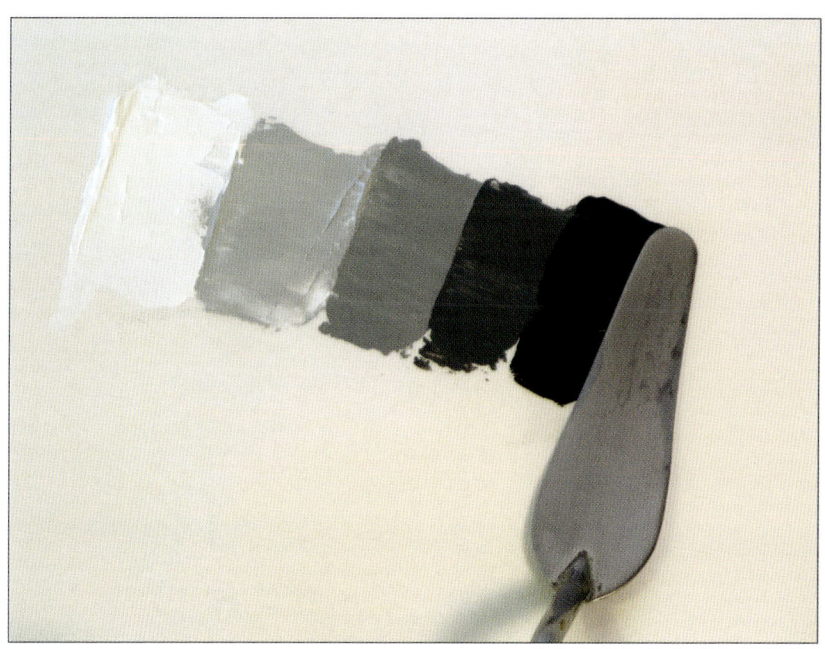

TIP

Value is relative, so the most reliable way to see if your mixtures are evenly stepped is to place tiny swatches side by side. You can do this on the palette or on a separate piece of paper.

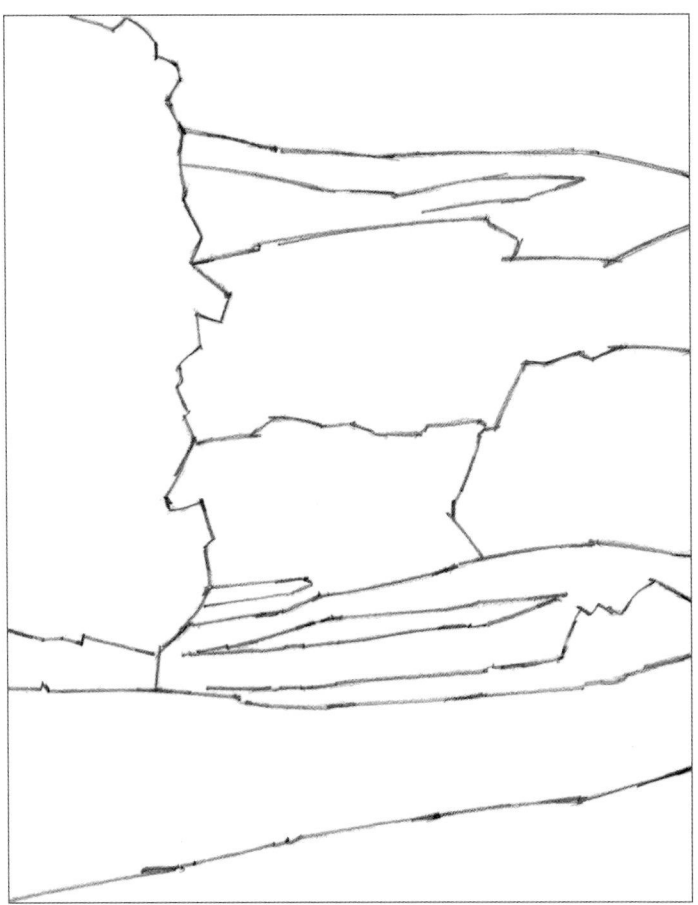

STEP 3: DRAWING

Work small, around 8 × 10 inches (20.5 × 25.5 cm). Begin by blocking in the *main* shapes—those that are foundational to the composition. This step is a challenge in itself, as the temptation will be to delineate minor shapes like branches, fenceposts, or leaves. Use a small brush or a pencil.

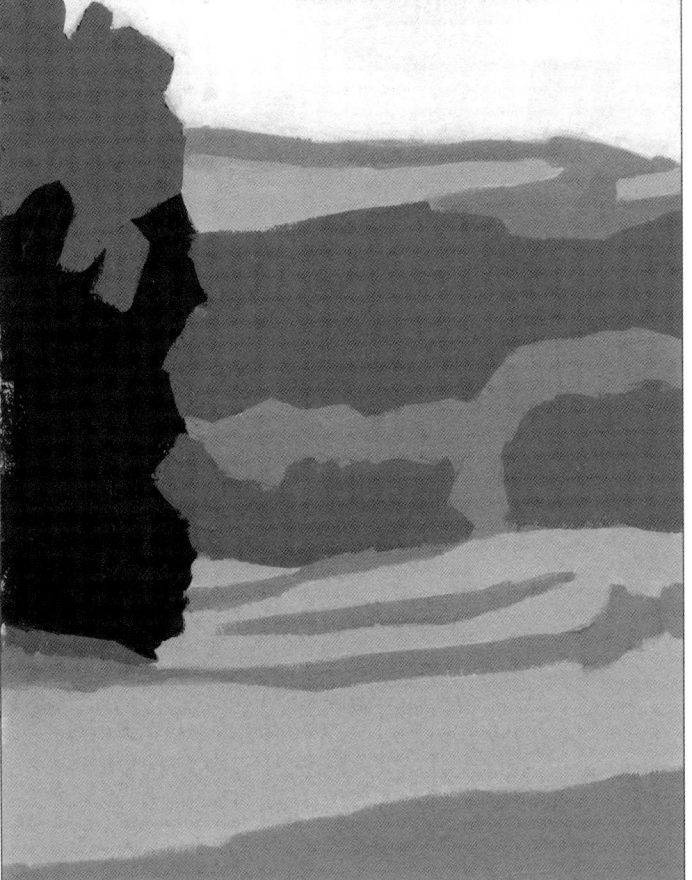

STEP 4: INITIAL BLOCK-IN

Begin blocking in the value zones. Squinting will help you see these zones. Because the photo has so many values, and you're limited to just five, you won't have every value you need. You'll be forced to make choices, which is part of the exercise. Keep the shapes and value zones as distinct as possible. This will encourage differentiation. Avoid a lot of blending. The acrylics will help with this because they dry so quickly.

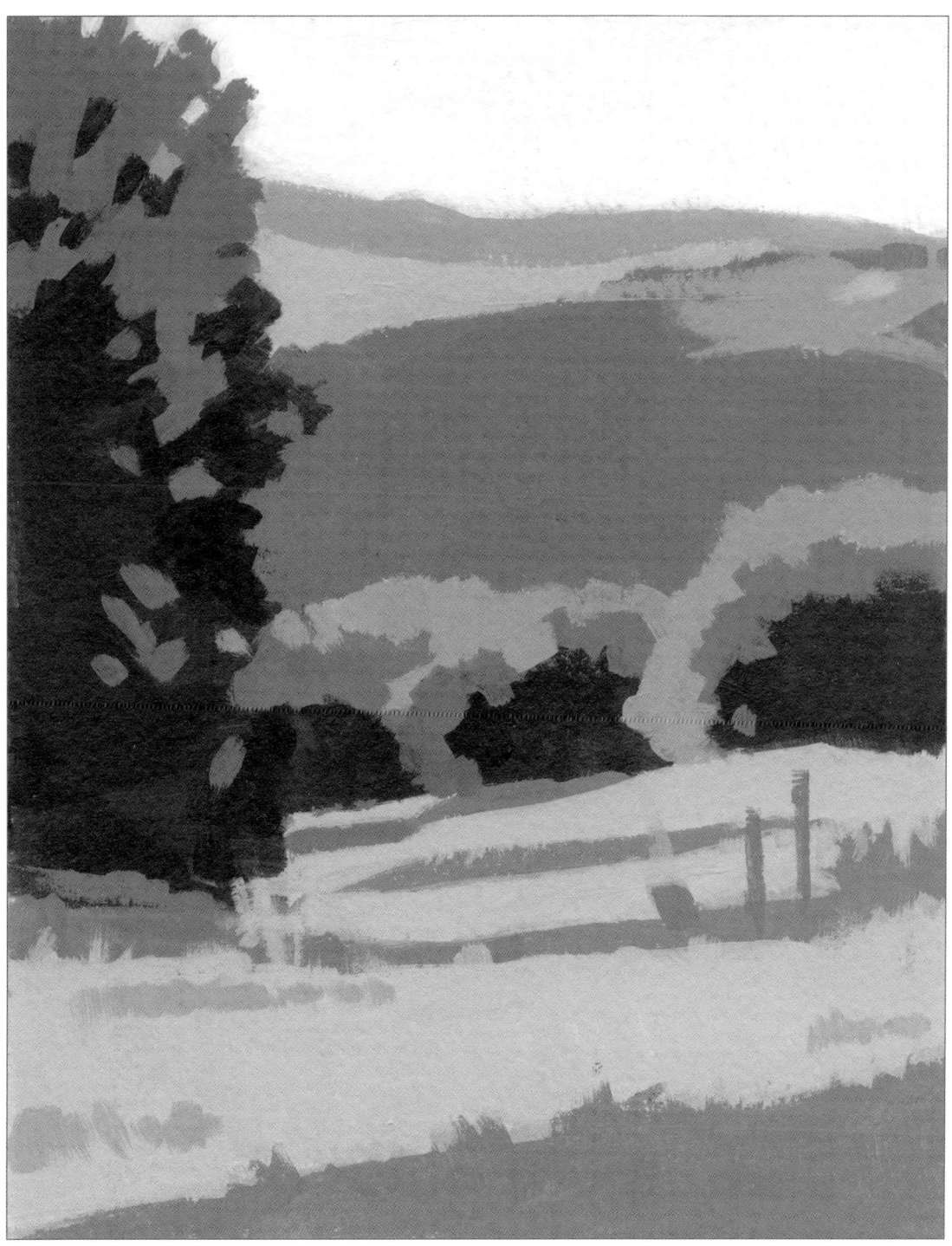

STEP 5: DEVELOPMENT AND FINISH

In order to achieve the necessary differentiation, you may have to make certain elements a different value than they appear in the photo. Here, the sky in the photo is value 2. If it were 2 in the painting, however, it wouldn't separate enough from the adjacent hills, so it becomes a 1 and the lightest value the painting. In the photo, the sunny foreground is nearly white, but as a 1 in the painting, it would have appeared too bright and competed with the sky, so it becomes a 2.

When you're done, ask yourself: If there is one additional value I could add that is *not* 1 to 5, which value would that be? Here, I would make the sun-struck foreground a little lighter, closer to a 1.5 than a 2.

EXERCISE:
SIMPLIFIED SHAPE PAINTING

OVERVIEW: One of the best ways to get a feel for shape interpretation is to work in a style of painting that simplifies in the extreme and defines shapes with distinct edges. Whether or not this is your preferred style, emulating it can be very instructive. You can experience how much can be conveyed through a small number of well-chosen shapes. For many, this must be experienced to be believed. In **Part 1**, you will do a master copy. In **Part 2**, you will try applying the same type of simplification and rigorous shape definition to your own painting.

PART 1: MASTER COPY

Do a copy of one or more of the paintings shown here by Sue Charles, Tony Allain, or Frank Hobbs. You can find additional examples of Charles' and Allain's work on pages 14 and 147, respectively, or online. Also look at the work of Fairfield Porter, a representational painter of the 20th century who worked in a similar shape-oriented way.

Work small, approximately 8 × 10 inches (20.5 × 25.5 cm). You may wish to capture the color, although color accuracy in this exercise is less important than experiencing what it is like to think in reductionist terms.

CONSIDER: The three examples shown here are in different media: oil, gouache, and pastel. But you can copy any painting regardless of your medium.

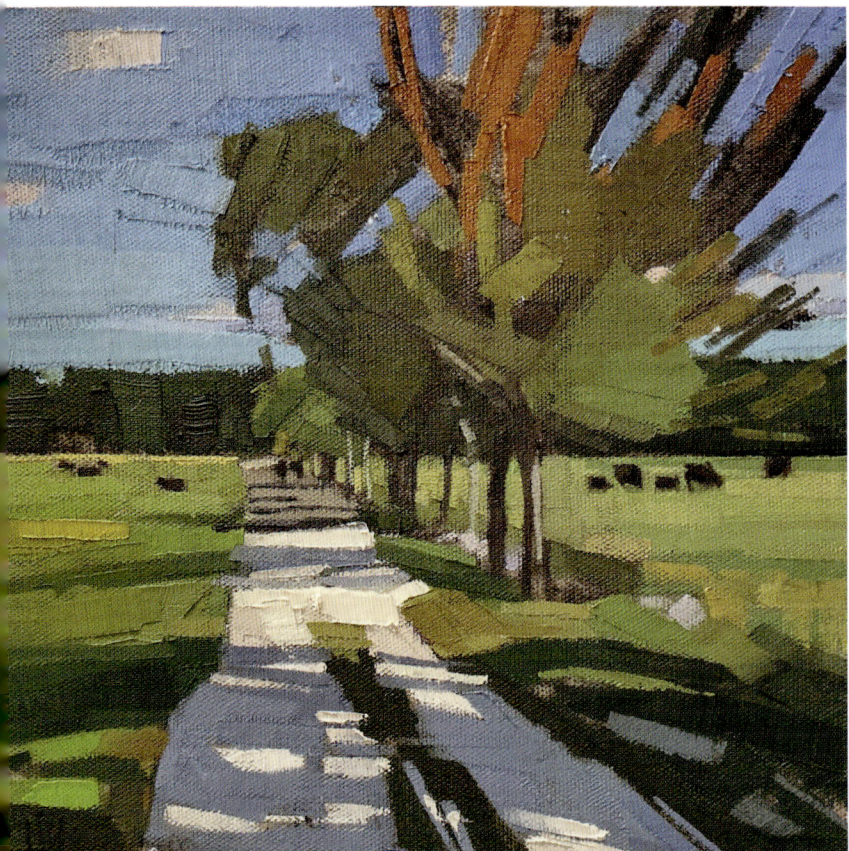

Sue Charles, *Fields in Summer*
Oil on cradled wood panel
10" × 10" | 25.5 × 25.5 cm

The degree of simplification in Charles' painting is the result of radical shape translation. The details of the original scene are consolidated into a much smaller number of clearly defined shapes. Despite the degree of consolidation, Charles conveys the essence of the original scene.

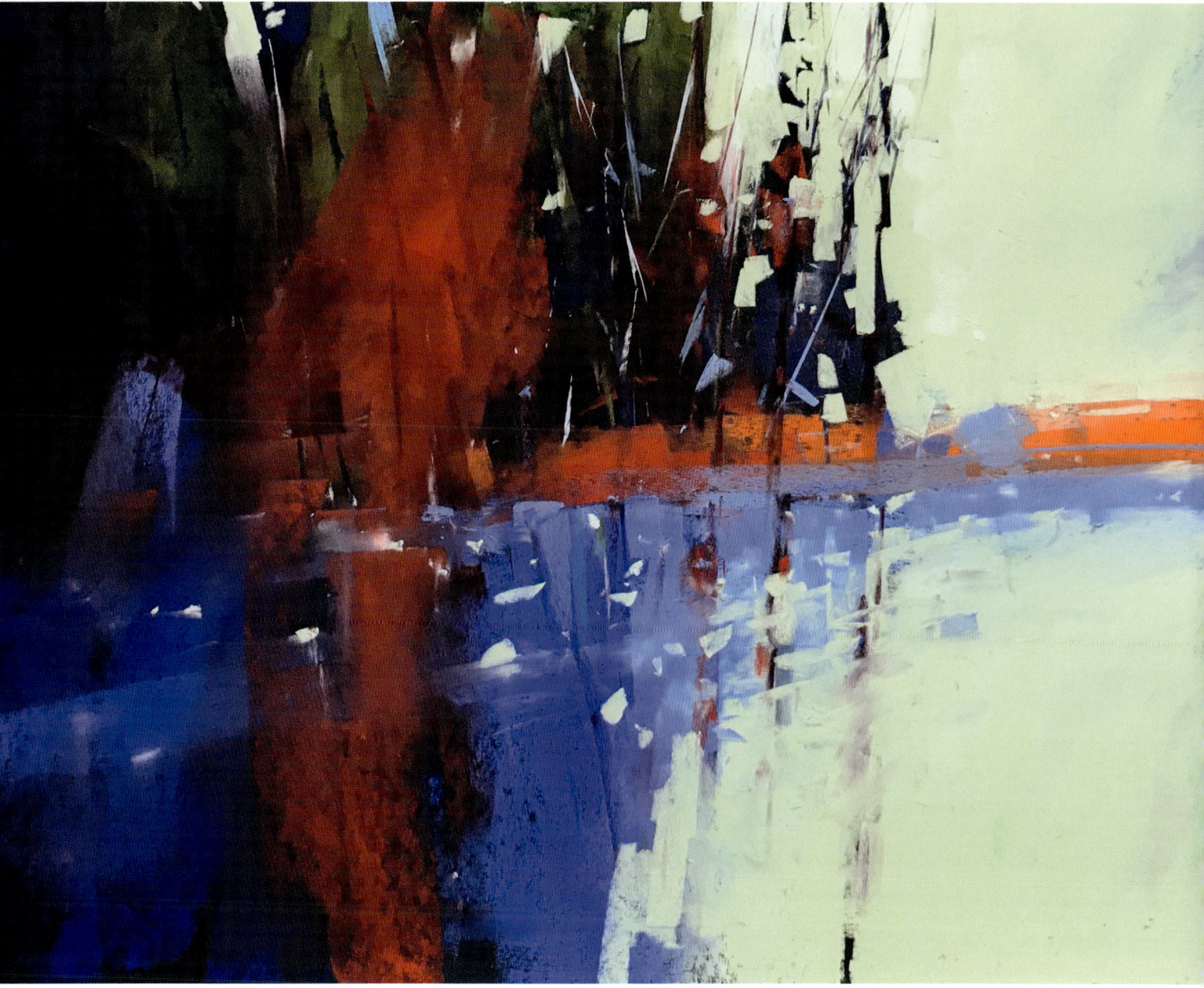

Tony Allain, *Sunburst*
Pastel on Canson paper, 11" × 14" | 28 × 35.5 cm

Allain handles his pastels like a painter using a very large brush. He uses the side of the pastel to create broad strokes, many of which correspond to the dominant shapes of the picture.

PART 2: TRANSLATION FROM LIFE

OVERVIEW: In the master copy you did in **Part 1** of this exercise, the shapes were already simplified and differentiated for you. Now, you will try interpreting the shapes in the same way on your own. Although this style of painting appears very graphic and simple, it is demanding. You are not performing a direct translation of every shape you see in the source. You are leaving out some shapes and perhaps combining several smaller shapes into one. Think of this study as a visual puzzle. What are the fewest number of shapes and strokes you can use to express the essence of the subject?

CONSIDER: Although you can do this exercise from life or a photo, you may want to do it from a photo first. This will give you extra time to consider your choices and perhaps revise the painting over the course of a few days.

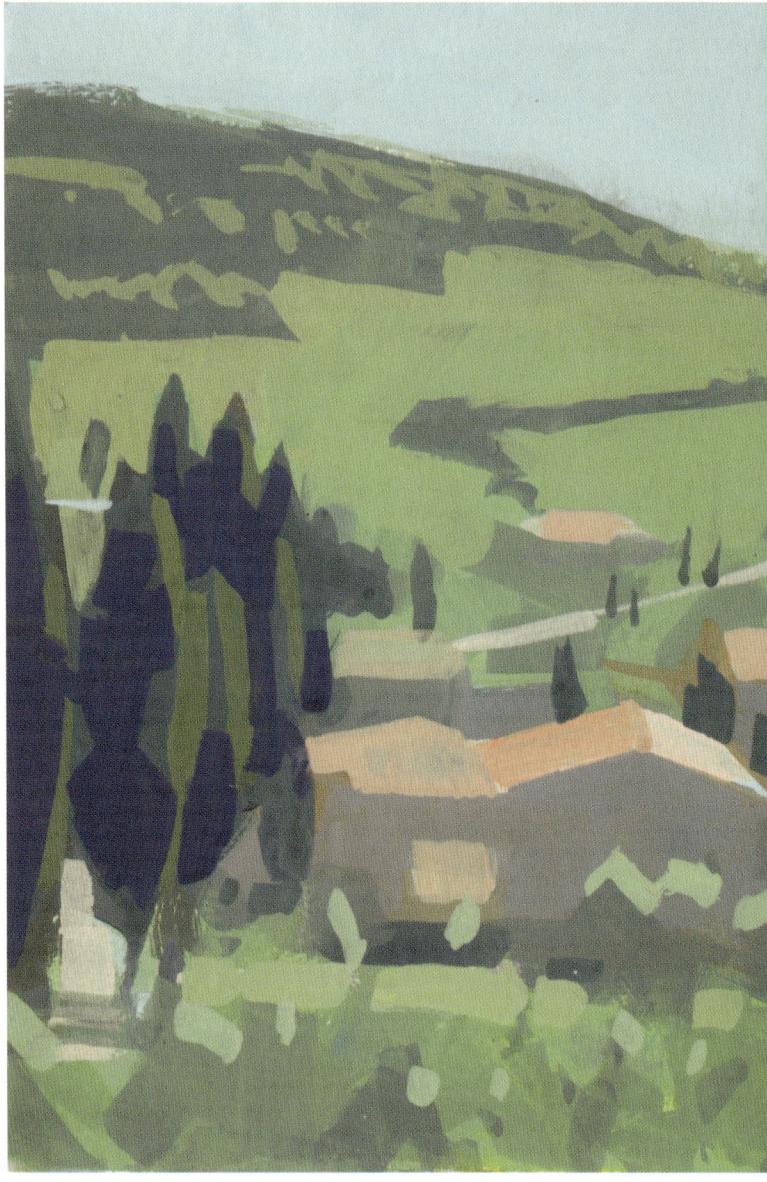

Frank Hobbs, *Monticchiello*
Gouache on rag paper, 9" × 6" | 23 × 15 cm

There are, of course, similarities between the painting and the photo reference. Yet, it is the differences that are enlightening. Allow your eye to jump back and forth between the painting and the photo, carefully comparing each area. What did Hobbs leave out? In complex areas, like the foreground trees and houses, how did he state them more simply? What details were absorbed into larger masses? "Simplification is about distillation," says Hobbs. "It's a search for the essential visual hierarchy—the main structural events; the strongest contrasts of darks and lights; the largest, most telling masses of color. An astute study can have a sense of completeness and unity that a more labored, detail-laden painting can lack."

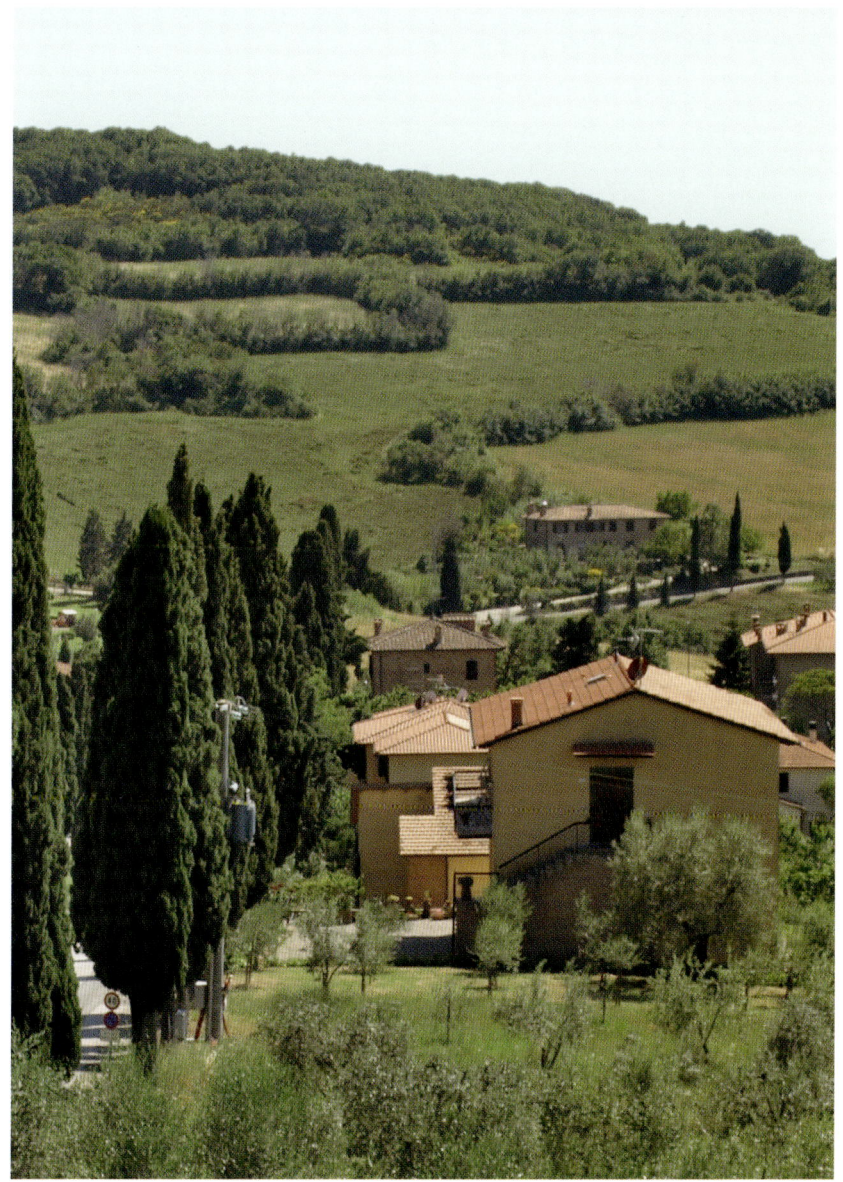

CONSIDER: Hobbs' crisp shapes are also the result of his media. Gouache, which dries quickly, allows him to work wet over dry. If you are working in oil and struggling to achieve crisp shapes, consider trying the exercise with faster-drying media like acrylic or gouache.

WHY SUBJECT SELECTION MATTERS

Hobbs is a skilled shape interpreter, yet his ability to perform such elegant shape translation is aided by the quality of his source material. *Monticchiello* was painted outdoors, but the photo shows that the scene has clear value patterns and well-differentiated shapes. Not all subjects do. If a subject is ambiguous in any way, if it has values that are indistinguishable from one another or unclear patterns of light and shadow, then how can we expect our painting to possess this necessary information? Whether working outdoors or from a photo, always begin by evaluating the quality of your subject. If the subject is lacking these necessary cues and you would have to make them up, then consider whether the subject is really a reliable starting point. The importance of selecting good subject matter cannot be underestimated.

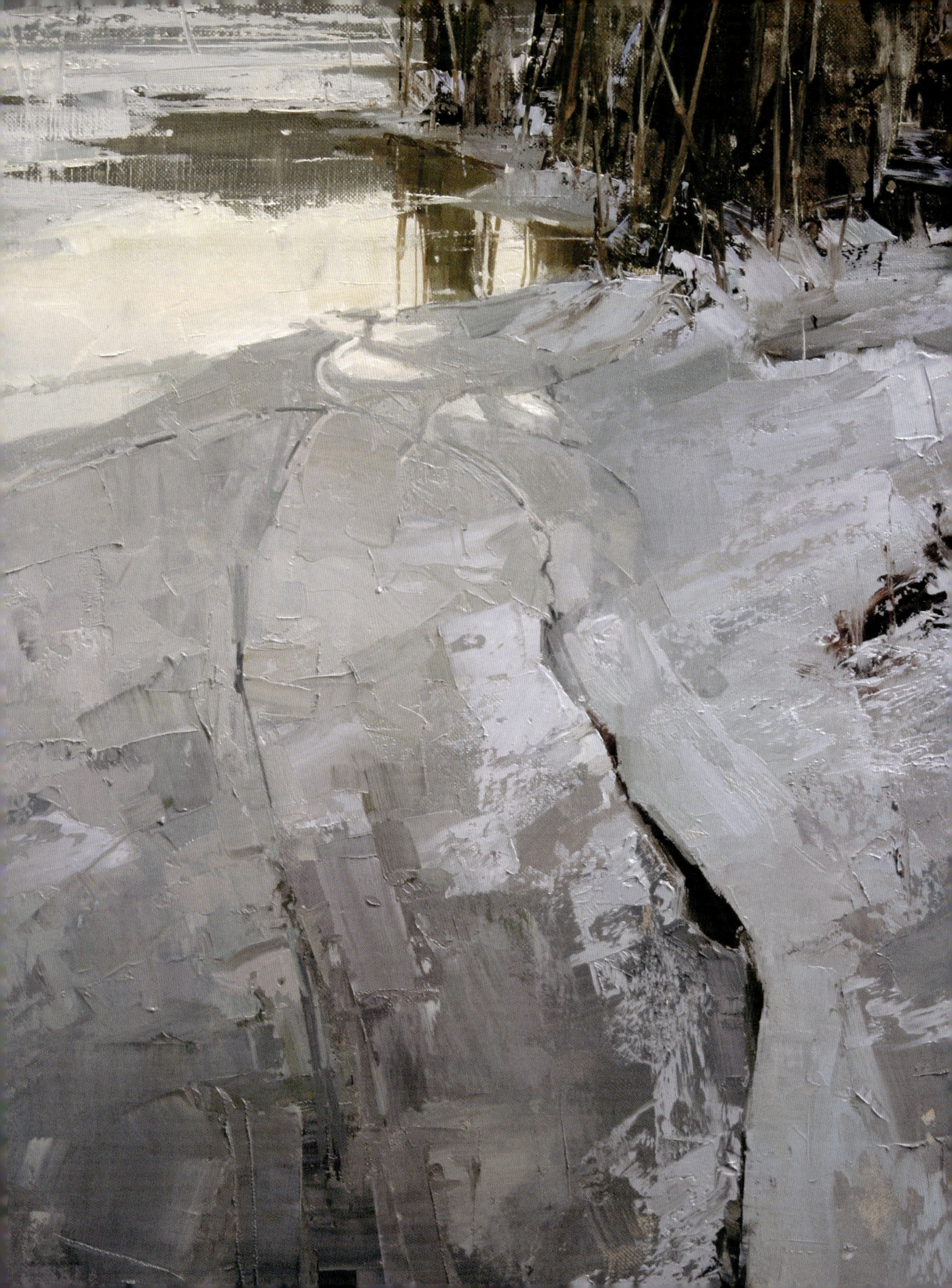

2

THE PICTURE WINDOW
AND ITS FORMAT

In the first chapter, we learned about the importance of converting nature's complexity into simplified and more visually concise shapes. Now, we turn our attention toward how those shapes are placed and arranged within our picture—otherwise known as *composition*.

The natural world is so vast and all-inclusive that it would be impossible to compose a landscape without limiting what we take in. The first act of composition, then, is to consider the rectangular paper or canvas that surrounds our subject—the *picture window*. How we position the window around our subject tells us what will be included in our composition and what will be left out. What small portion of the world will become the subject of our picture? The shape, or *format*, of the window itself—be it horizontal, vertical, or square—also imposes its own type of directional energy onto a composition.

In this chapter, we will look at the picture window as the first step in composition and in particular the unique attributes held by each of the formats.

◄ Tibor Nagy, *Fading Light*
Oil on linen, 16" × 12" | 40.5 × 30.5 cm

Each picture format—horizontal, vertical, or square—imposes its own type of directional energy on a composition. *Fading Light* is framed within a vertical format. The format itself imposes a directional movement—inward and upward—that supports the sense of deep space.

LIMITED FOCUS AND THE PICTURE WINDOW

The rectangle, or *picture window*, we impose around our subject is essentially the framing device for our composition. The picture window (or cropping, if we are to use the less formal term) determines which parts of the subject will be included in our composition, how those parts relate to each other, and how they relate to the four sides of the picture window itself. *Limited focus* is an apt term. It wonderfully describes the dual nature of the picture window: it *limits* what we include in our painting, but improves the composition by *focusing* our visual intent.

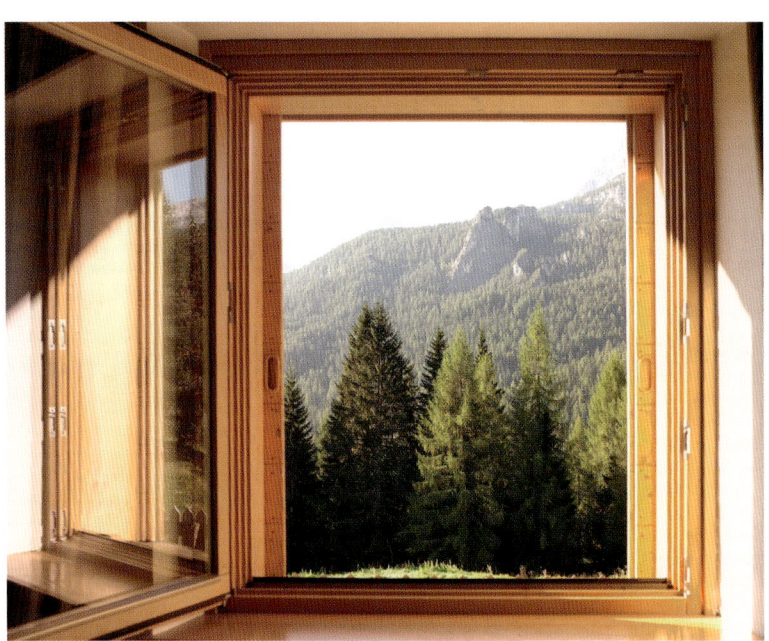

THE PICTURE WINDOW

When we look out a window, we see only a small portion of the wider world outside. Similarly, the rectangle, or *picture window*, we impose around our subject is the framing device for our picture. A composition cannot exist independent of the window that surrounds it.

LIMITED FOCUS IN ACTION: LESS IS MORE

Mitchell Albala, *Ascension, North Cascades*
Oil on panel, 18" × 18" | 46 × 46 cm

The original subject, as seen in the photo, holds the seed of a visual idea—the snow-capped mountain catching the light and the mist rising into the sky. But that idea is lost in a sea of excessive, repetitive information that adds nothing to the visual story. A limited focus allows us to decide what the visual story is and eliminate everything that doesn't contribute to it.

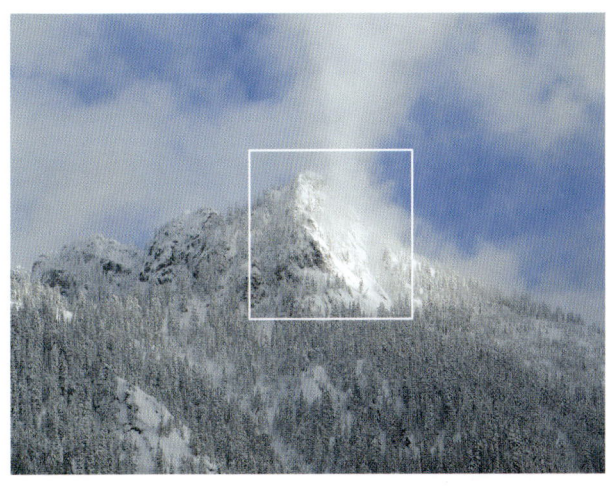

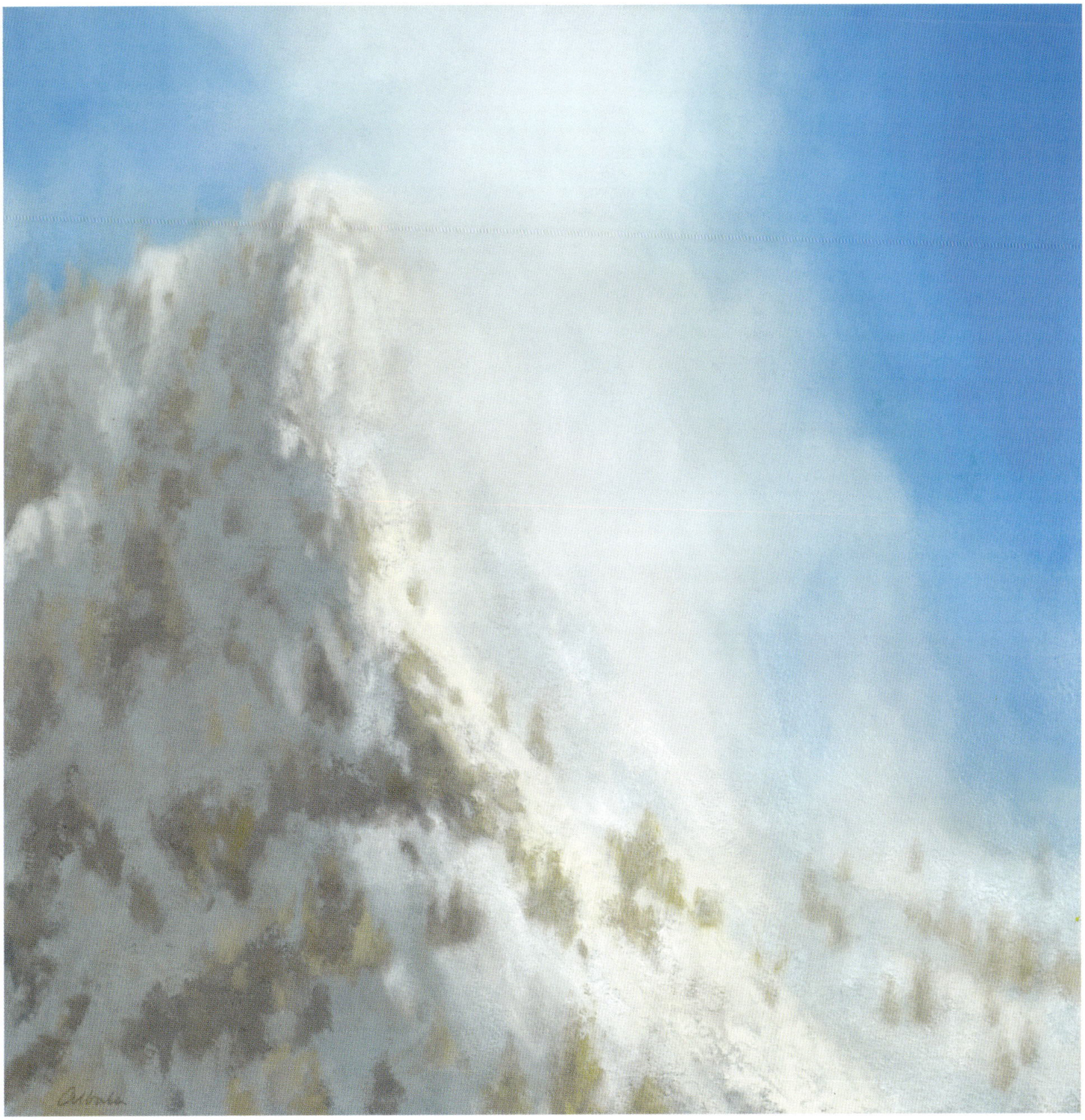

WAYS OF APPLYING A LIMITED FOCUS

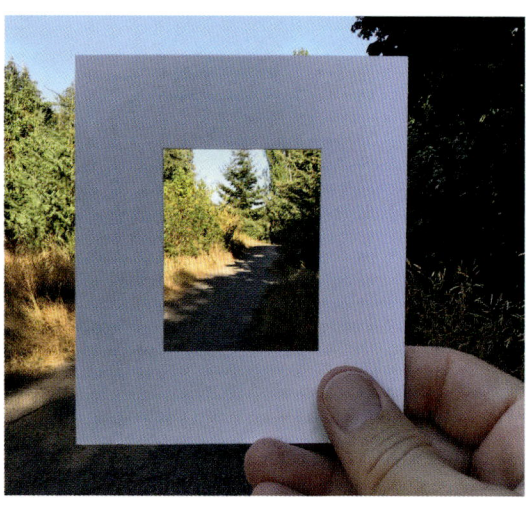

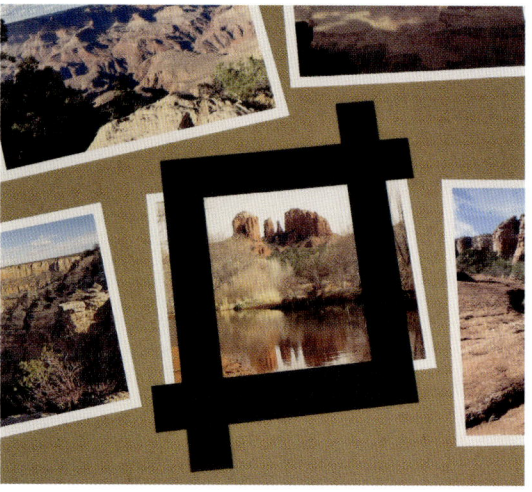

LIMITED FOCUS IN *PLEIN AIR*

When working outdoors, a limited focus can be applied by using a plastic or cardboard viewfinder. Any type of camera can be used in the same way. For a more hands-on approach, consider a traditional thumbnail sketch. Unlike a viewfinder, which frames the subject, a thumbnail requires you to position the subject within an *existing* window drawn on the paper. This is more challenging because you have to decide how the elements will be positioned relative to the boundaries of the window. (See the exercise "Notan from Observation" on page 98.)

LIMITED FOCUS IN THE STUDIO

When working from photos in the studio, you can use a pair of L-shaped cropping devices to experiment with different compositions. You can also crop images digitally with an image editing app.

TIP

When shooting photos, feel free to take a "postcard" shot, composing it as perfectly as you want—*but always shoot one that includes more real estate than you think you would ever need*. This is your *non-composed* work photo from which you can extract multiple compositions. A good source photo will preserve your options, not eliminate them. (See the exercise "One Subject, Different Formats" at the end of this chapter.)

PHOTOS: PREPARING FOR LIMITED FOCUS

It is a curious artifact of the digital age that when working with photos, painters often don't question the composition captured by the camera. Why? When they look through the viewfinder and press the shutter, they are in effect asserting that as the final composition. Then, when the photo is printed out with its crisp edges, it is a further assertion of the inviolability of the composition. One of the many ways we can misuse a photo is to assume it is a fully resolved composition. It *may* be, but in most cases, it is not.

PICTURE FORMATS AND DIRECTIONAL ENERGY

Because the picture window is such a key determinant of a composition, it stands to reason that the shape, or *format*, of the window—horizontal, vertical, or square—will also have an effect. And indeed, it does. Each format asserts its own type of directional energy. The "landscape" format reinforces horizontal movement. The vertical format encourages inward and upward movement. And the square, with its symmetrical sides, does neither; it asserts uniform pressure on all sides.

If the same subject were composed within each of the formats, you would get three very different compositions. This is the exercise you will do at the end of the chapter.

When we understand the properties of each format, we realize that format is not arbitrary. We choose the format that best suits our compositional intent for each particular subject.

PICTURE FORMATS AND MOVEMENT

Picture formats have a direct effect on one of the most important aspects of composition—movement. Movement is guided by the interior elements of the composition, but it is also influenced by the shape of the picture window itself, which asserts its own directional energy. This is why the picture format is so important and should never be chosen arbitrarily.

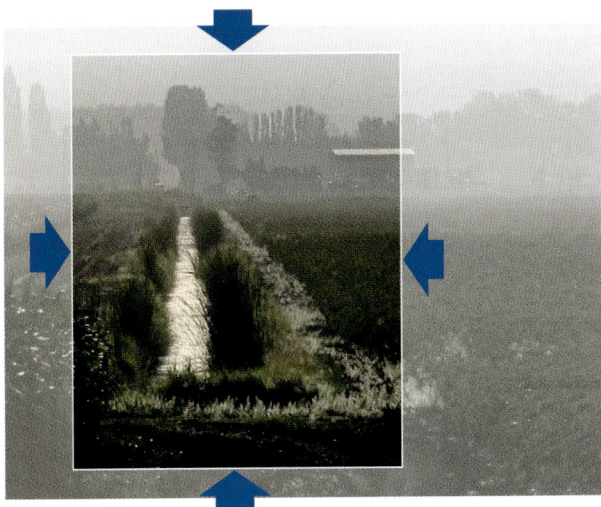

THE STRONGEST FORCES

When I discuss composition in my workshops, I often point to the painting in question and ask, "What are the strongest compositional elements in this picture?" The answers are always things like "the perspective of the road," "the contour of the hill," or "the visual weight" of a particular element. Although these do affect the composition, the correct answer is not always obvious. The most important forces in the composition are formed by the top, bottom, left, and right sides of the picture window.

THE "LANDSCAPE" FORMAT: HORIZONTAL MOVEMENT

The horizontal format—aptly named "landscape"—is the most frequently used picture format in landscape painting. When we survey the history of landscape, even as far back as the eighteenth and nineteenth centuries, we find that most landscape paintings are horizontal. Why is this the case?

A wider format is a natural "fit" for the horizontal character of the landscape itself. We are surrounded on all sides by landscape elements, both natural and man-made. Some elements are nearer to us and some elements are farther away. Yet when we consider the totality of all that surrounds us, the predominant directional energy is horizontal—from left to right, east to west, and back again.

Furthermore, our own natural tendency is to scan the landscape horizontally, from left to right, across some segment of the 360 degrees that surround us. The horizon line, a strong presence in many landscapes, also reinforces horizontal movement. Even if the horizon line is obscured, it is always implied by the elements that rest upon it and follow its course.

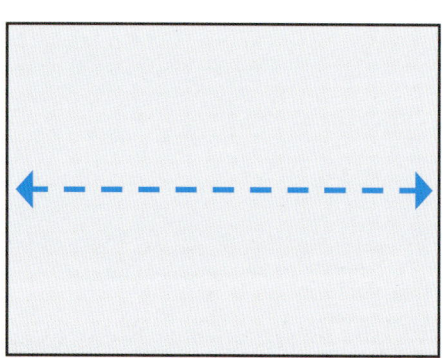

EAST TO WEST

The horizontal format asserts directional energy along the horizontal axis. This tends to reinforce any horizontal movement the subject itself may contain.

HORIZONTAL REWARDS, HORIZONTAL RISKS

A painter may choose a horizontal format for various reasons. Some subjects are so expansive that they simply won't fit well in a vertical or square format. The greatest strength of the horizontal format is its stability. Because humans are so grounded to the horizontal plane, the format can have a steady and calming effect, like a river flowing lazily past. However, one can also have too much horizontal energy.

When a subject that flows horizontally is placed within a format that reinforces horizontal movement, one can get an excess of horizontal energy.

This can inhibit the ability of the composition to suggest depth. The key to avoiding this is to add verticals and/or diagonals to the composition.

COUNTERACTING HORIZONTAL MOVEMENT WITH VERTICALS

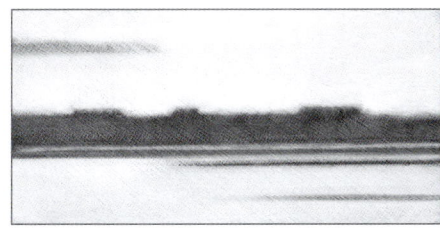

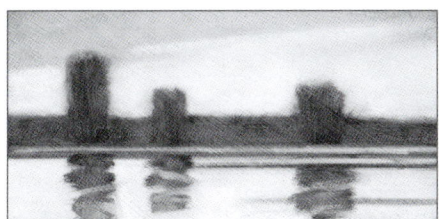

One way to counteract excess horizontality is with verticals. Each of these wide compositions is anchored to a long horizontal shoreline. On the left, the thin cloud, the reflections in the water, and the shoreline all flow from left to right and back again. It is calm and stable, but without any verticals or diagonals, the composition is static. On the right, larger trees and their reflections form three vertical axes. It is still a relatively calm composition, but it is now more active. The eye can move in different directions.

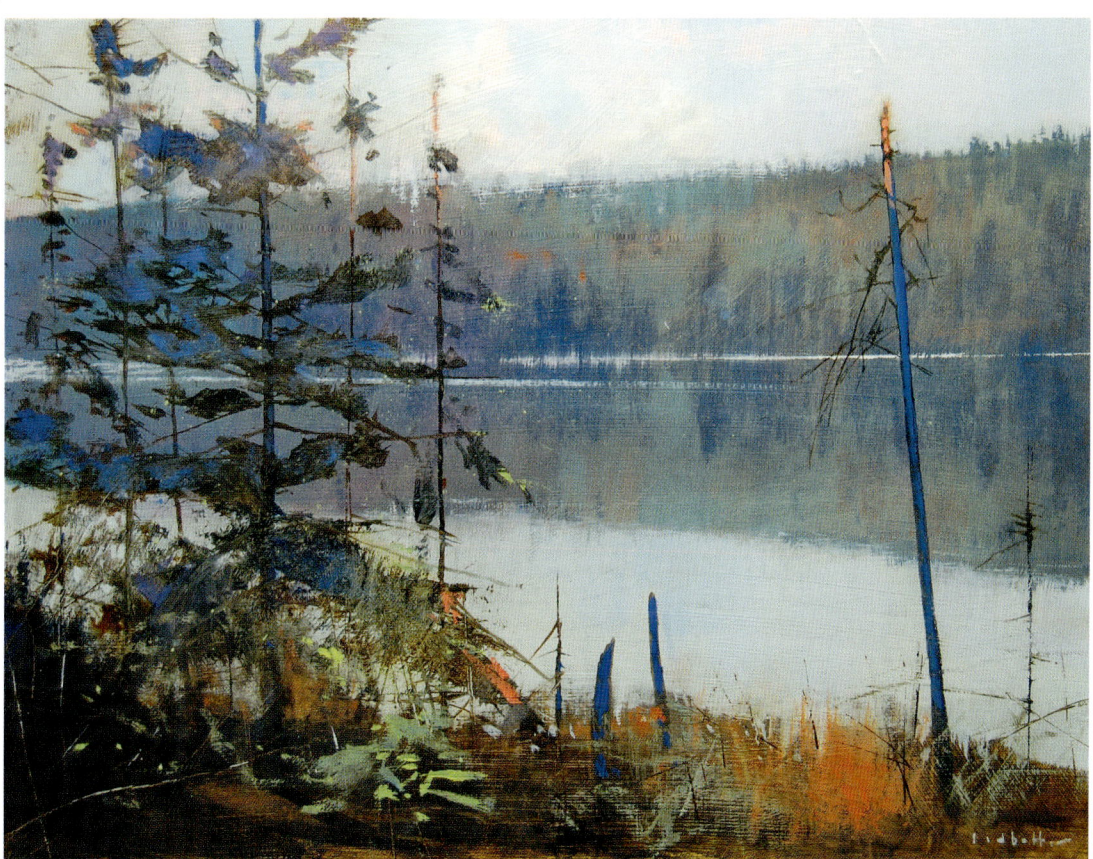

David Lidbetter, *Morning, Brewer Lake*
Oil on panel, 12" × 16" | 30.5 × 40.5 cm

Morning, Brewer Lake is a good example of how a painter can use verticals to counteract the horizontality asserted by the subject and the format. The vertical axes formed by the trees run in opposition to the horizontal axis of the shoreline. Also note the slight deviations from these horizontals and verticals: the tilt of the thin blue tree on the right and the subtle diagonals of the shoreline and foreground. Though shallow, these diagonals add a welcome note of variation to the strict horizontal structure of the composition.

COUNTERING HORIZONTAL MOVEMENT WITH LINEAR PERSPECTIVE

Kim Matthews Wheaton, *The Promise of Abundance*
Oil on canvas, 24" × 48" | 61 × 122 cm

Matthews Wheaton frequently works with an extended horizontal format. In less skilled hands, this format could be a recipe for excess horizontality. However, she provides a dramatic counterpoint to both the format and the many horizontal lines of the subject. Like an arrow, a vast green field pierces the horizontal space in dramatic perspective. Also note how the alternating patterns of light and dark in the fields keep our eye jumping back and forth from one side of the painting to the other.

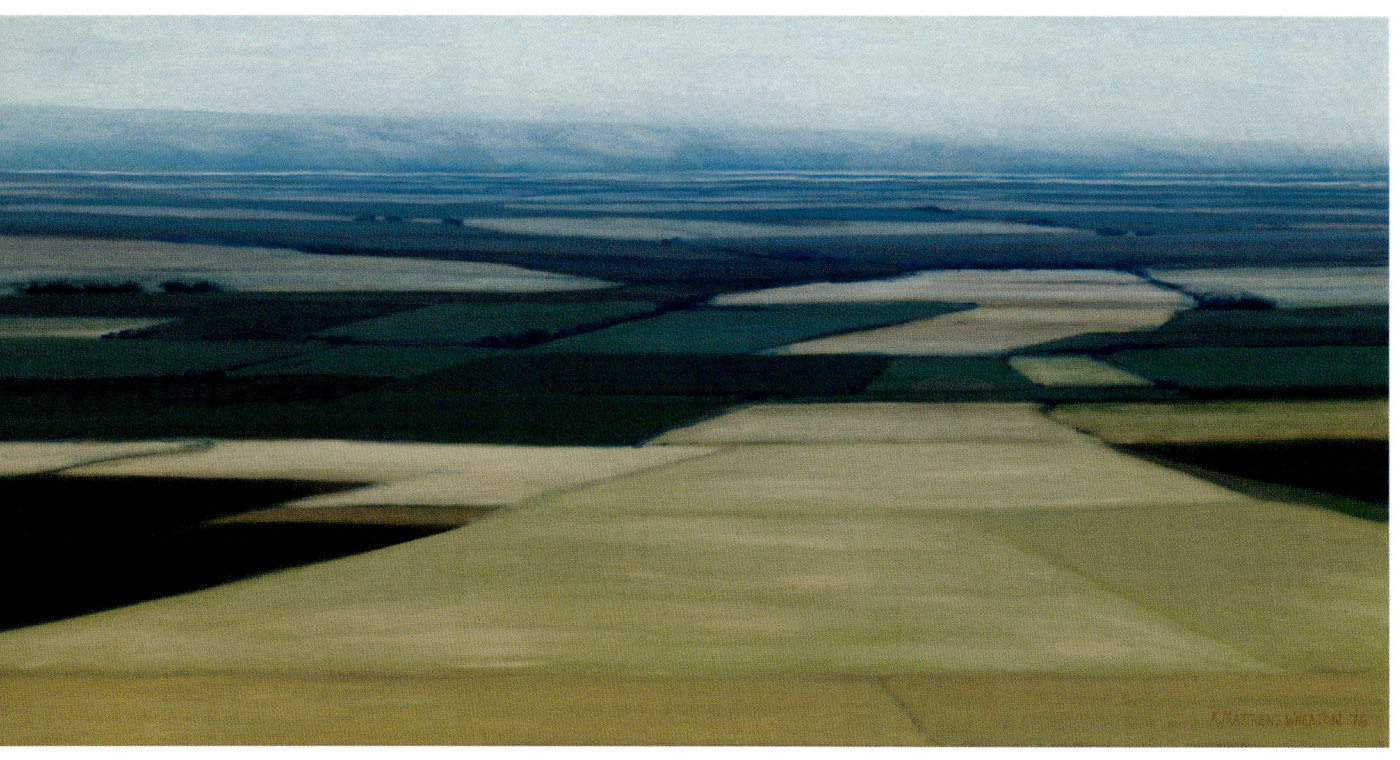

THE VERTICAL FORMAT: INWARD AND UPWARD

Just as the horizontal format reinforces movement along the horizontal axis, the vertical format reinforces movement along the vertical axis. In terms of composition, this translates as *inward and upward* movement—which on a flat picture plane can help suggest depth. This makes the vertical format particularly useful for the landscape painter who might be struggling with a composition that has too much horizontal movement or lacks depth. By positioning the subject within a vertical format, we allow the format to perform some of the depth-inducing work not provided by the subject.

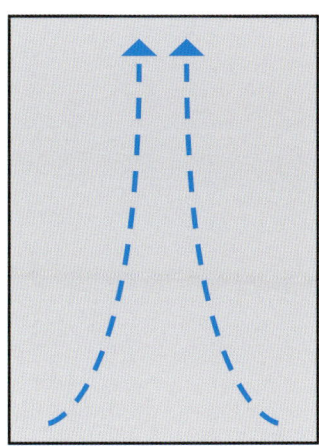

INWARD AND UPWARD

The directional energy imposed by the vertical format is inward and upward. This effect is especially pronounced when the subject has elements of linear perspective.

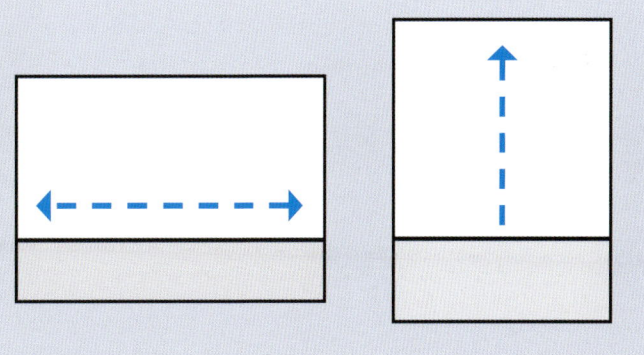

HORIZONTAL AND VERTICAL

A side-by-side comparison of the horizontal and vertical formats demonstrates how they affect movement. When a horizontal ground plane is contained within a horizontal format, the sense of movement along the horizontal is reinforced. When the same ground plane sits within a vertical format, its horizontality is counteracted by the verticality of the format and movement is redirected upward.

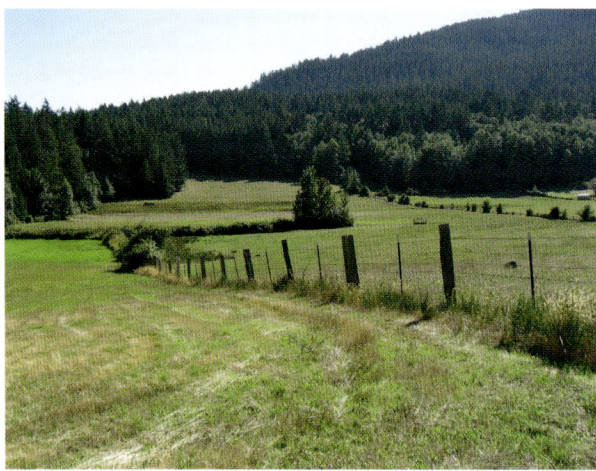

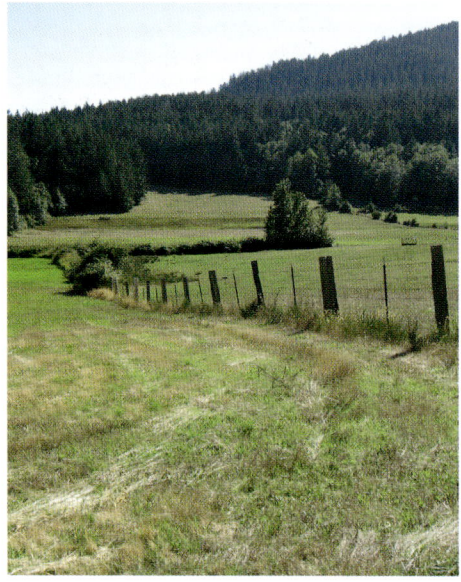

The main event in this subject is the ground lines and fence sweeping back in perspective. This is evident in both the vertical and horizontal formats. In the vertical, however, the sense of depth is heightened. It's as if the vertical sides of the picture squeeze the subject inward and push it upward. This action of the vertical format is particularly heightened in subjects that have a lot of linear perspective.

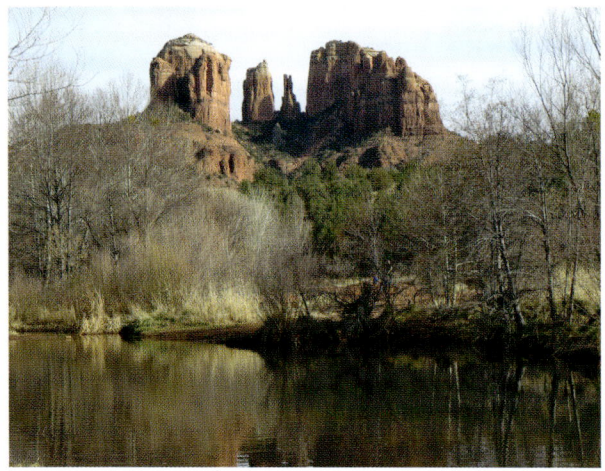

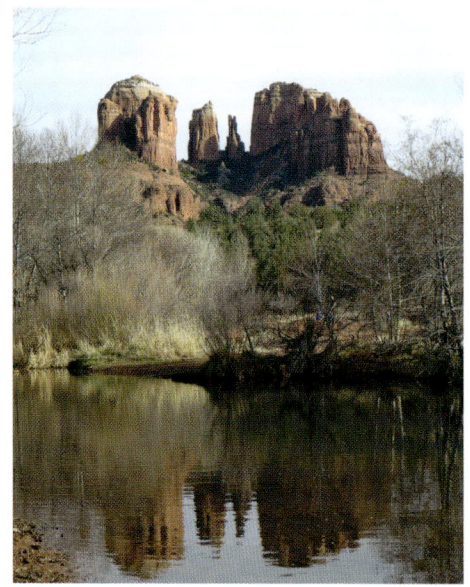

The focus of this subject is the formation of red rocks towering in the distance. In the horizontal format, we feel their upward thrust, but that feeling gets diluted because most of the directional energy is from left to right. In the vertical format, horizontal movement is curtailed. The eye is pulled inward and upward, increasing the sense of height in the rocks.

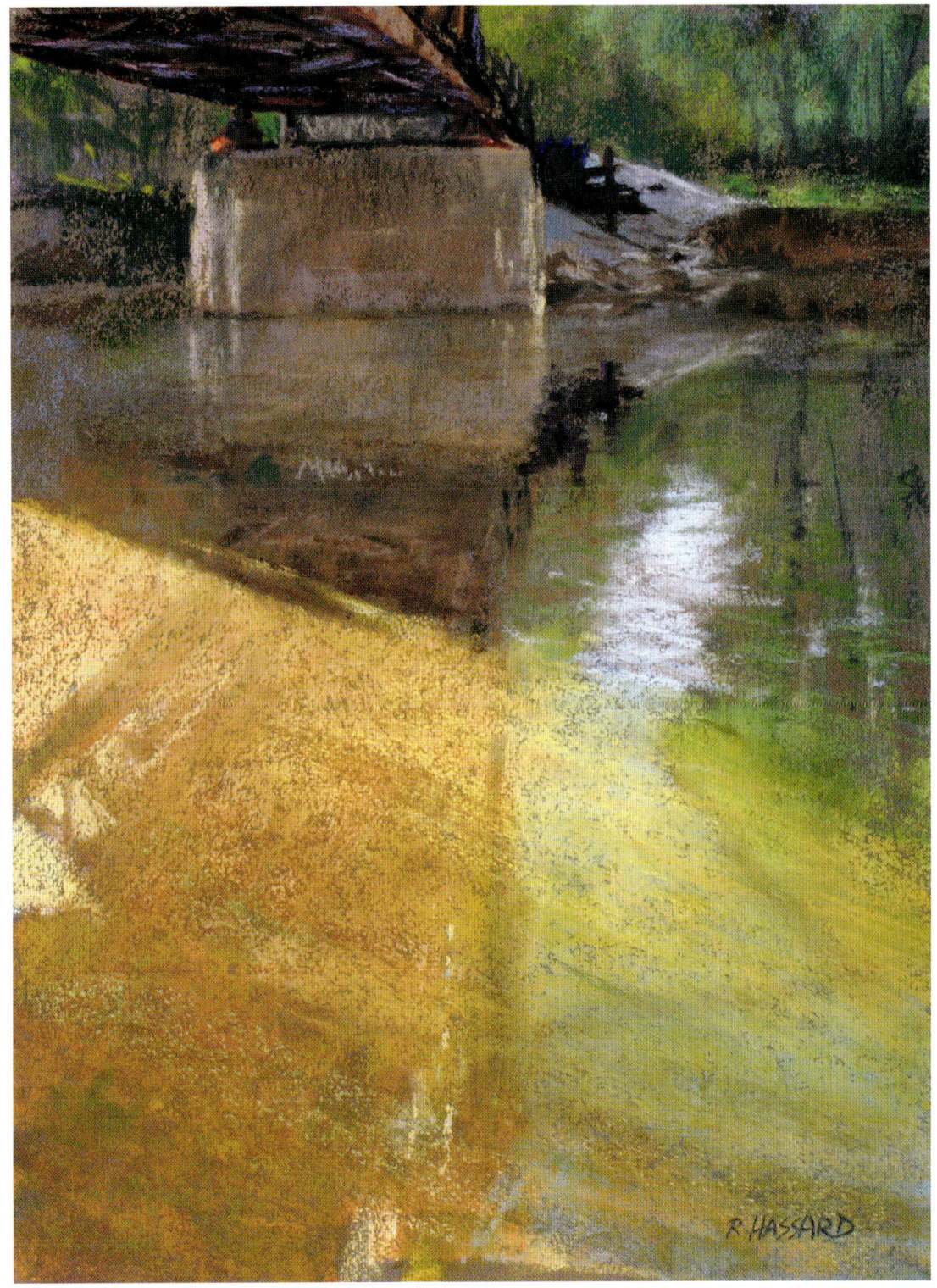

Ray Hassard, *Flood of Light*
Pastel on sanded panel, 16" × 12" | 40.5 × 30.5 cm

In *Flood of Light*, Hassard uses a series of diagonals and lines of perspective to create a strong sense of depth. The broad yellow plane of light (which occupies more than half the area of the painting), draws us sharply into the space. Note the subtle lines of perspective Hassard adds to that area. Then, by placing his composition within a vertical format, which lends inward and upward movement to the subject, he further reinforces the illusion of depth.

THE SQUARE FORMAT: CONTAINMENT

If the landscape format reinforces horizontal movement and the vertical format suggests inward and upward movement, then what does the square format do? As you might expect, it does neither. It exerts a uniform pressure on all sides and so lends no directional energy of its own to the composition. To suggest movement, therefore, a painter must rely entirely on the internal elements of the composition.

Scott Gellatly, whose work appears on page 107 and 160, says, "The allure of the square is its neutrality. It does not come with preconceived notions of the restful horizontal or the upward thrust of the vertical format. The square elevates the painting into an object, not just a window. The square format firmly supports the abstract nature of painting."

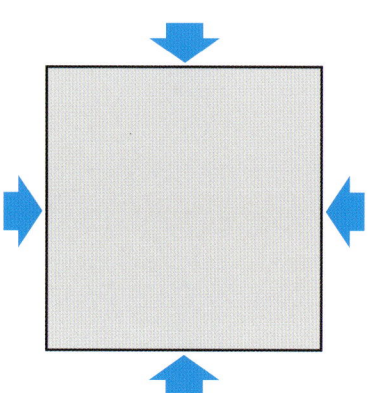

CONTAINMENT

Unlike the horizontal and vertical formats, the square exerts a uniform pressure on all sides. This acts as a force of containment. Movement is focused toward the center and, in some cases, can even be suppressed.

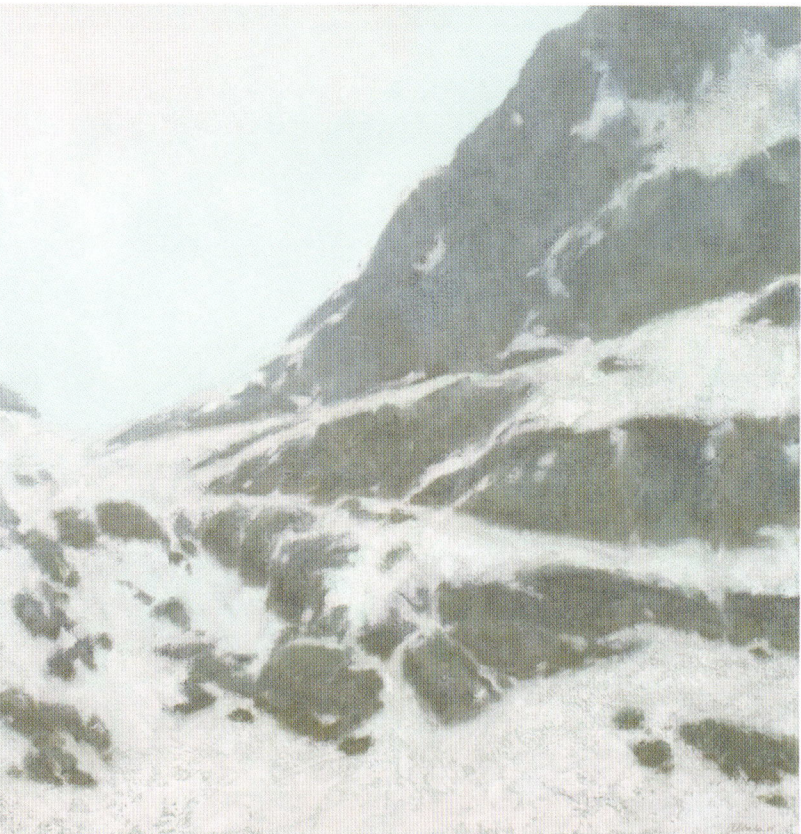

Mitchell Albala,
Upper Ridge in Snow
Oil on panel
18" × 18" | 46 × 46 cm

If this subject had been framed within a horizontal format, there would have been greater movement from left to right. But in a square, the movement created by the patterns of snow and rocks is constrained by the symmetrical confines of the square. The sense of stillness in *Upper Ridge* is, in part, conferred by the square itself.

THE SQUARE FORMAT: INTENTIONAL OR ARBITRARY?

The square format has become increasingly popular in recent decades. Painters are drawn to its balance and symmetry. It's different. The availability of ready-made square panels and canvases has also contributed to its wider usage. Many websites and social media platforms constrain users to square thumbnails, which further standardizes the neat formality of the square.

As appealing as the square may be, it should never be chosen arbitrarily. The painter should always ask, "How does the square format serve my intent for this composition?"

Choosing a square simply because it's available or because you *like* it is not a compelling enough reason. As with any format, the square should be chosen because it supports your compositional intent. Don't force a subject into a square if it will work better in a horizontal or vertical format.

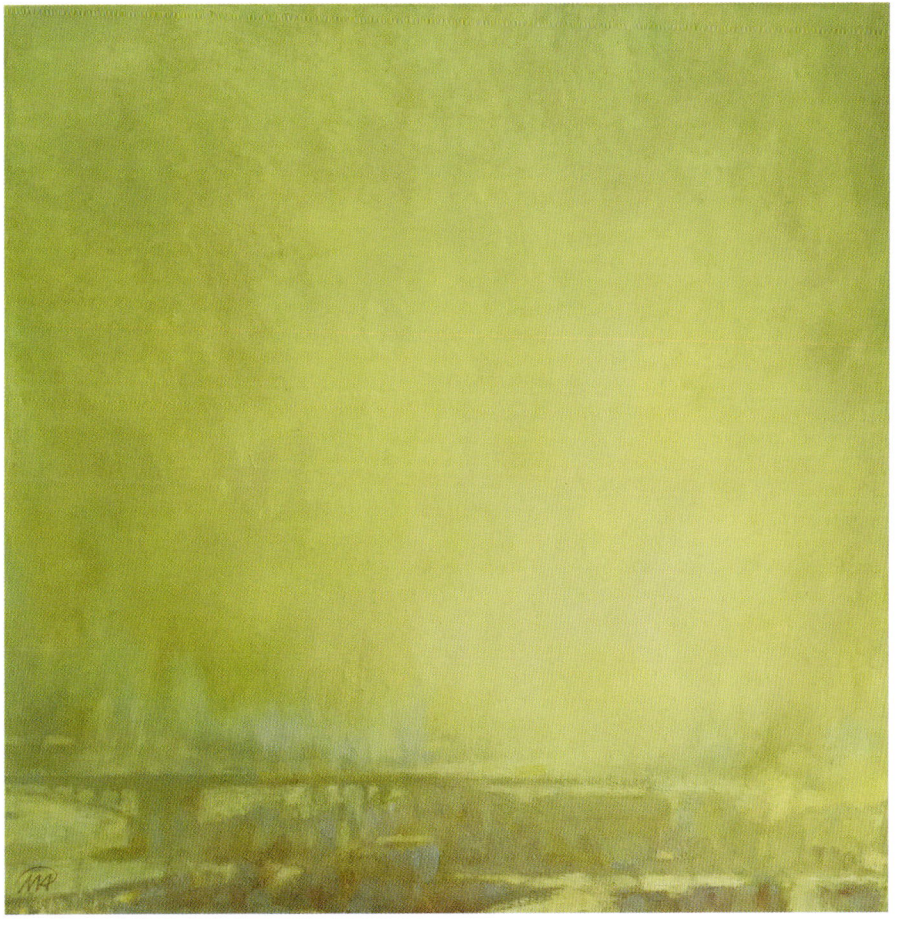

Mitchell Albala, *Ballard Bridge, Under a Golden Light*
Oil on paper
12" × 12" | 30.5 × 30.5 cm

In *Ballard Bridge*, the sky is the main compositional event. The darker tones around the periphery form a circle, drawing our eye toward the center. The square format acts as a force of containment and pulls the eye inward, reinforcing the centeredness of the subject.

If working from a photo, are you accepting its composition as final?

There are many potential compositions hidden within every scene. By working with a limited focus and testing different formats, you can often find better compositions than what was captured in the initial photo. See "Photos: Preparing for Limited Focus" on page 42.

Have you considered other formats besides horizontal?

The horizontal format is the most frequently used, but it isn't ideal for every subject. How would your composition react in a vertical format? A square? Is one better suited to your intent for the composition?

How is movement within the subject affected by the picture format?

Each format has its own directional energy that can work to encourage or suppress movement.

When working within a horizontal format, are there also vertical and/or diagonal lines to counteract the horizontality of the format?

The landscape format exerts strong horizontal directional energy. What compositional elements allow the eye to move in other directions?

Would a vertical format help suggest greater depth?

The vertical format has an inherent ability to suggest inward and upward movement.

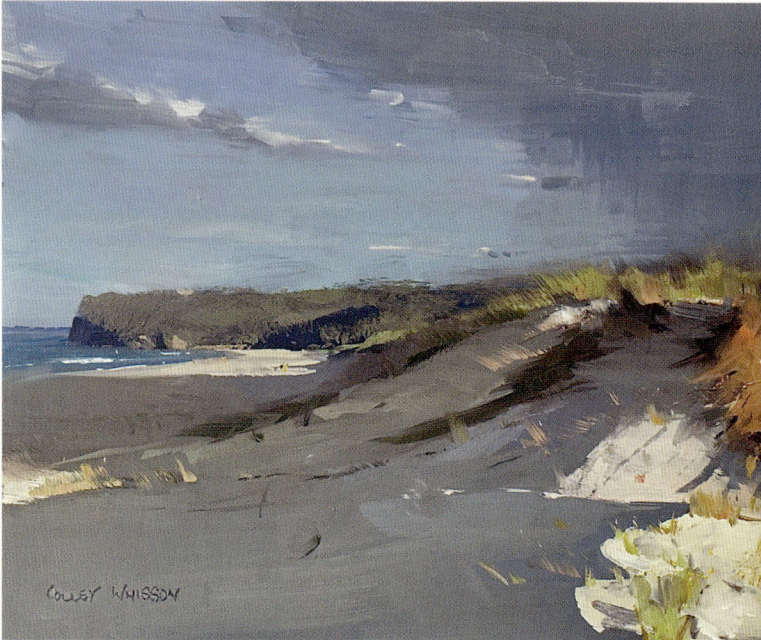

Colley Whisson, *Rain Showers Approaching, Australia*
Oil on panel, 10" × 12" | 25.5 × 30.5 cm

If choosing a square format, have you considered its unique qualities?

The square format has no directional energy of its own. It exerts a uniform pressure on all sides. Does it suppress movement within the composition? If so, would a vertical or horizontal format work better? Don't select a square format arbitrarily.

EXERCISE:
ONE SUBJECT, DIFFERENT FORMATS

OVERVIEW: A seasoned landscape painter may be able to identify a good composition quickly, with a single thumbnail study or one glance through the viewfinder. But most of us will find it revealing to discover that a single subject can often yield many potential compositions. In this exercise, you will develop three compositions from the same subject, in each of the three formats: horizontal, vertical, and square. By developing multiple options, you'll see the effect each format has on the composition, allowing you to select the one that works best.

MATERIALS: Reference photo | Tracing paper | Soft 2B to 6B pencil or markers | Tape | L-shaped cropping tool

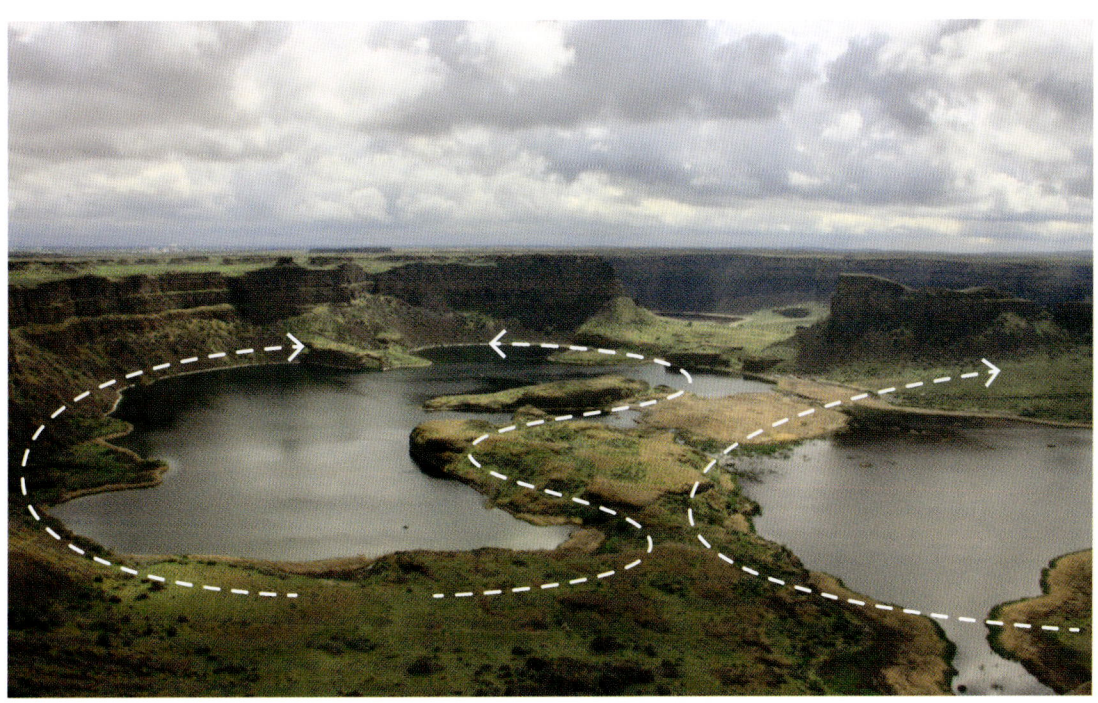

STEP 1: SUBJECT SELECTION

Don't choose a "postcard" subject that is already perfectly composed. Choose one that has more real estate than you would typically include in single painting. This will give you more options to explore various compositions. This expansive, wide-angle subject offers many options, indicated by the movement lines.

Photo: Charles Sharpe

TIP

Don't work with overly large photos (8½" × 11" [21.5 × 28 cm]). Using a smaller photo (5" × 7" [13 × 18 cm]) will make for smaller thumbnails, which are quicker and easier.

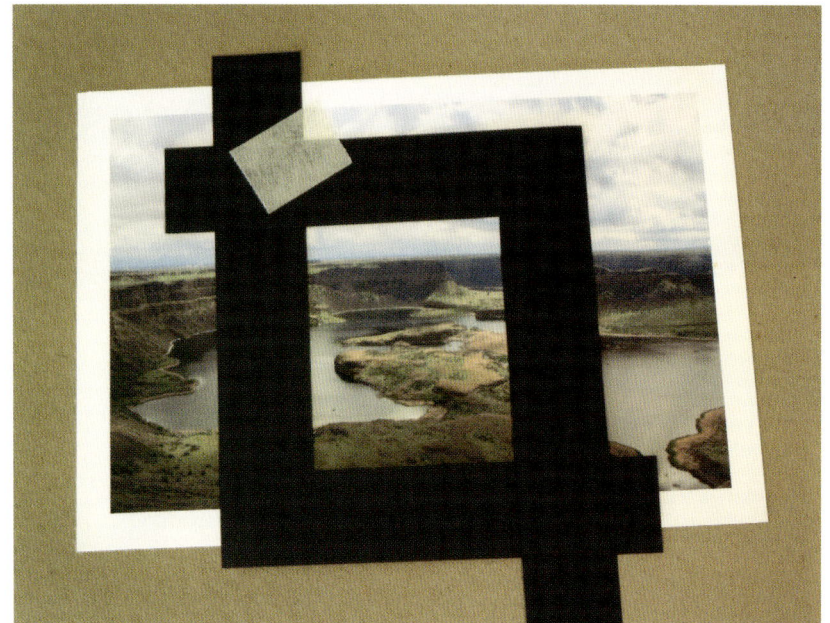

STEP 2: COMPOSING

Place the L-shaped cropping tool over the photo and begin to look for a **vertical** composition. Position the window over different areas of the subject, opening and closing the window. For a better idea of the aspects of composition to look for, see chapter 3. As you explore different compositions, you'll arrive at one that rings true. Tape the cropping device in place.

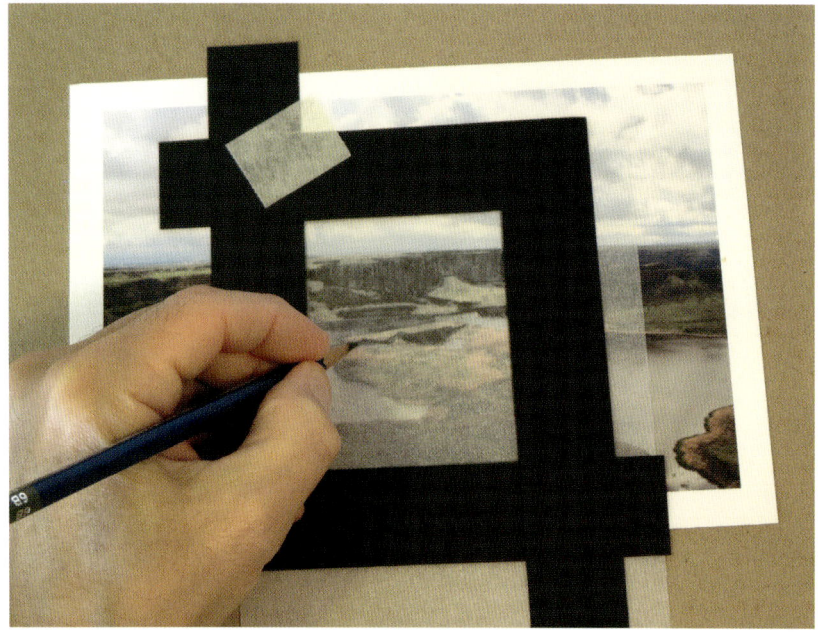

STEP 3: TRACING

Slip a piece of tracing paper beneath the cropping device and then draw the edge of the picture window, defining the format. Then, in a shape-oriented thumbnail style, using pencil or marker, trace the composition. Don't get bogged down in articulating details or every single value. Two or three values are enough to define the main shapes and the broad areas of light and dark. Here, I worked in notan-style thumbnail, using just two values. (For tips on doing thumbnail studies, see "Building a Better Study: Notan Technique" on page 91.)

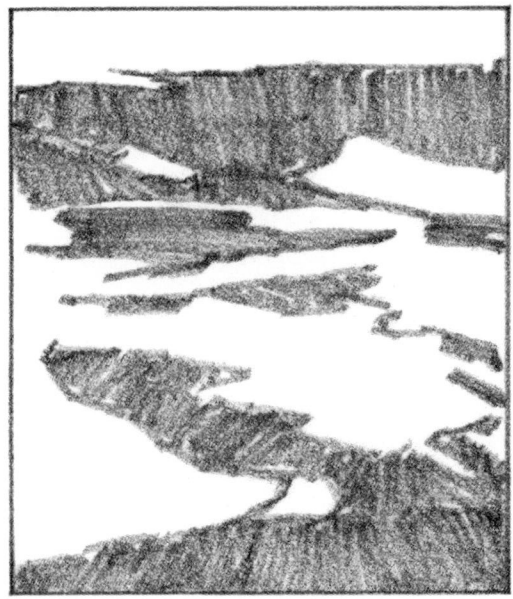

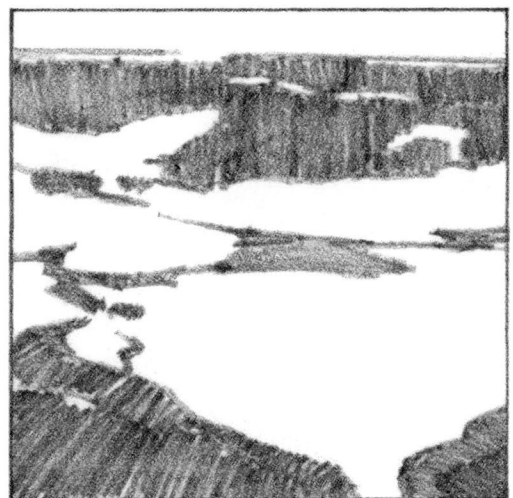

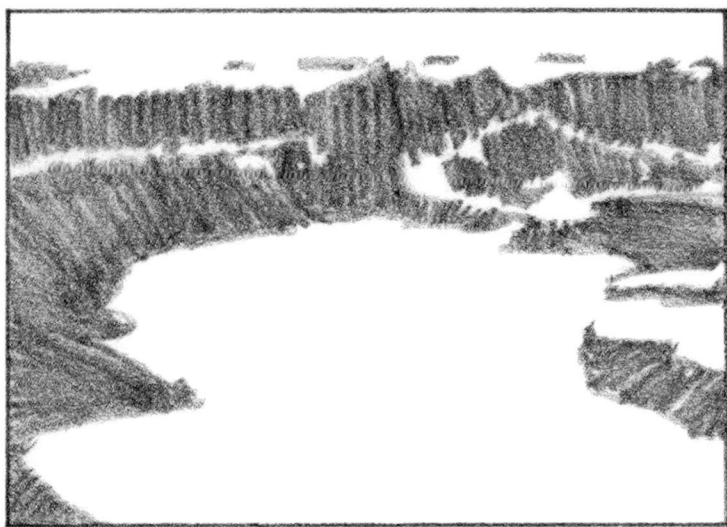

STEP 4: ALL FORMATS

Also do studies in **horizontal** and **square** formats and then evaluate each. How do the different formats affect the composition? Is one stronger? If so, why? The square captures the movement with the downward-pointing triangular shape formed by the water. The horizontal is the simplest of the three and best conveys the distance of the cliffs. The vertical format has a zigzag that draws the eye upward, but it is not as simple as the horizontal and square compositions. All three capture the curvilinear movement and depth found in the original scene, but in different ways.

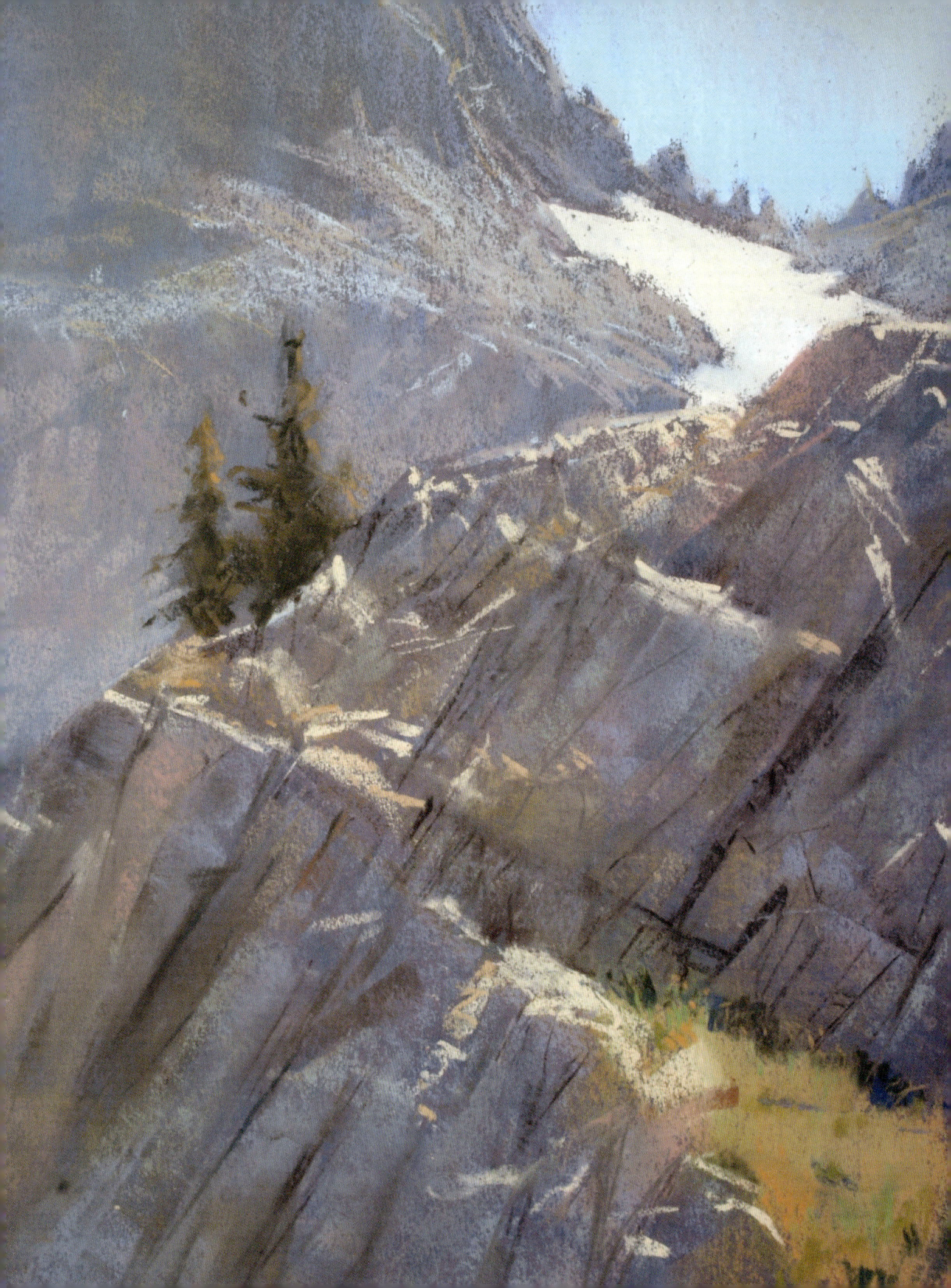

3

COMPOSITION IN ACTION

In the last chapter, we learned about the picture window and how using a limited focus determines what portion of the world will become our subject. Now, we turn our attention toward what goes on *inside* that window. How do the elements we typically associate with a composition—the various parts of the subject—relate to one another? How do they keep a viewer engaged? How do they suggest movement?

For many, composition remains the most elusive area of our practice. This isn't because we can't tell the difference between good and bad composition. We have an innate sensibility that allows us to do that. The problem is that we haven't trained ourselves to approach each aspect of composition as an inquiry. When we do, we inevitably find the answers we seek. In this chapter, we will cover three main areas of compositional inquiry: variation and differences, movement, and active negative space.

◄ Bill Cone, *Looking Up*
Pastel on paper, 12" × 9" | 30.5 × 23 cm

The main goal of composition is to keep the viewer's eye active and engaged. One of the most effective ways of doing this is through movement. In *Looking Up*, a zigzag pathway carries our eye upward. So decisive is this movement, it becomes the main event of the composition.

VARIATION: THE CARDINAL RULE OF COMPOSITION

As in so many aspects of life, the differences are what make it interesting. We are averse to boredom and seek variety wherever we can find it. And so it is with pictorial composition.

There are many aspects of variation, all of which conspire to do the same thing: *keep the viewer's eye active and engaged.* Without adequate variation, viewers can lose interest very quickly. They instinctively know the difference between a composition that speaks in a monotone and one that varies its pitch and volume.

If there is a cardinal rule of composition, it is this: variation and differences keep a composition alive and interesting.

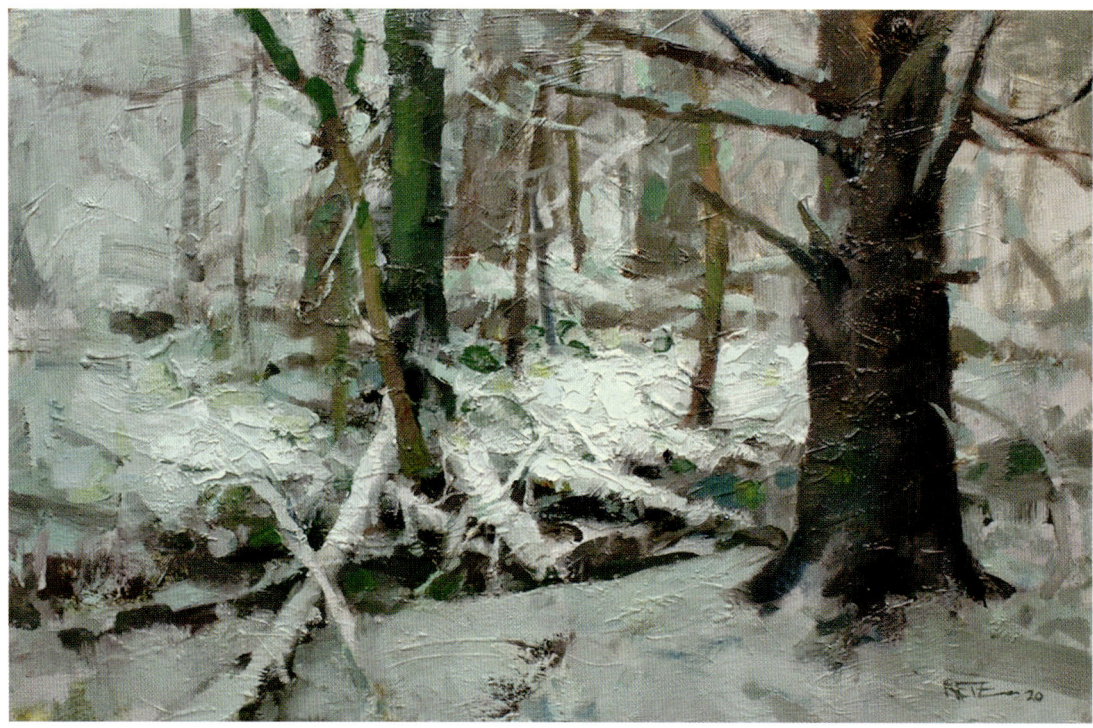

Tad Retz, *Light Covering*
Oil on board, 12" × 18" | 30.5 × 46 cm

The aspects of variation in the "forest" thumbnails on the next page come to life in this painting by Tad Retz. In this forest, every aspect of variation is at play. There are marked differences in the thickness (visual weight) of the trunks and limbs. There are differences in the angles of the limbs, including the downed trees in the foreground. There are differences in the heights of the trees and the intervals between them. And there are differences in color and value. Some trees are very dark, some medium value, and others as light as the snow.

ASPECTS OF VARIATION

The more aspects of variation that are at work within a composition, the more engaging the composition will be. In this sequence of thumbnails of a group of trees, the composition becomes progressively more interesting as aspects of variation are added.

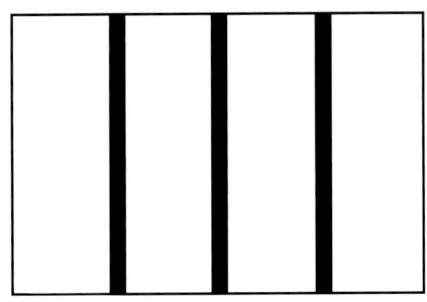

NO VARIATION

In the first sequence, everything is the same. The spaces in between each bar or tree are the same, as are their thicknesses, angles, and lengths. The result is balanced and symmetrical, but it is a static composition.

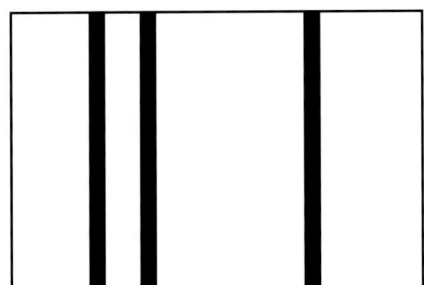

INTERVALS

Intervals are the "spacing and pacing" between elements. Are they the same or do they vary? By varying the intervals, our "forest" becomes slightly less static.

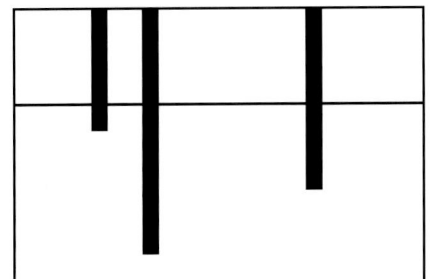

LENGTH AND HEIGHT

By changing the length of the trees and adding a ground plane, the composition begins to suggest depth. Now, there are different intervals and lengths, as well as depth.

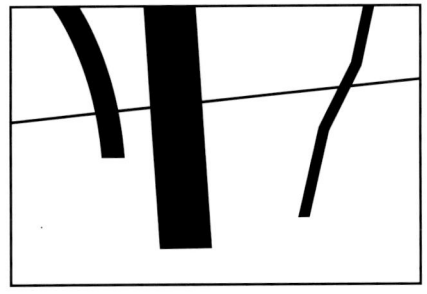

ANGLES AND WEIGHT

Two aspects of variation are added. The thickness (visual weight) of each tree is different. And each element (including the ground plane) is at a different angle. Now, we have variation of intervals, lengths, visual weight, and angles.

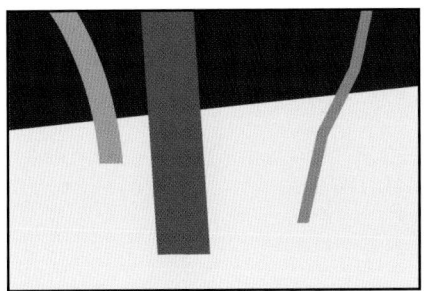

COLOR AND VALUE

In the final sequence, the color of the elements change. Note how the gray and black negative spaces that surround the trees all vary in size and proportion. Variation of intervals, lengths, visual weight, angles, shapes, and color makes for the most interesting composition.

VARIATION IN ACTION

Greg Hargreaves, *Winter Fields*
Acrylic on canvas, 30" × 24" | 76 × 61 cm

Variation and differences are just as important in an abstract landscape painting as they are in a representational one. The biggest aspect of variation in *Winter Fields* is the different amount of area allocated to the lights and the darks. A lot more area is allocated to the lighter color. The darker bands at the top are made up of a patchwork of irregularly sized shapes. They flow roughly from left to right, but they also shift vertically. The bottom half is one large zone, but it is far from empty. It is divided into four smaller shapes, each one a different size. (See "Active Negative Space" on page 70.)

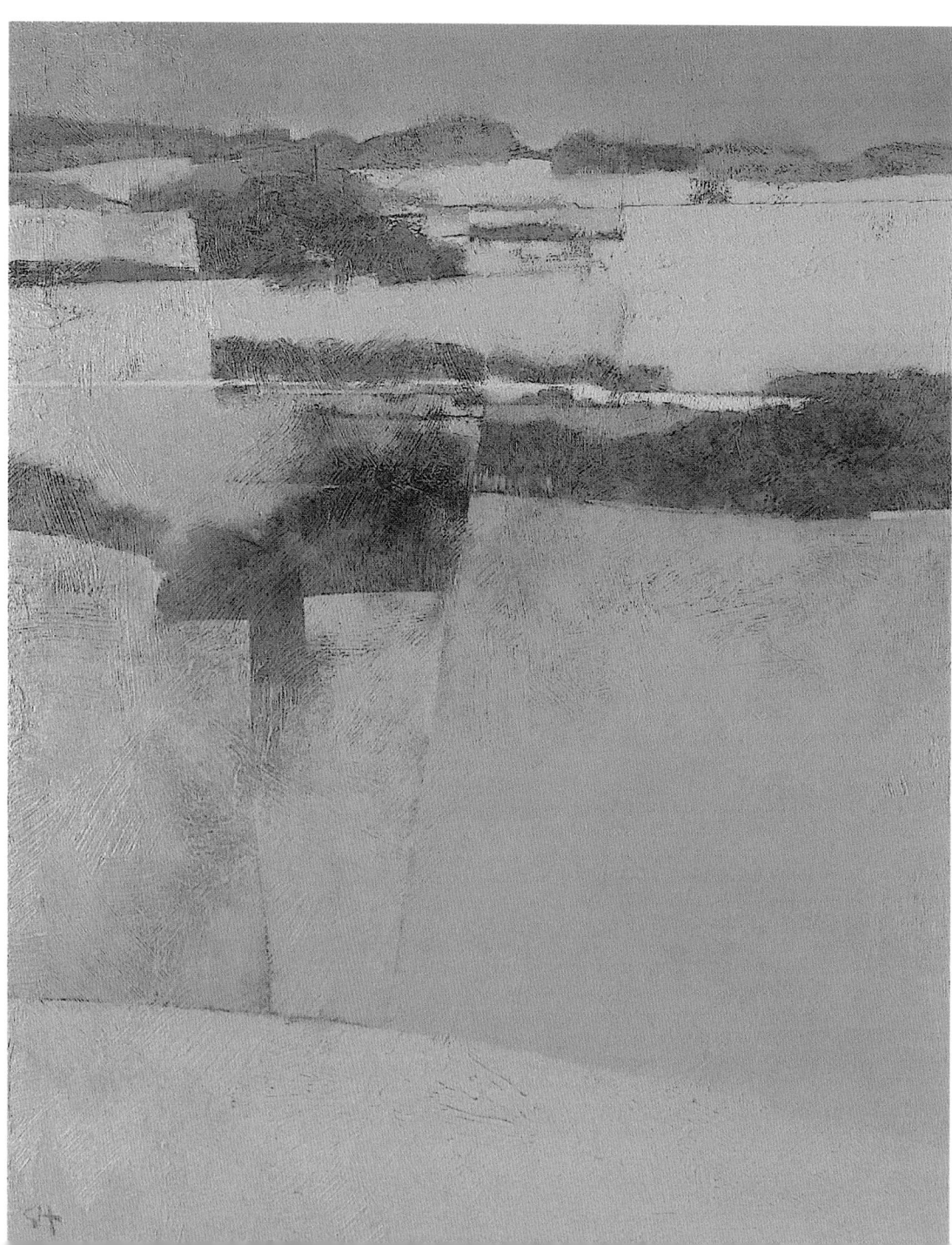

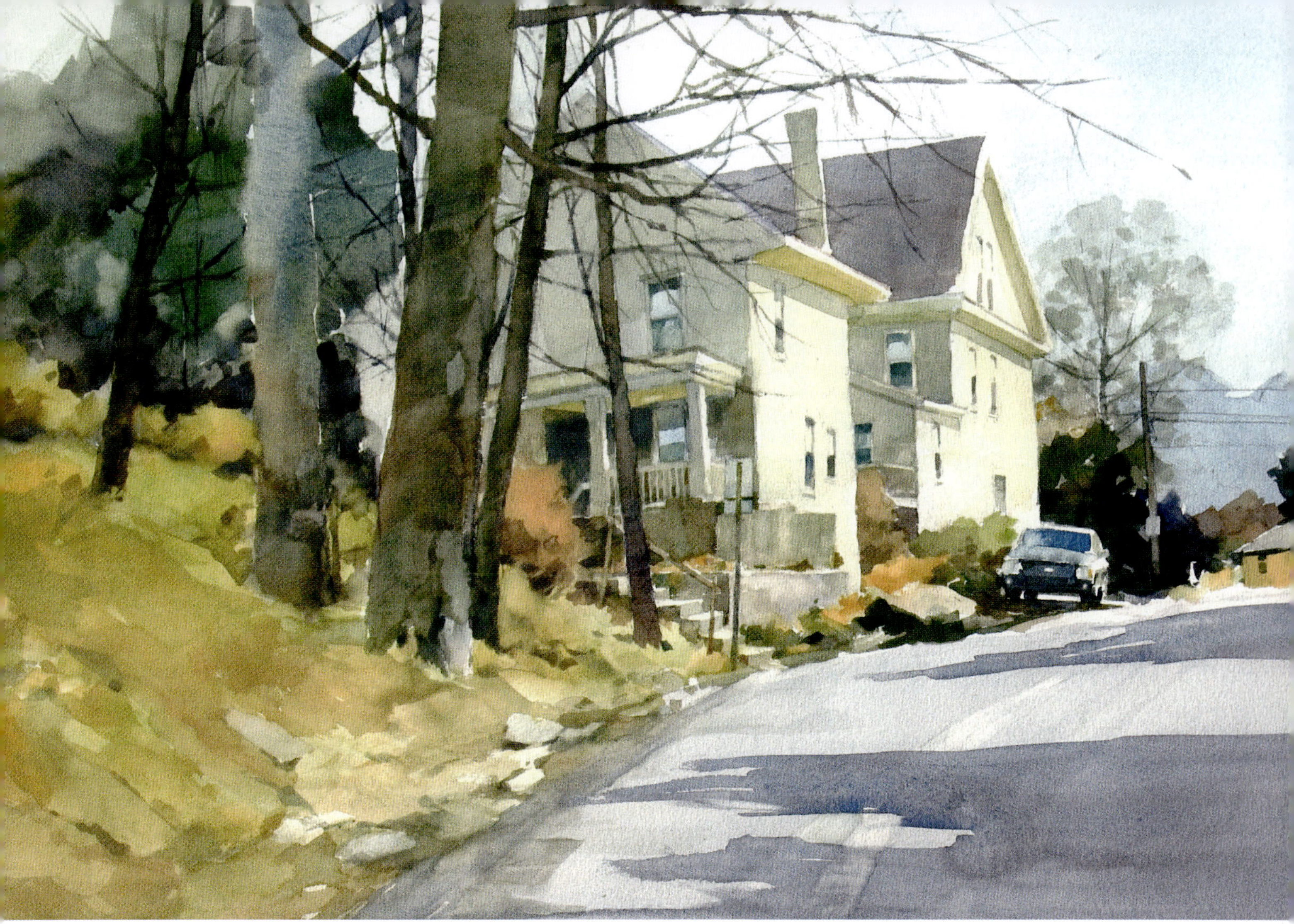

Bill Vrscak, *Mostly Sunny, High 76*
Watercolor, 17" × 23" | 43 × 58.5 cm

Variation and differences abound in Vrscak's beautifully executed composition. One aspect of variation in *Mostly Sunny* is in the *type* of shapes: irregular organic forms on the left are played against the architectural forms on the right. Shape sizes vary as well : the large shapes of the grassy slope and the street contrast with the smaller shapes of the houses, the car, and the details at the far end of the street. These scale differences set up a sense of near and far. The *amount* of color used is also a form of variation. The yellow-green color group is most dominant in the foreground. A smaller instance appears in front of the houses and finally, there's a tiny dash in the house at the far end of the street.

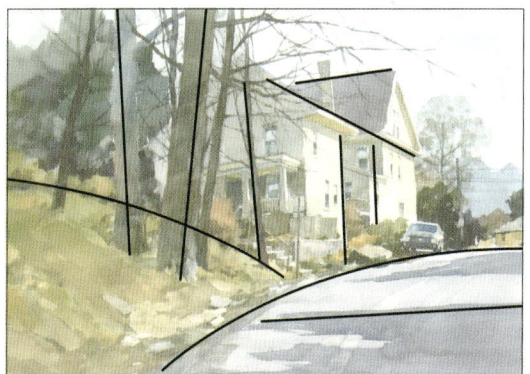

ANGLES

There is a lively interplay of angles in *Mostly Sunny*: the slightly angled trees, the arcing diagonals of the street and the grassy slope, and the diagonal perspective in the houses. The entire scene is offset slightly from the rigid verticals and horizontals of the picture window. Not a single angle in the picture is strictly horizontal or vertical.

DEMONSTRATION:
BALANCING LAND/WATER AND SKY WITH SIZE VARIATION

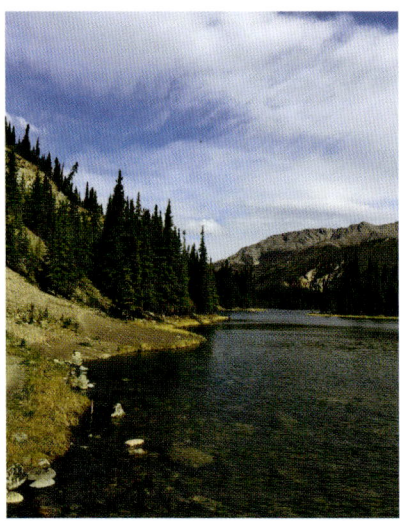

The greatest potential for size variation in landscape is often found through the difference in the amount of area devoted to the sky and the ground. A subject like this, with well-differentiated shapes and dramatic content, can easily convince us that a composition is fully resolved. However, in the original photo, the major areas of the picture compete for attention. Will the painting be about the water? The sky? Or the middle ground trees and hills? A lack of variation leads to a lack of focus. A painting, of course, can have several foci, *but one must have priority*.

Photo: Dirk Greeley

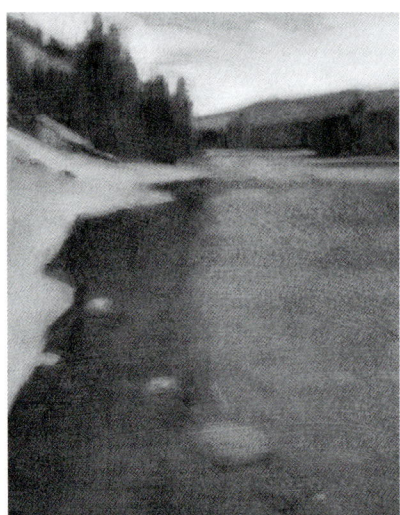

LAND/WATER-DOMINANT

In this version, the water occupies about 80 percent of the picture. By focusing on this area, we pick up several dynamic points of interest: the linear perspective of the shoreline, the arc of the shadow in the water, and the implied movement along the rocks.

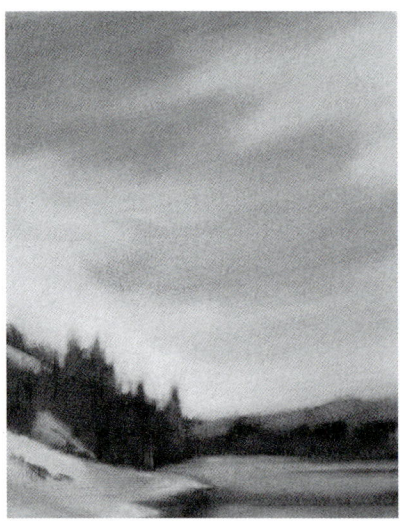

SKY-DOMINANT

In this version, the sky is the main event. The large difference in size between the sky and the water lends a dynamic tension to the composition. When considering the relative size of the sky and the land or water, always look to make one noticeably larger than the other.

MOVEMENT: ANIMATING THE COMPOSITION

Movement is what animates a composition and brings it to life. Our eye remains active and engaged as it moves around and through the picture. Only a blank painting surface, absent of any mark or shape, would have no movement at all. But as soon as we add shapes and colors and lines, our eye naturally begins to find pathways and seek connections between elements. Movement in landscape painting may be fast or slow, strong or gentle, steady or halting, but it is always desirable.

Almost anything within the picture may be used to suggest movement. The most common generators of movement are lines, the visible pathways that fall along the edges of picture elements.

Our eye glides along the mountain's edge or follows the arc of a tree limb. It follows the bend of the river or flies up a rock face. This is called *direct* movement. Less obvious, but of equal importance, is *implied* movement. Implied movement doesn't follow visible contours or edges, but is created as the eye makes connections between different spots within the picture, in a connect-the-dots fashion.

One criteria for selecting a subject is whether it suggests enough movement. Some subjects have obvious pathways of movement. All we need to do is make sure we include them in our composition. Other subjects suggest less movement. We may choose to reject that subject, or perhaps we can amplify the movement by slightly shifting elements around or modifying colors and values to accentuate an edge or contour.

FOCAL POINT VS. MOVEMENT

One of the pithy rules of composition says that every painting should have a focal point, one area that is the primary focus. Yet that would seem to contradict the idea of movement, which says that our eye should move around the picture, never stopping or resting in one spot for too long. However, a painting can have a focal point *and* movement as long as the focal point doesn't hold the eye in one place and prevent it from traveling elsewhere. Instead, it is a spot that we can travel from and return to repeatedly, as our eye moves around the painting.

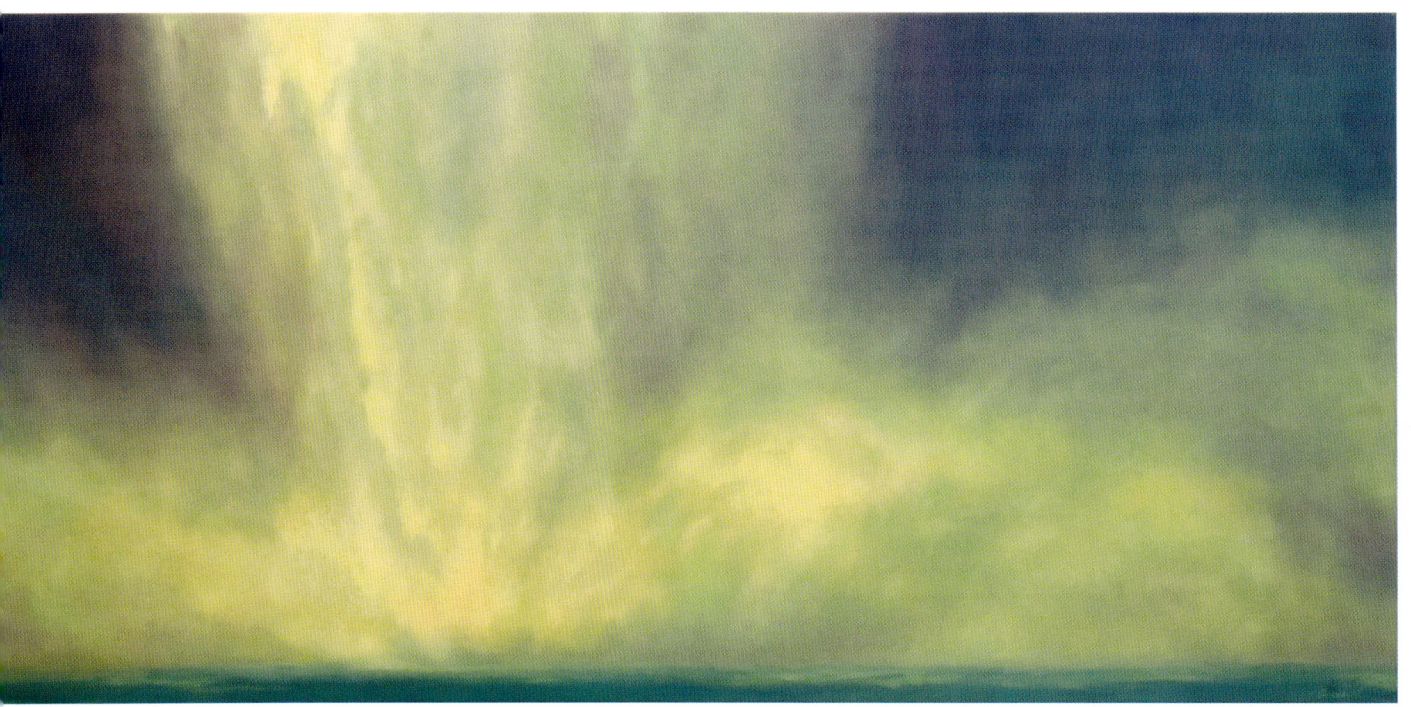

Mitchell Albala, *Cascadia*
Oil on canvas, 20" × 42" | 51 × 107 cm

The movement in *Cascadia* flows in two directions: vertically, through the downward thrust of the waterfall; and horizontally, as the water expands outward to the left and right. The vertical column of water serves as a counterpoint to the extended horizontality of the format. While movement often flows along hard edges or lines, in *Cascadia*, there are only soft edges. The lines in the diagram don't correspond to hard edges, but indicate the direction in which the water flows.

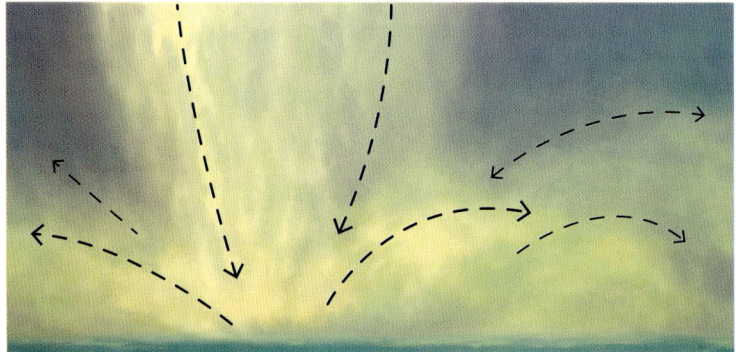

INTO THE THIRD DIMENSION:
DIAGONALS AND LINEAR PERSPECTIVE

As we learned in chapter 2, horizontal lines carry the eye from left to right. Vertical lines carry our eye up and down. And the built-in horizontal or vertical thrust of the picture format reinforces these movements. These are essential directional energies in composition—but they only move us in two dimensions.

To experience a full range of movement within a picture, we also need *diagonals*. In a flat two-dimensional picture, diagonals break away from the rigid horizontality and verticality of the picture window itself and allow us to move at any angle, in any direction. We would be hard put to achieve dynamic movement in our pictures without diagonals.

Diagonals also form lines of perspective. The technique is the single most powerful way to foster the illusion of depth, to lead the eye into the third dimension.

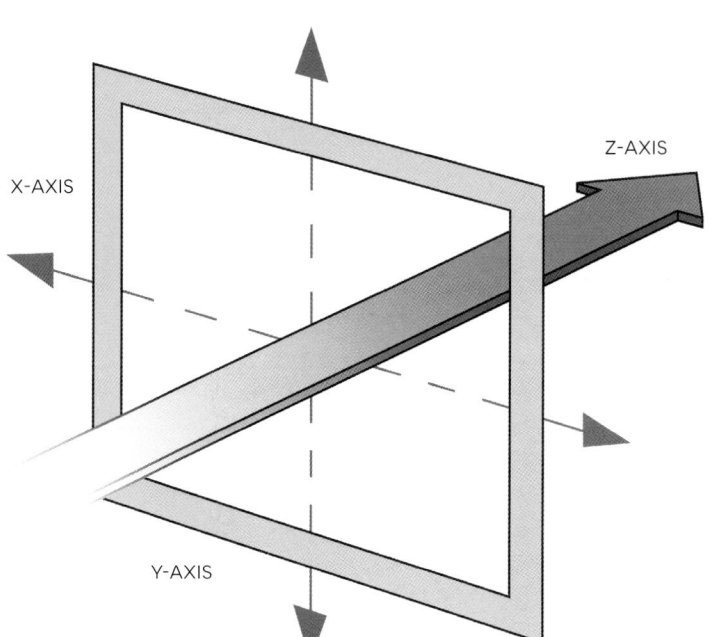

DIAGONALS AND THE Z-AXIS

A painting is flat and two-dimensional, so any suggestion of depth is always an illusion. We can imply movement into the third dimension with diagonals and linear perspective. In geometry, the X-axis represents the horizontal, and the Y-axis represents the vertical. They define movement in two dimensions. The Z-axis—corresponding to lines of perspective in our paintings—passes *through* the flat picture plane defined by the X- and Y-axes and carries the eye into the imaginary third dimension.

DEPTH THROUGH LINEAR PERSPECTIVE

David Lidbetter, *Trickle Down*
Oil on panel, 12" × 9" | 30.5 × 23 cm

Nothing counteracts the flatness of the two-dimensional picture plane and suggests depth more effectively than linear perspective. Starting in the lower-right corner, Lidbetter pulls us sharply into the space with the steep perspective of the stream. The depth suggested through the linear perspective is also reinforced by the vertical picture format, which lends an inward and upward movement to the composition.

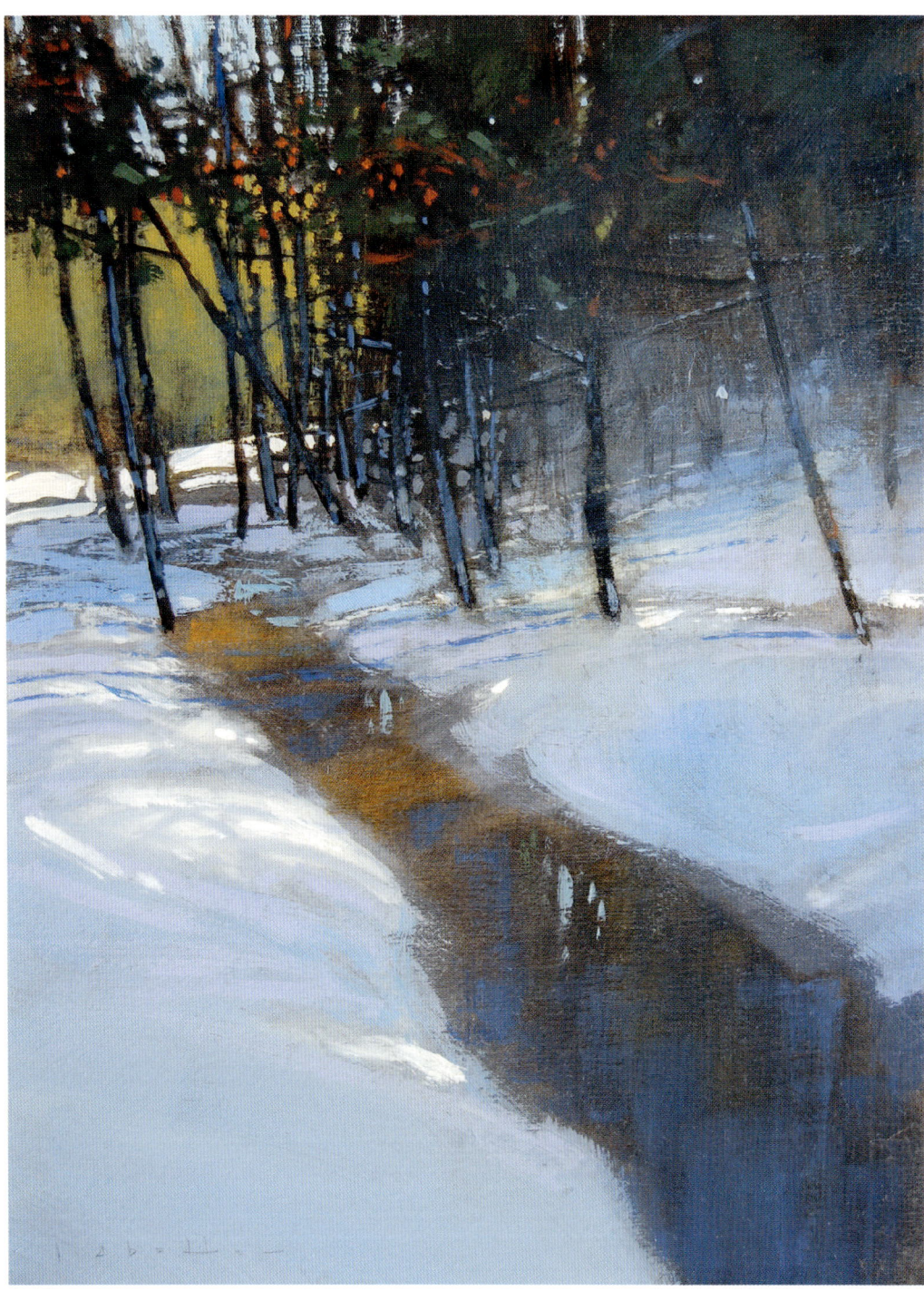

MOVEMENT THROUGH DIAGONALS

Cindy Baron, *Spring Passage*
Watercolor, 15" × 9½" | 38 × 24 cm

Linear perspective is achieved with diagonal lines, but not all diagonals create linear perspective. In Baron's majestic piece, we find a series of diagonals that, through multiple pathways, carry our eye to the uppermost peaks. In combination with the extended vertical format, Baron achieves a strong upward movement. Other than the tiny trees at the bottom, there is not a single horizontal or vertical line in the painting or even a horizon line.

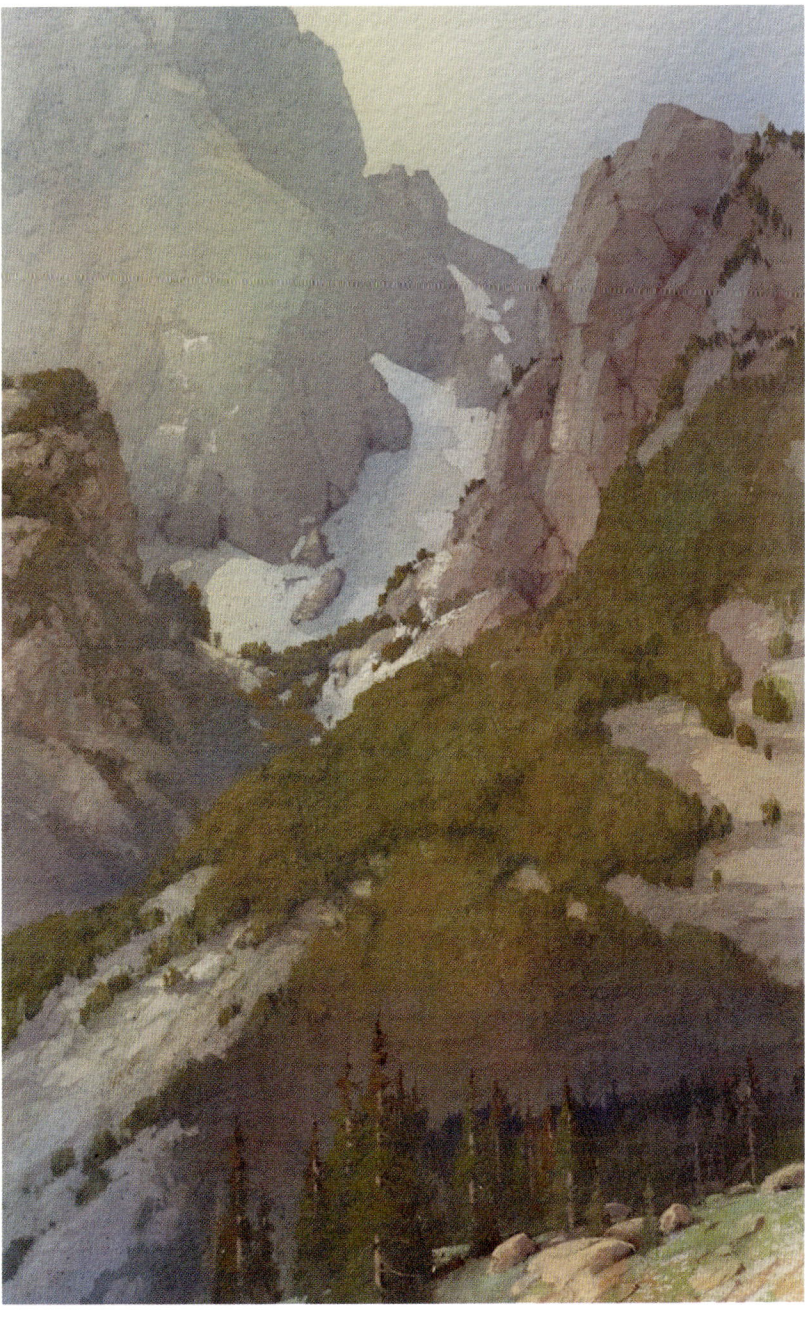

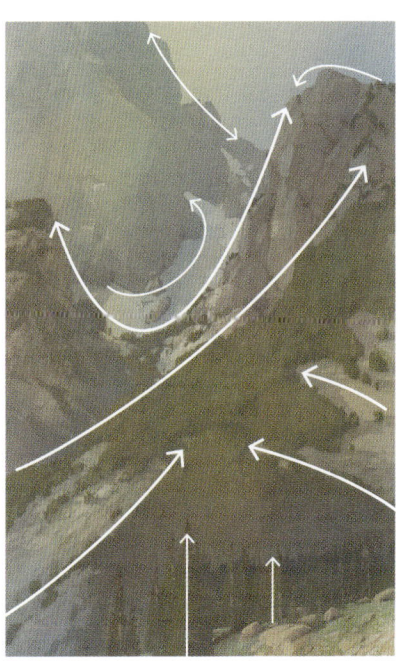

DIRECT AND IMPLIED MOVEMENT

Mitchell Albala, *Pathway to the Canal*
Pastel on paper, 5" × 8" | 13 × 20.5 cm

With *direct* movement, the eye follows a continuous path, such as the contour of a mountaintop or the edge of a road. *Implied* movement, on the other hand, forms an implied connection between two or more points in a connect-the-dots fashion. In *Pathway to the Canal*, the direct pathway is indicated by a solid line. Our eye moves up the vertical street on the right, turns sharply left, up again along a diagonal, and then back toward the right. Implied movements are indicated by the dotted lines. Our eye jumps from rooftop to rooftop until it arrives at the canal in the upper right.

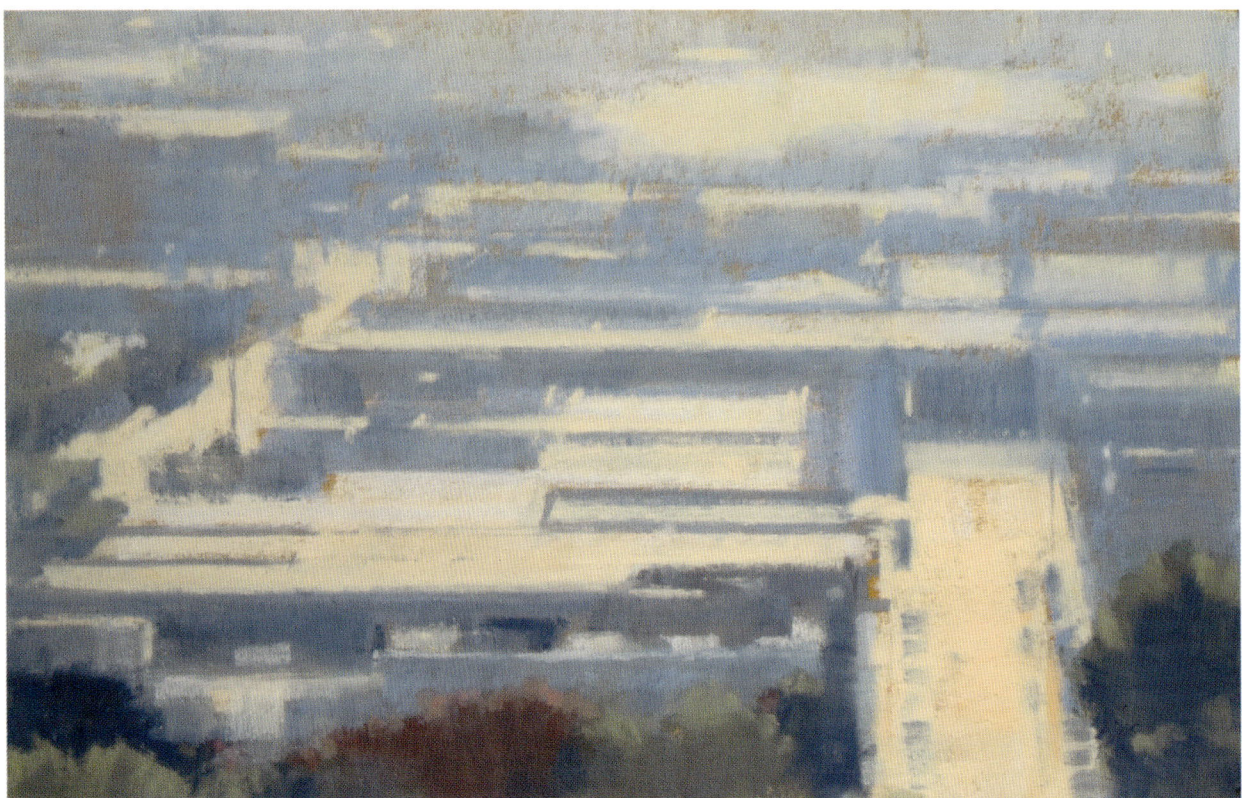

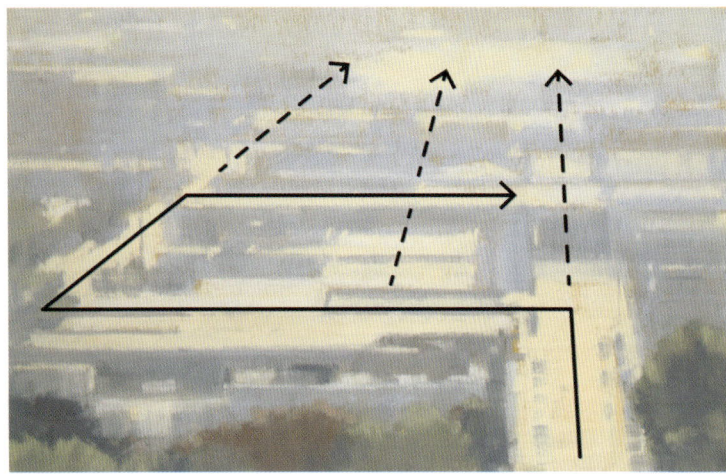

CIRCULAR MOVEMENT

The circle is a tried-and-true compositional armature, in which the eye follows a complete, or nearly complete, path around the painting. Circular movement doesn't have to be an actual circle, however. It may be oval, triangular, or even rectangular, as longs it carries the eye in a full course around the painting. Circular movement keeps the eye contained within the bounds of the composition.

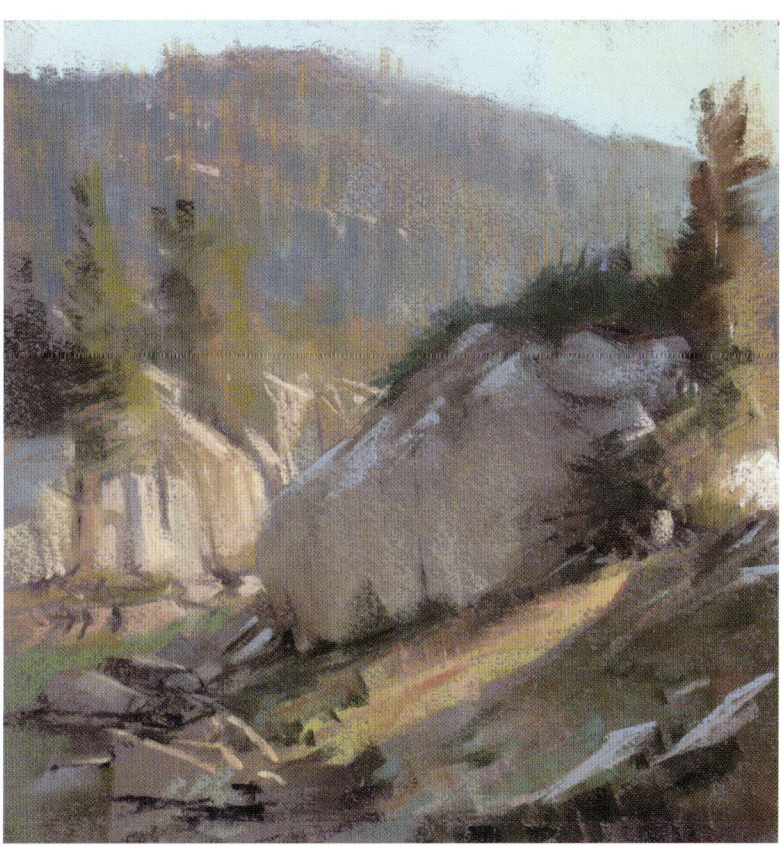

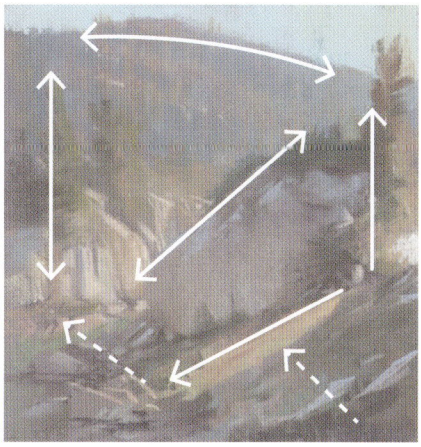

Bill Cone, *Garnet Pond*
Pastel on paper, 9 ³⁄₁₀" × 9" | 23.5 × 23 cm

In *Garnet Pond*, direct pathways are indicated by solid lines: along the mountain ridge, up and down the trees on the sides, and along the slope in the foreground. Together, these pathways form a roughly circular course around the picture. The diagonal across the center connects the upper right and lower left. The implied pathway, indicated by the dotted line, doesn't follow a continuous line or contour, but hops across the rocks in a connect-the-dots fashion.

ACTIVE NEGATIVE SPACE

Negative space is typically defined as the area *in between* or *around* the "positive" elements of a subject. In figurative or still life painting, for instance, the negative space is usually the space *behind* the subject, in the background. In landscape, the sky comes closest to behaving in this way, sitting like a vast backdrop behind all the land-based elements. But, there are other large spaces in landscape composition that behave similarly, such as large bodies of water, fields, or empty streets that advance toward the viewer. These are not negative spaces in the traditional sense—they are "positive" forms—but because they are so large and often uniformly colored that they effectively behave like negative spaces.

If these areas are not properly *activated*— if they are treated like "empty" spaces—they won't feel like a fully integrated part of the composition. We never want one part of the painting to feel separate from any other part. Negative spaces can be activated in several ways:

- Varying the color and/or value within the negative space
- Dividing the negative space into smaller portions (closed negative space)
- Adding spatial cues to the negative space, such as clouds in the sky, furrows in a field, or reflections in the water

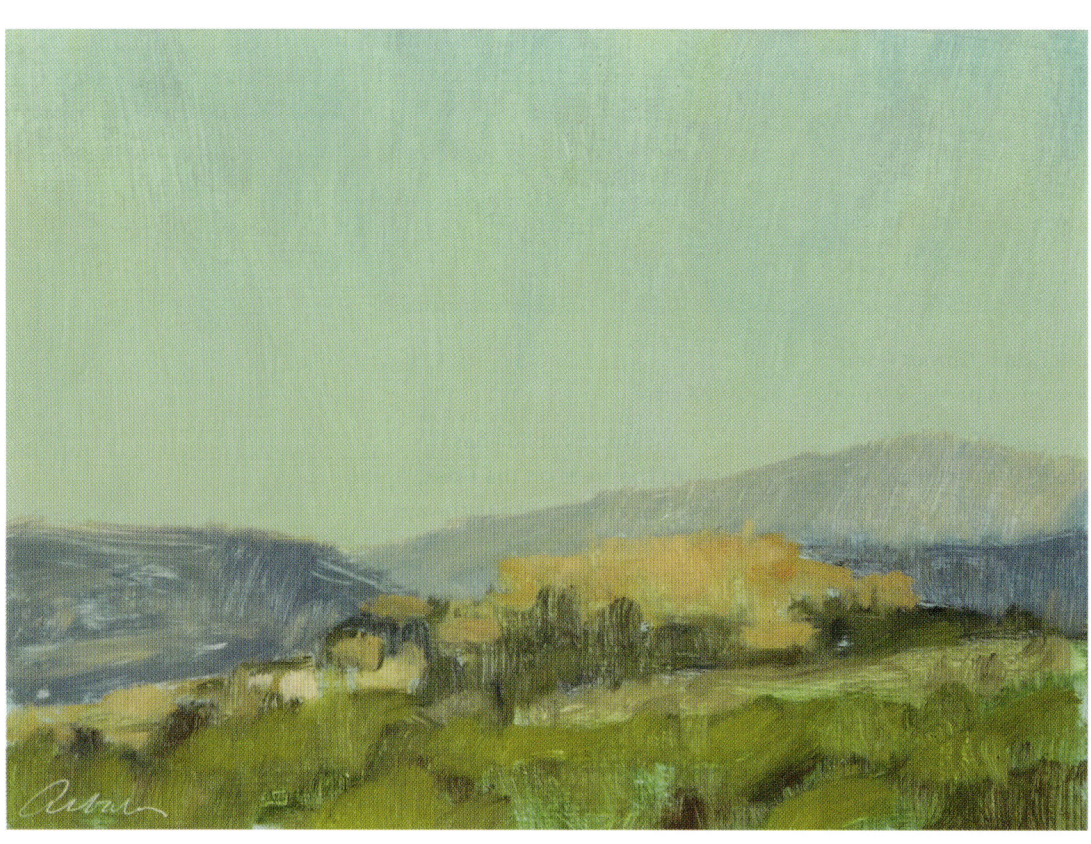

ACTIVATING SKIES WITH COLOR AND TONAL VARIATION

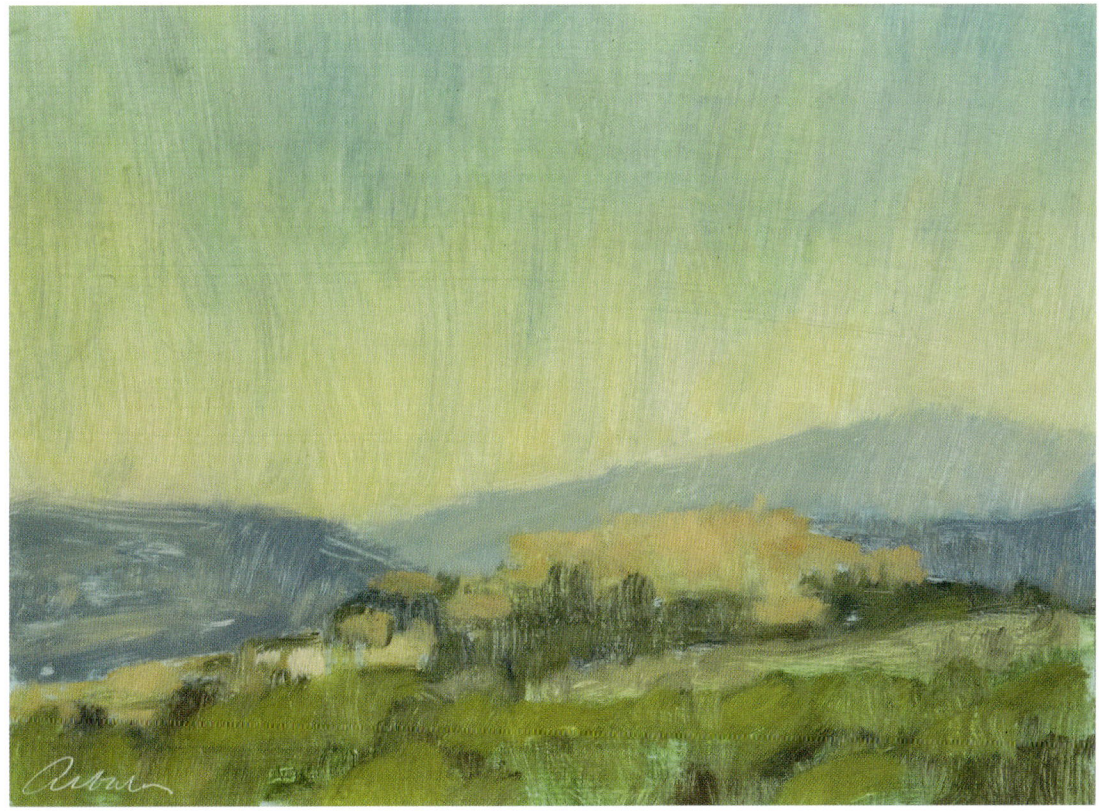

Mitchell Albala, *Montegabbione, Umbria*
Oil on paper, 5" × 7" | 13 × 18 cm

How do we activate a cloudless sky so it becomes more than just an empty blue backdrop? In the original *Montegabbione* painting on the previous page, there is no color or tonal variation in the sky. It is flat and uninteresting. In the improved version, above, the sky has a noticeable shift in hue, temperature, and value. This activates the sky and gives it more dimension and life than the original version. As a general rule of thumb, avoid painting a sky as a flat, unvarying color.

OBSERVE: Color and tonal variation in the sky is not an artistic invention. Skies actually do have these gradations, and we should always look for them. The closer to sunrise or sunset it is, the more apparent they are.

ACTIVATING SKIES WITH CLOSED NEGATIVE SPACE

Alvaro Castagnet, *Montevideo Urban Series*
Watercolor, 40" × 26" | 101.5 × 66 cm

Skies can also be activated by using *closed* negative space. When parts of the subject—such as a tree, a telephone pole, or a rooftop—touch or nearly touch the edge of the painting, it breaks up the negative space into segments. Two or three segments of negative space are more visually interesting than a single space. Here, Castagnet allows the uppermost corner of the building to touch the top edge, dividing the sky into two major segments of different sizes. The telephone lines and street light break up the larger negative space even further.

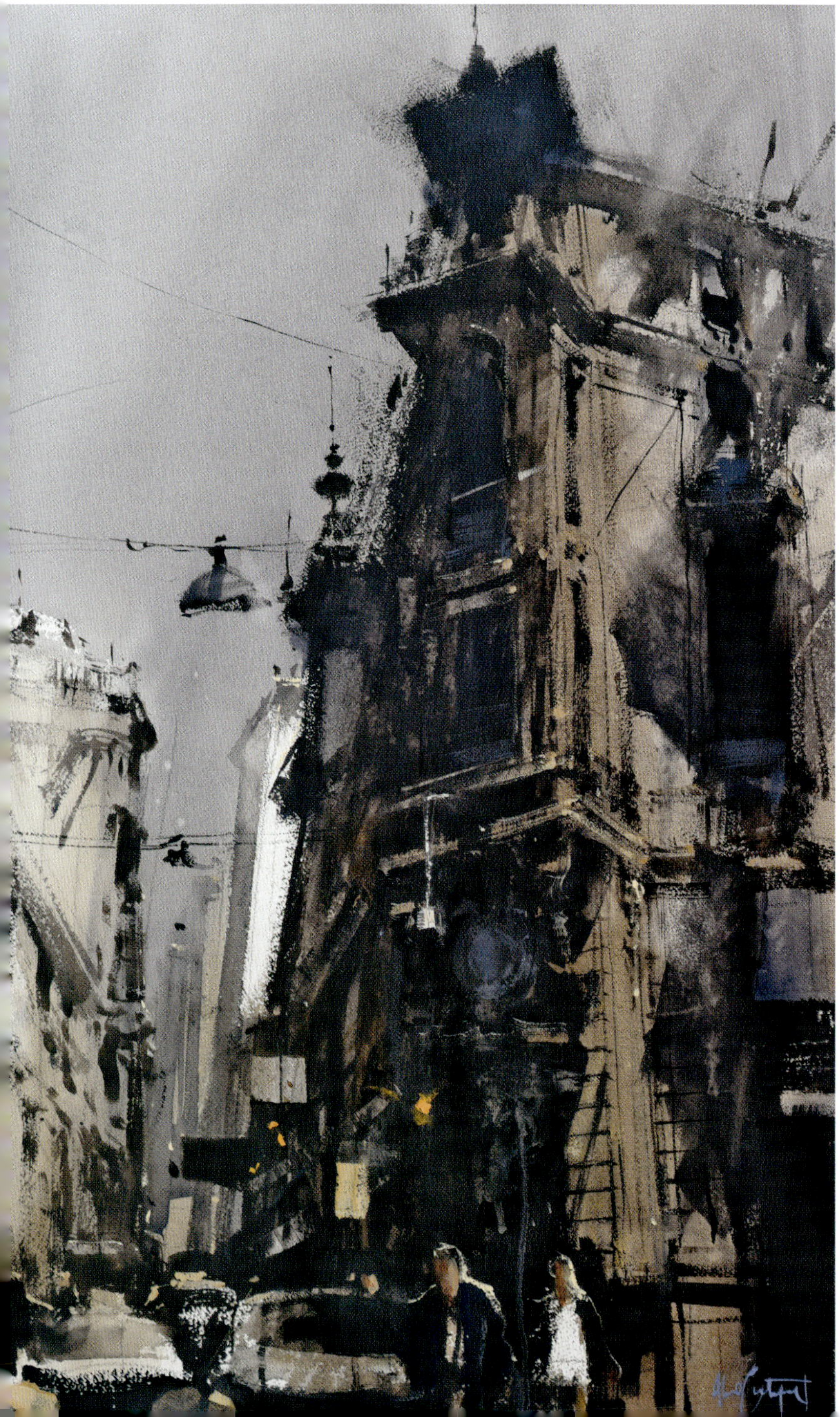

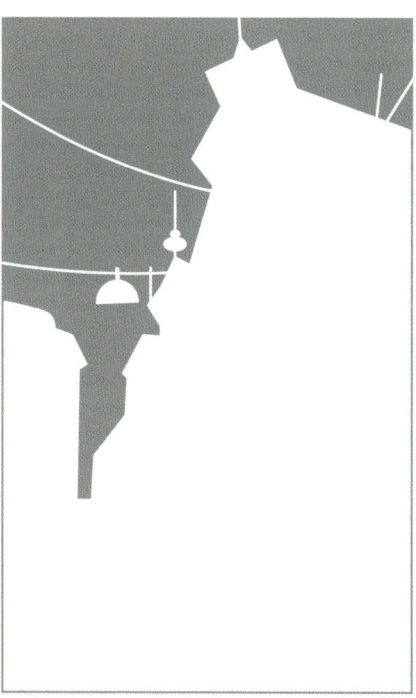

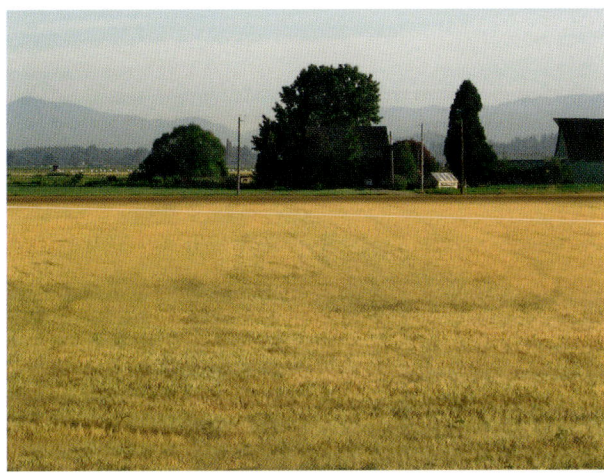 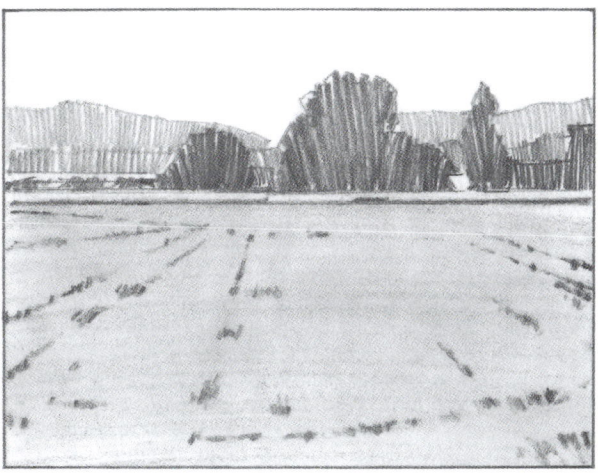

ACTIVATING THE GROUND PLANE IN A NATURAL SETTING

The dominant event in this subject is the field, but it lacks visual cues that carry the eye *over* the field and *into* the distance. By bringing out the subtle ground lines and furrows and accentuating the linear perspective, the field becomes much more interesting. In some subjects, it is necessary to take existing cues and exaggerate them. In others, you may have to invent new cues. The trick is not to overdo it. A few accents or spatial cues can be enough to bring the negative space to life.

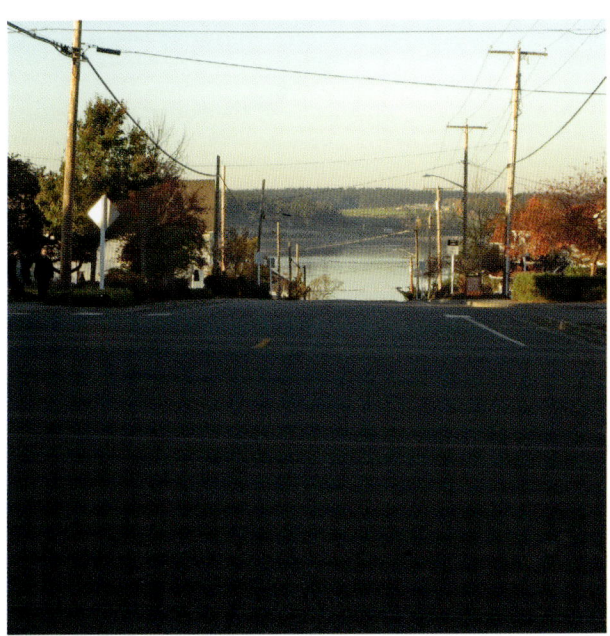 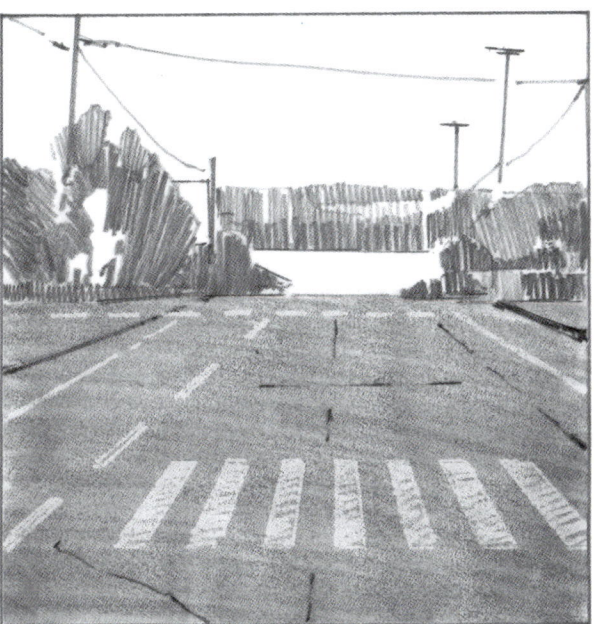

ACTIVATING THE GROUND PLANE IN AN URBAN SETTING

Roads that advance toward the viewer can offer a dramatic entry into a painting. In this scene, though, the negative space of the road is empty and appears to drop down at the bottom edge, like an upright plane. By adding perspective cues—cracks, a crosswalk, and white lines—the road becomes more active. It becomes as much a part of the composition as the upper portion. Note how the addition of the crosswalk raises the portion of the road closest to us so it no longer feels like an upright plane.

REVIEW QUESTIONS:
COMPOSITION IN ACTION

VARIATION

How do the sizes of the shapes differ?

Big shapes versus small shapes; major shapes versus minor shapes. Differences in size make a composition more varied and engaging. Can you compose the picture in a way that amplifies the size differences?

What is the relative area devoted to the sky versus the ground or water?

The relative area devoted to the sky versus the ground or water often accounts for the biggest size differential in a composition. Is the subject sky-dominant or land- or water-dominant? How big of a size differential is there? Can it be greater? How would that affect the reading of the space?

Do the spaces in between shapes vary enough?

Are the intervals the same, or are there differences in the "pacing and spacing" between elements? The more the intervals vary, the more compelling the composition will be.

How does the visual weight of elements vary?

Visual weight may be affected by size, value, color, or position. Avoid having too many elements with the same visual weight.

Is there an adequate difference in the amount of light and dark values?

Having a different proportion of light and dark is a means of applying variation across the overall composition.

How do the colors in the painting affect the composition?

Size affects the visual weight or density of a shape, but so does its color. Variation of color adds interest to the visual tapestry.

MOVEMENT

What are the pathways of movement in your subject?

One of the criteria for a good subject is whether it has pathways of movement that will allow the eye to move around the picture. Is there naturally occurring movement in the subject? Can you heighten the effect of movement by emphasizing or exaggerating certain elements?

Is there any linear perspective in the subject that you can capitalize on?

Diagonals that form linear perspective not only serve as a counterpoint to horizontal and vertical movement, they are the most direct means of suggesting depth. Even small angles and shallow perspective can instigate movement.

Is movement direct or implied?

Is movement *direct*, found along the contours and edges of elements? Or is it *implied*, formed by connecting various points within the composition in a connect-the-dots fashion?

ACTIVE NEGATIVE SPACE

Are the negative spaces in your composition fully activated?

Skies, bodies of water, fields, or empty streets can occupy large areas of a subject. Are they inactive, empty, or flat? How can you add interest to these areas?

Is the sky an active part of the picture or is it treated like an empty blue backdrop?

Would introducing variations of color and/or value into the sky make it more active? Is there a way to apply *closed* negative space? Allowing a tree, a mountain, a telephone pole, or a building to touch the edge of the painting will break up the sky into smaller segments, which is more interesting than one single sky shape.

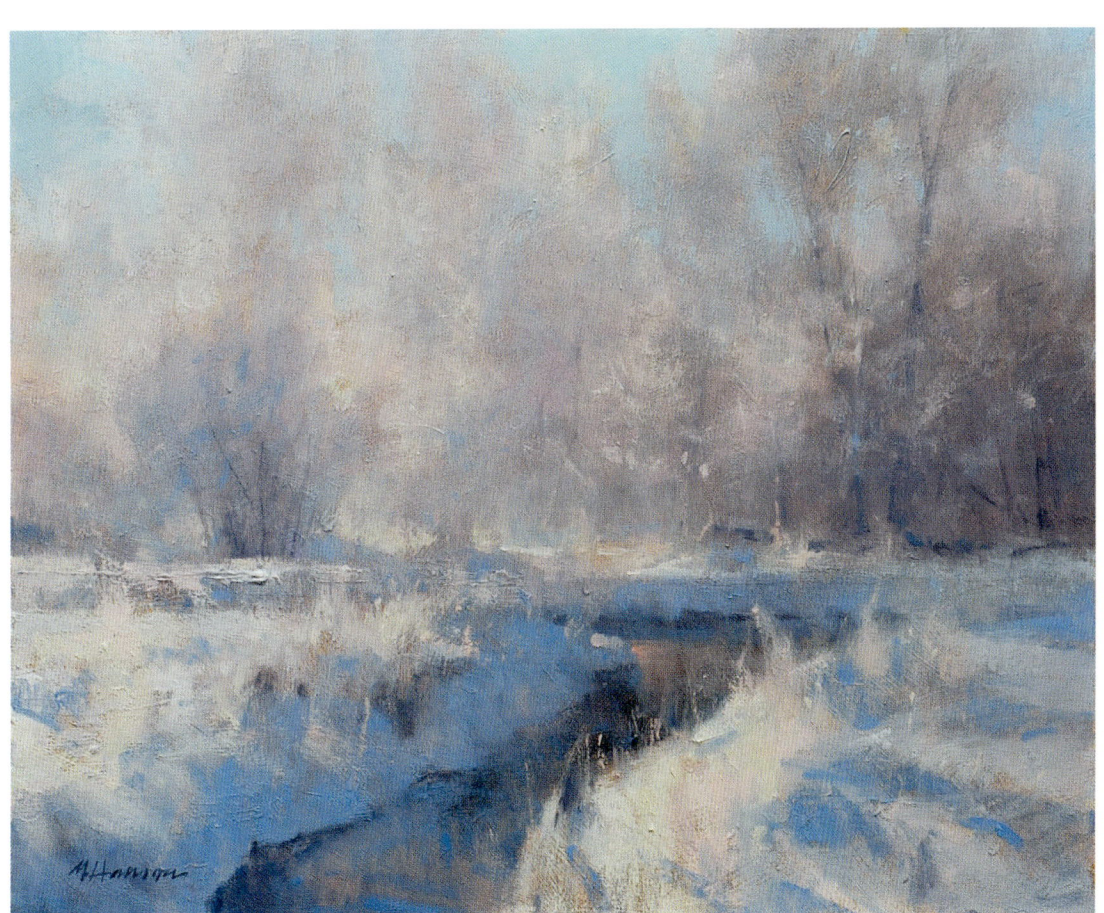

Marc Hanson, *A Quiet Frost*, oil on linen, 16" × 20" | 40.5 × 51 cm

What is the direction of the movement?

Is the movement mostly horizontal or vertical? Are there diagonals to counteract horizontal and vertical movement? Can the eye move around the composition in a circular fashion? In a zigzag? Generally, a composition is more engaging if there is a dynamic interplay of horizontals, verticals, and diagonals.

EXERCISE: **CUT PAPER: ASPECTS OF VARIATION**

OVERVIEW: In this exercise, you will create a flat, simplified composition of a "forest," using as many aspects of variation as possible. You'll use cut paper, in collage-like fashion, with only three values: black, white, and middle gray. Use five, six, or seven trees and one ground plane. This exercise looks simple and unrefined, but it isn't easy. You'll find it challenging to assert variation at every level.

NOTE: The more trees you include, the more challenging the exercise. The more intervals there are, the harder it is to make them all different.

MATERIALS: White, black, and gray paper (inexpensive craft paper or toned charcoal paper) | Scissors and/or hobby knife | Glue stick or transparent tape (removable) | White craft glue | Metal straightedge or ruler

TIP

In this exercise, there is a tendency to not take variation far enough. Students make the trees different thicknesses—but not enough. Or, they vary the intervals—but only slightly. *More variation is better.* As you move toward greater variation, you'll notice that the composition becomes stronger and more dynamic.

STEP 1: SET THE STAGE

Begin with a sheet of paper approximately 8 × 10 inches (20.5 × 25.5 cm). Starting on a white foundation is easiest, but you can also start on gray or black. The format can be horizontal, vertical, or square. Although the composition loosely resembles a forest, avoid high representation or detail. A high degree of craft or polish is not required here.

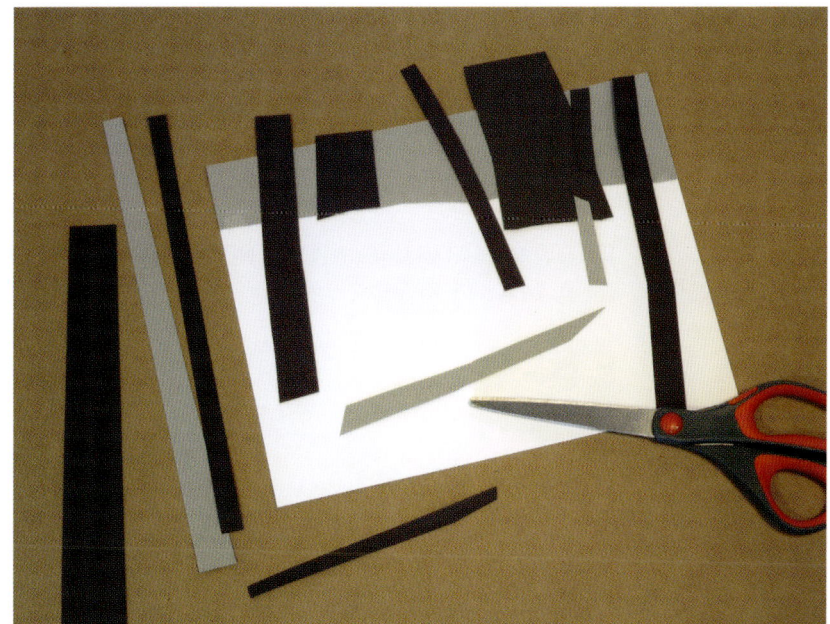

STEP 2: DESIGN

Begin by cutting out strips of paper of varying thicknesses and different tones. (You can also tear the paper, which will give a different edge quality.) Create a ground plane and decide whether it will sit above or below the midline. As you position the shapes, continually ask yourself: How does the thickness of *this* tree differ from *that* one? How do their angles differ? Their heights? Be especially conscious of the intervals (spaces) *between* the trees. No two should be the same. At every turn, assert variation and avoid sameness. Temporarily hold pieces in place with a glue stick or removable transparent tape. Take photos of your progress so you can refer back to earlier versions of your design.

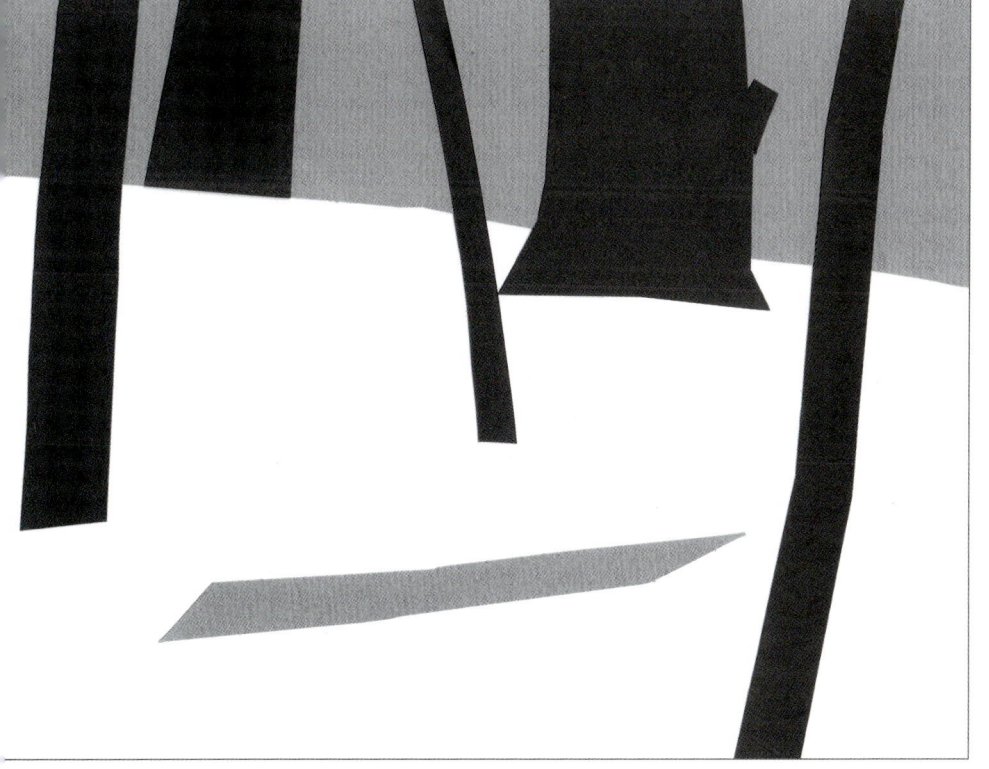

STEP 3: FINAL COMPOSITION

When you're done, affix the pieces into place with a glue stick or a bit of white glue. Notice that each tree has a different visual weight, as indicated by its thickness. One tree is a different value. Each tree is at a different angle, including the fallen tree that is nearly horizontal. Each of the gray intervals between the black trees at the top is also different.

EXERCISE: **MAPPING PATHWAYS OF MOVEMENT**

OVERVIEW: Movement is a powerful way to keep the viewer's eye active and engaged. This exercise is designed to build your awareness of movement. In **Part 1**, you'll diagram or "map" the pathways of movement you find in an existing painting. In **Part 2**, you'll do the same with one of your own subjects. These movement maps will be drawn by hand, but they are similar to the diagrams for Bill Cone's *Garnet Pond* (page 69) and Cindy Baron's *Spring Passage* (page 67).

MATERIALS: Tracing paper | Soft pencil (2B to 6B) | Tape | Eraser

Place arrowheads on the lines to indicate the direction of movement. If it flows in both directions, put an arrowhead on each end.

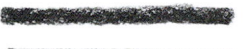

Make bolder lines for strong movements and thinner lines for subtler movements.

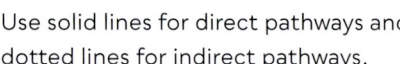

Use solid lines for direct pathways and dotted lines for indirect pathways.

PART 1: MAPPING MOVEMENT IN A MASTERWORK

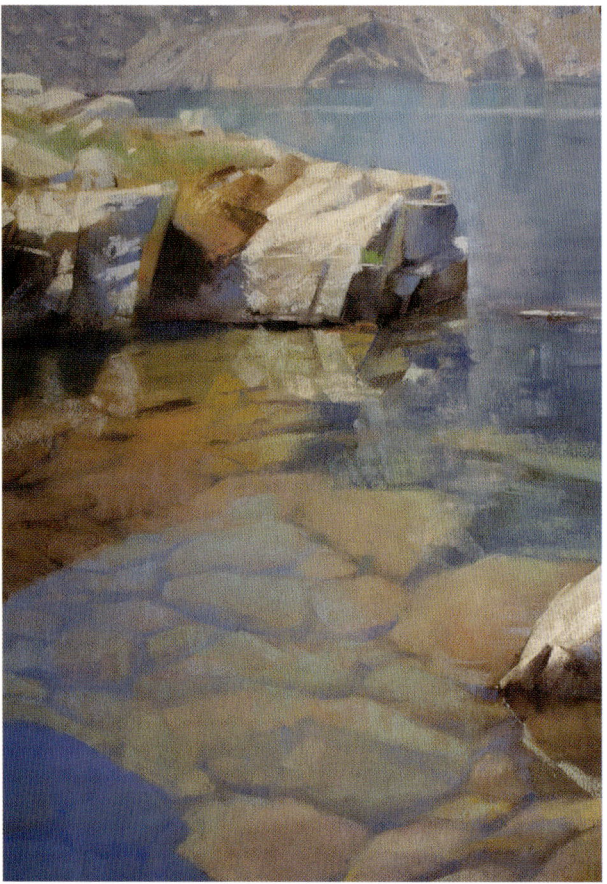

Bill Cone, *Iceberg Shore,* Pastel on paper
20" × 14" | 51 × 35.5 cm

STEP 1: PAINTING SELECTION

Select a classic or contemporary painting, in any medium, that suggests movement. For this exercise, I've chosen Bill Cone's *Iceberg Shore*. There are several paths of entry along the rocks at the bottom. There are also clear jumps from the foreground to the middle ground and then to the background, through both direct and indirect pathways.

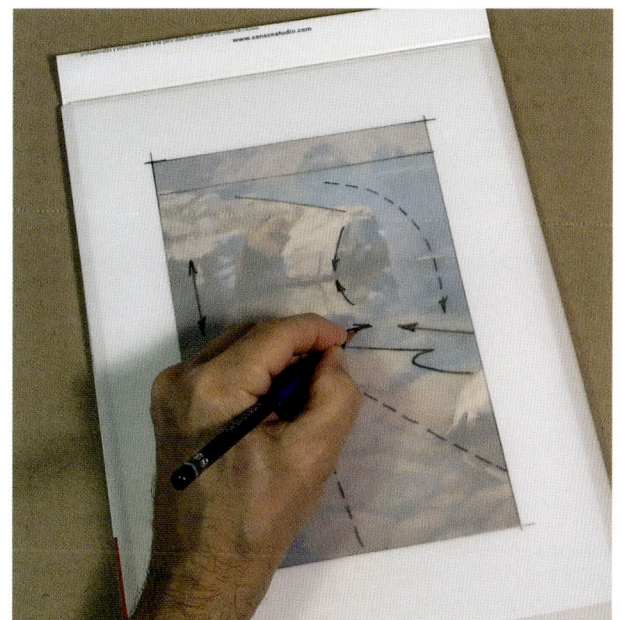

STEP 2: MAPPING

Tape a piece of tracing paper over your example. Begin drawing lines that suggest the pathways of movement you see in the painting. Use a soft pencil so you can erase and make adjustments. Some pathways may fall along the edges of elements, others may not. Your lines should indicate the direction and flow of the movements.

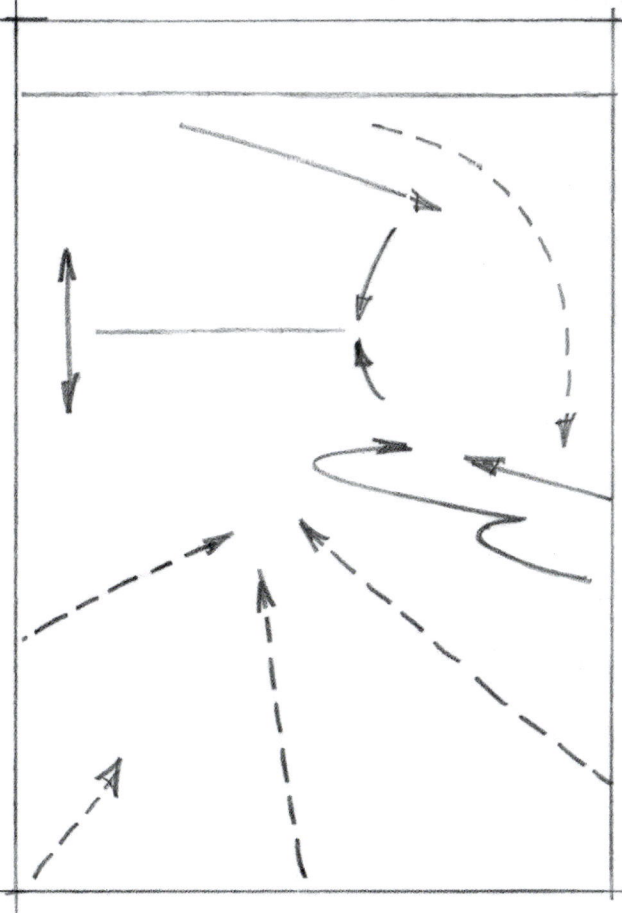

STEP 3: COMPLETED MAP

If we think of our diagram as a weather map, then our movement lines are like indications of the wind direction. The most dynamic movements in *Iceberg Shore* are found in the lower portion, where several pathways skim over the submerged rocks. Note how the energy of the movement calms down as we move upward (further back in space). At the very top, the horizontal line of the shore is the quietest movement of all and is therefore indicated with a lighter line. Although some movement lines fall along the edges of elements, your map should not look like an outline drawing of the painting. If it does, you may be too focused on shapes and contours and not enough on the pathways the eye naturally follows.

PART 2: MAPPING MOVEMENT IN YOUR OWN SUBJECTS

Part 1 of this exercise was a warmup for the real challenge: finding movement in your own compositions.

EXAMPLE 1

In terms of movement, the most interesting thing about this composition is how the silhouetted trees connect with the shoreline to form a roughly circular (oval) pathway. The bottom rim of the clouds echoes this. Shorter arrows on the left tree and on the building in the middle indicate smaller, but important movements.

CONSIDER: If five different painters created a map of this subject, each map would not look identical. When it comes to movement, there is room for interpretation.

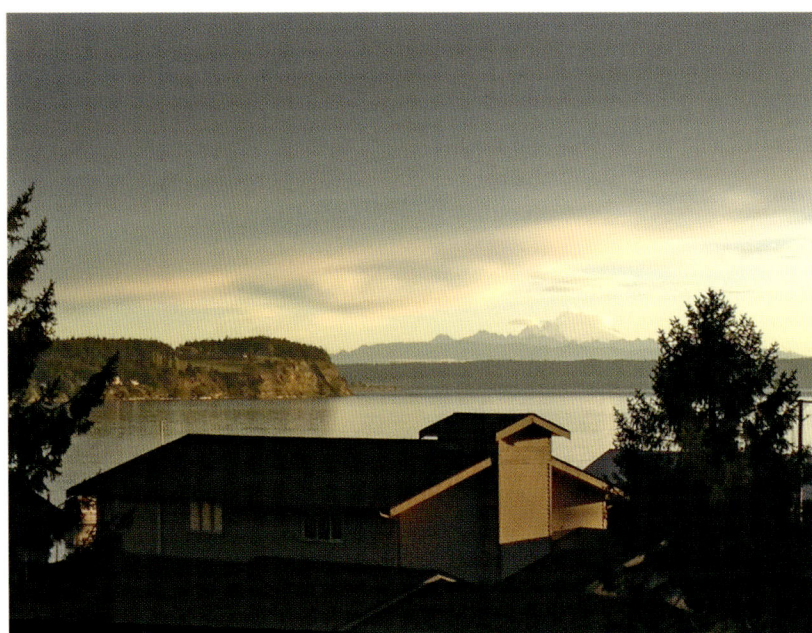

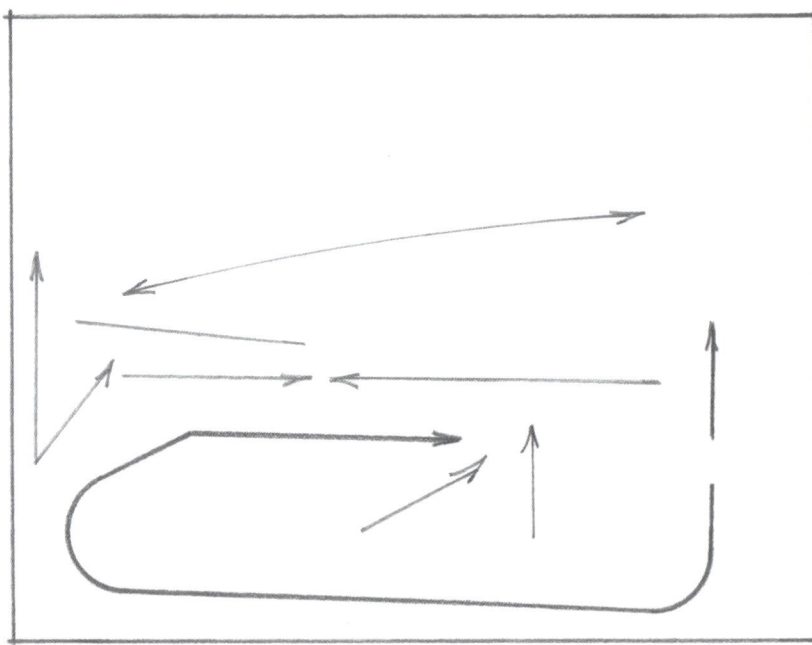

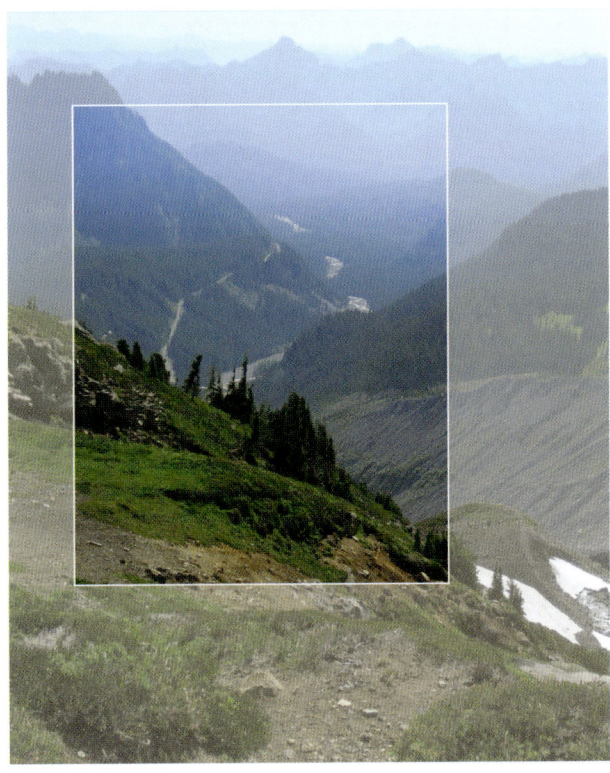

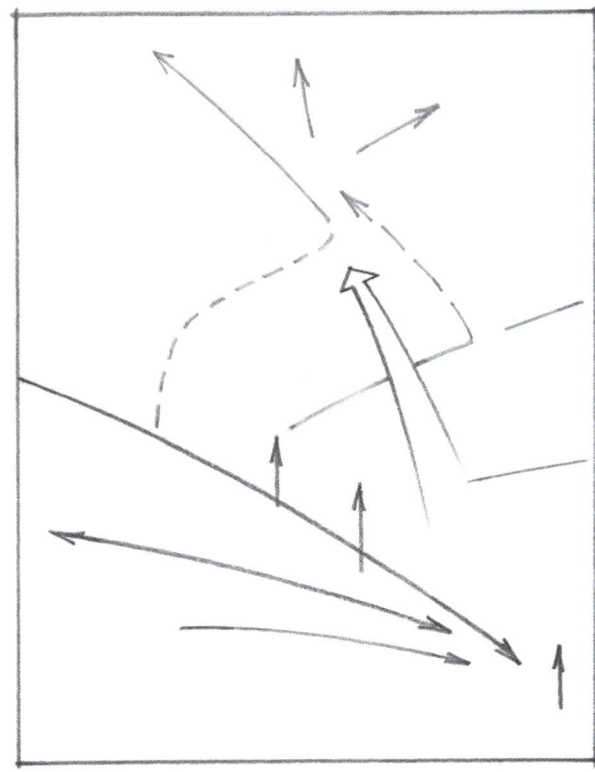

Photo: Carol Sandor

EXAMPLE 2

We can often bring greater attention to movement within a scene by how we position the landscape within the picture window. The original "pre-composed" scene certainly suggests an expansive and deep space, but it devotes nearly equal amounts of area to the foreground and the blue background, which weakens the impact of both. By tightening the focus, and allowing the background to become the dominant area, greater attention is drawn to the main event of the scene—the deep blue space and atmospheric perspective beyond the foreground.

This scene has many diagonals, which are a direct means of suggesting movement. However, the strongest movement in the final composition is entirely implied. Our eye is pulled over the foreground ridge, across the diagonal edges of the mountaintops, and deep into the space beyond (indicated by the broad arrow right of center). Implied pathways can sometimes provide the strongest movement in a composition.

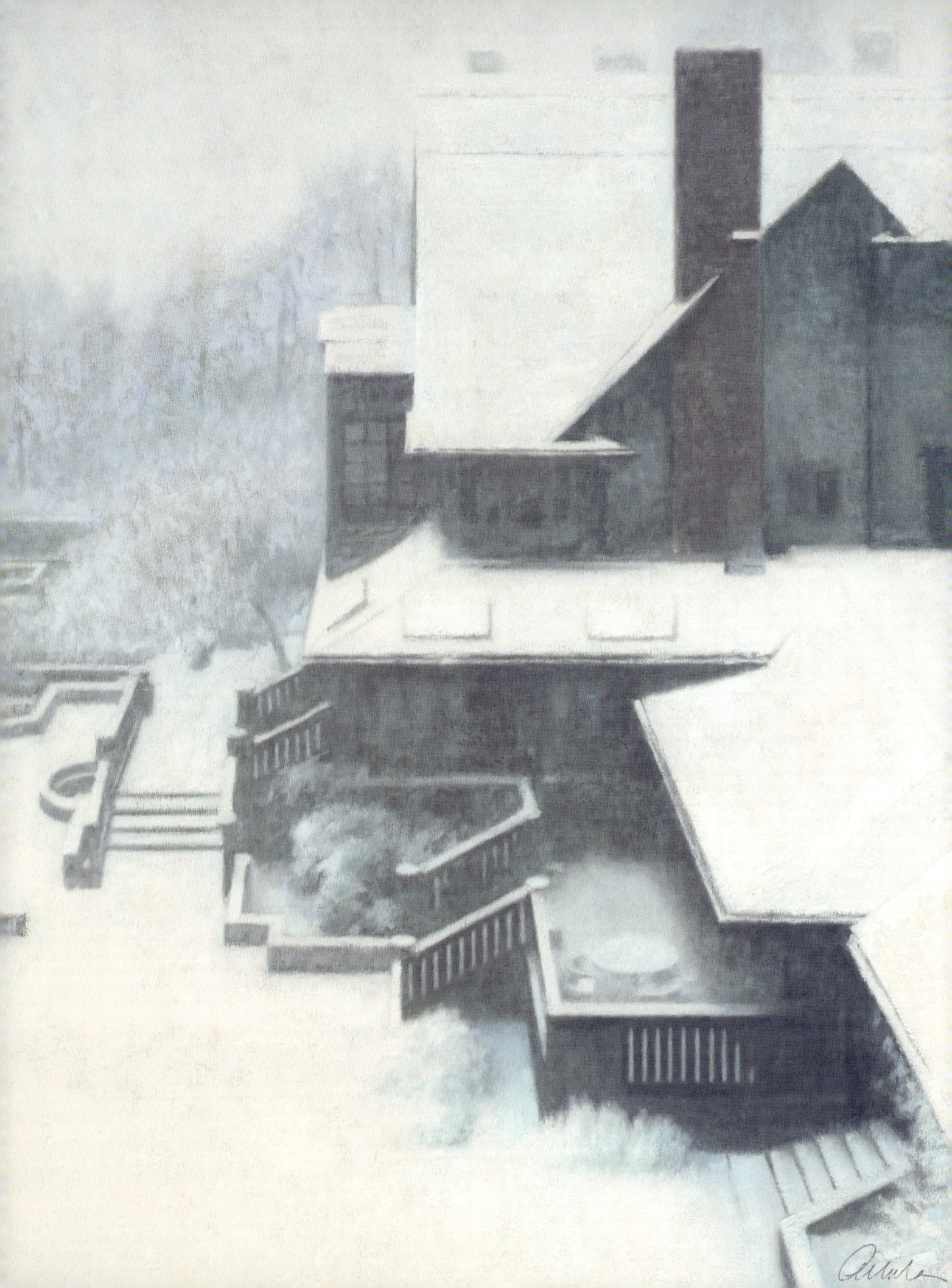

4

NOTAN AND THE COMPOSITIONAL STUDY

Good composition isn't an accident, but the result of deliberate decisions about the structure of the painting. We have to consider the picture window that surrounds the subject and then how the parts of the subject we include relate to one another. The best time to consider these options is at the outset, when the painting is in its most formative stage. Just as a map is an invaluable aid to the explorer heading into unfamiliar territory, so too is a compositional study a way for painters to explore their options before they begin.

Shapes are the building blocks of composition, so any type of compositional study must also be shape-oriented. And no type of study is more shape-oriented than notan. In this chapter, we explore the contemporary approach to notan, which positions it as a tool for identifying shapes and patterns. This will be followed by exercises that show you how to use notan studies in your own work.

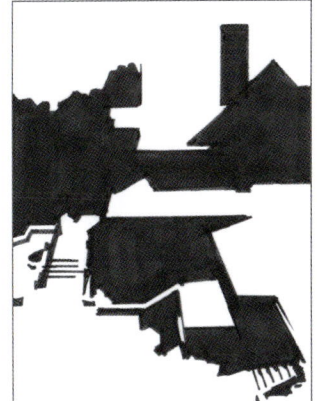

◄ Mitchell Albala, *Garden Steps in Winter*
Oil on canvas, 28" × 21" | 71 × 53.5 cm

A notan defines the essential shapes and patterns of a composition. When the underlying notan is strong, then the painting that is built upon it, with all its color and detail, is also strong.

DEFINING NOTAN

The notan is a bit mysterious. It has an exotic name and is often misinterpreted as a value study—which it is not. *Notan* is a Japanese word that translates as "light-dark balance." It is a design principle that suggests that strength and balance in composition are found through a harmonious relationship between light and dark shapes.

Most descriptions of notan are just like the one above. It is defined in terms of "light and dark"—which to painters is the same thing as "values" or "tones." In my own work with notan, both inside and outside the classroom, I have found that seeing the notan simply as a value study can prevent us from fully appreciating its broader application as a means of defining shapes and patterns, which are the building blocks of composition.

HOW THE NOTAN WORKS

The landscape is a busy place, with elements of all shapes and sizes, innumerable gradations of value and color, and endless detail. All this has bearing on the final painting, but it can also obscure the underlying shapes and patterns that we need to identify at the outset.

In chapter 1, we learned that when we limit ourselves to five values, shapes become more clearly differentiated. With notan, we push the exercise one step further. By using just two or three values, the foundational shapes become even more clearly defined. And the more clearly defined our shapes are, the more we will be able to see aspects of composition such as variation, movement, and negative space. The notan is like a perceptual lens that allows us to explore the composition in its most basic, irreducible shape-terms. It is the most direct method of accessing the underlying energies that animate a composition.

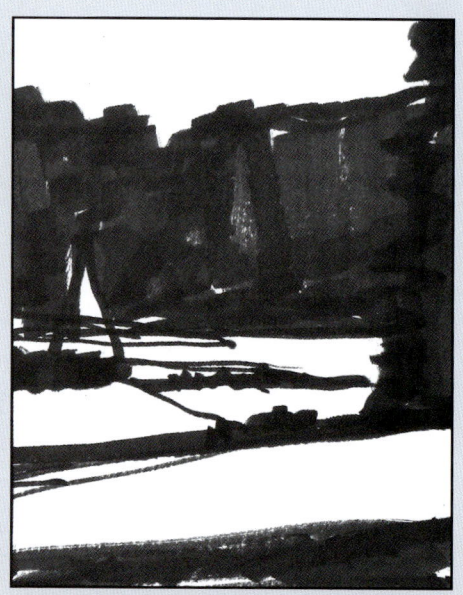

NOTAN AND THE LANDSCAPE

The notan's ultra-simplified visual shorthand may seem an unlikely choice for the landscapist, whose world is brimming over with content and detail. Yet it is *exactly* the kind of study we need. For landscape painters, simplification and massing are visual imperatives. Without the ability to simplify, we are at a loss to distill the landscape's myriad shapes into organized patterns. The notan encourages us—indeed forces us—to think in terms of shapes and patterns, the building blocks of composition.

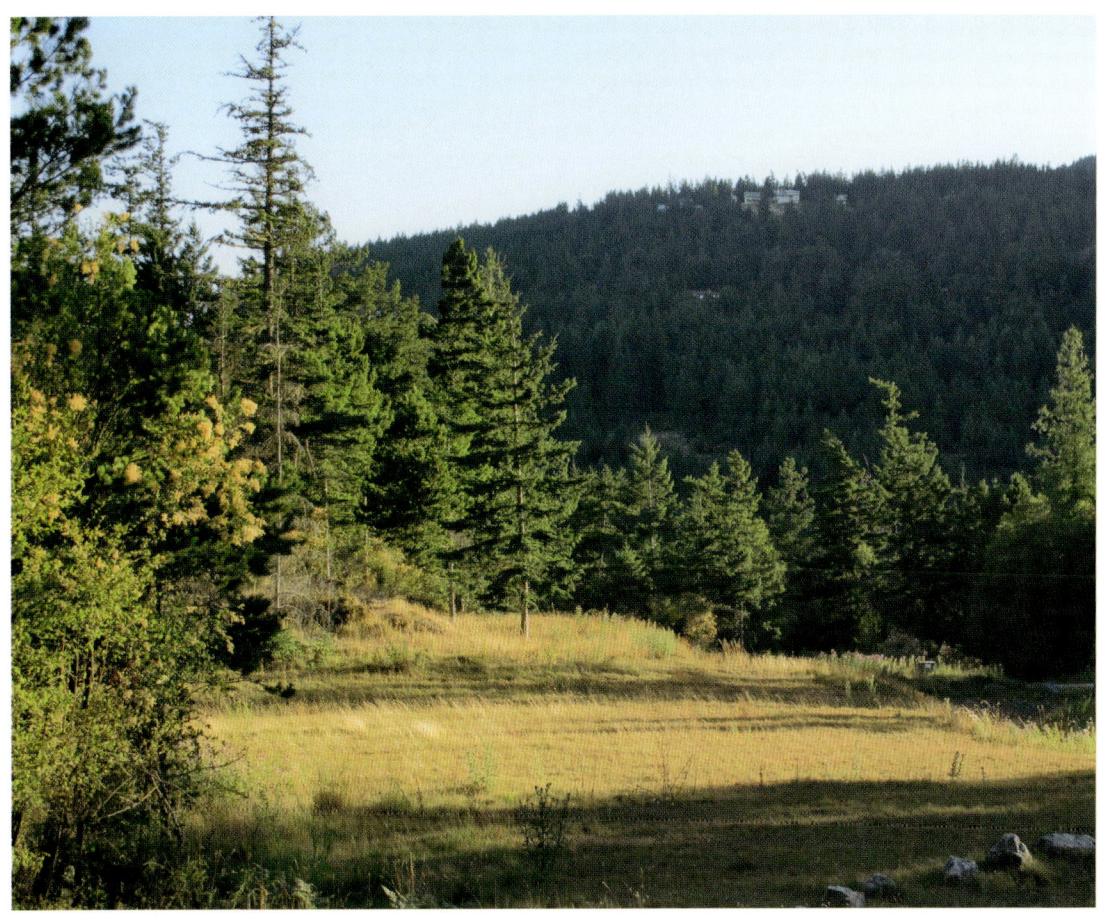

NOTAN IN ACTION

Whenever a student is wrestling with a compositional problem, I do a quick notan study. With a soft pencil, a marker, or a brush, I do a small study with a simplified arrangement of light and dark shapes. Whenever I demonstrate this for the first time, I hear "ah-ha" as they see the basic structure of the composition in a way they could not before. In this scene, the mass of trees on the left is quite busy, with many small shapes and values. My goal isn't to capture every bit of it, but to reduce it to its most fundamental shape-terms. This means I have to make compromises. The many midvalues will have to be pushed to either white or black, and I have to simplify in the extreme, eliminating nearly all detail.

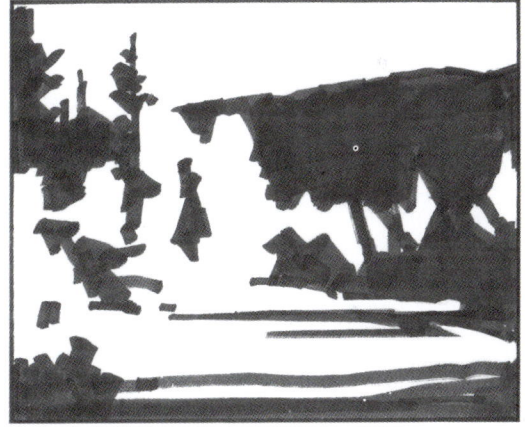

CONSIDER: A notan study is the first test of the integrity of a composition. If you can't express the essence of the composition in notan form, that's valuable feedback from your subject. Is it too complicated? Would another view of the scene offer a better arrangement of shapes?

SHAPE AND PATTERN DEFINITION, NOT VALUE

When most artists are first exposed to notan, they assume it is simply a high-contrast value study, a map of the patterns of light and shadow. This is an easy assumption to make. After all, notan is always defined in terms of "light and dark," which for painters is synonymous with "values." In subjects with strong patterns of light and shadow (think: bright sunny days), the black and white of the notan *will* neatly correspond to the patterns of light and shadow. *But most subjects don't present their values in binary fashion.* There are intermediate values that must be considered.

How can a notan study, with just black and white and possibly a middle gray, ever hope to convey all the values in any given subject? *It can't.* This is why the notan is not a value study in the traditional sense.

With its ultra-simplified visual shorthand, the notan is more effective at defining the basic shapes and patterns of a composition than it is at articulating a full range of values.

If a composition has a soul, then the notan is the doorway to that soul.

PROGRESSION: FROM NOTAN TO VALUE STUDY

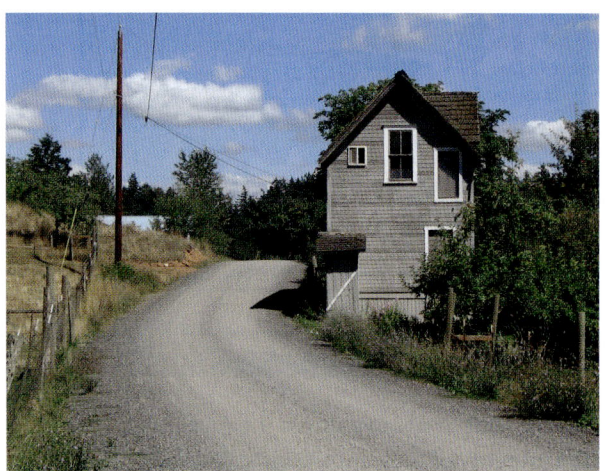

The notan is not a traditional value study. It is best suited to defining the underlying shapes and patterns that drive a composition. This progression shows that as the number of values increases, the study takes on a different meaning.

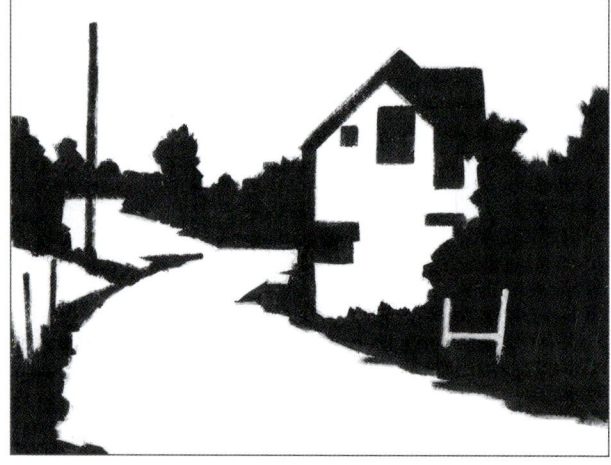

2-VALUE NOTAN

A black-and-white notan isn't capable of expressing the range of values found in nature. But it is extremely effective at suggesting the "bones" of the composition, the underlying armature upon which additional colors and values will be laid. Note that some midvalues have been assigned to white and others to black.

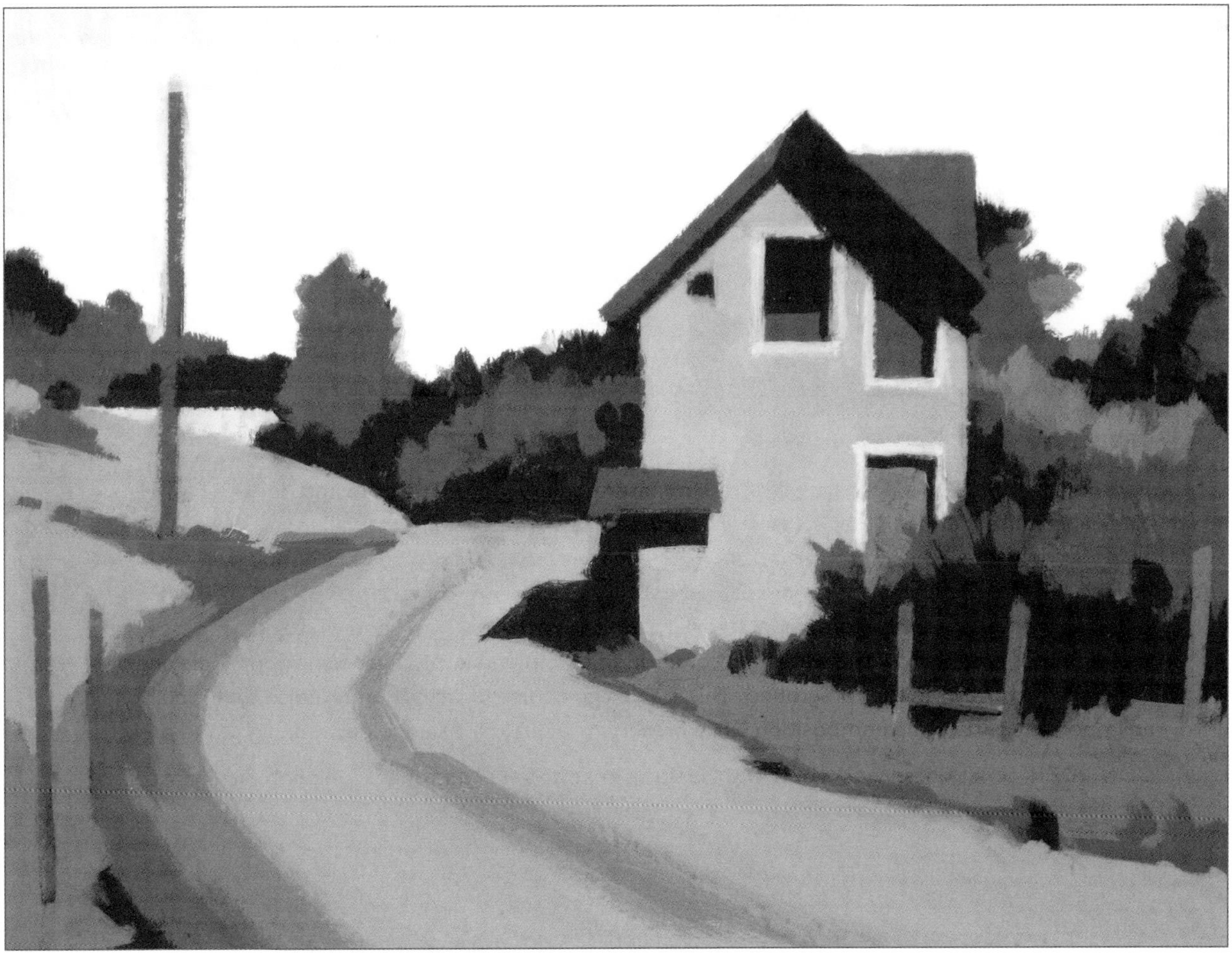

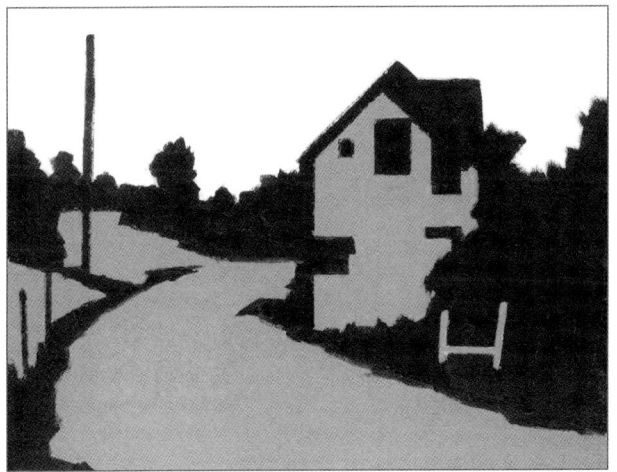

5-VALUE STUDY

With 5 values, the study graduates from notan and becomes a full value study. It expresses the value range, structure, and depth found in the subject. We don't see the foundational structure as readily as we do in the 2- or 3-value notans, but it exists beneath the surface and guides the overall composition. If we begin with a strong notan design, then the painting that is based on it will also have a strong composition.

3-VALUE NOTAN

The addition of a third value makes the study more descriptive, but not by much. A black, white, and gray notan is still "bare bones" enough to effectively express the underlying foundation of the composition.

STRICT AND LIBERAL FORMS OF NOTAN

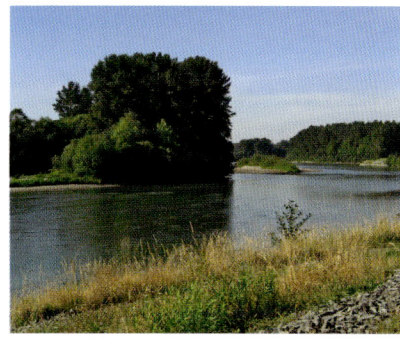 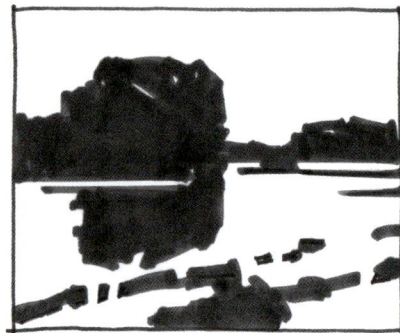

STRICT NOTAN: BLACK AND WHITE

Traditional notan uses black and white with no intermediary grays. The pure and poetic beauty of black and white is undeniable; however, this *strict* form presents a design challenge. What does a painter do with all the intermediary values, those that are not white or black? Should they be assigned to the white areas or to the black areas? If you squint at the photo, you can see that the values in the water and the foreground are very similar. With only black and white, it's impossible to separate these. So, I allow the water and foreground to join and imply the separation by playing up the diagonal furrows in the foreground. This is a design choice, a visual compromise that is clarifying an important part of the composition while preserving a healthy balance between light and dark.

CONSIDER: Strict notan works best with subjects that have very strong value contrasts, rooted in clear patterns of light and shadow.

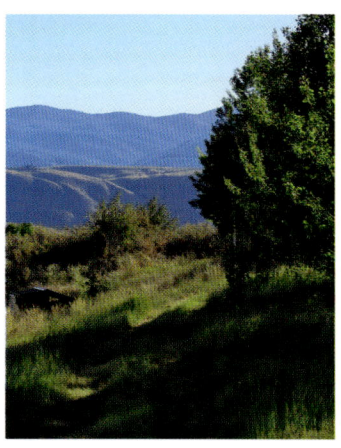 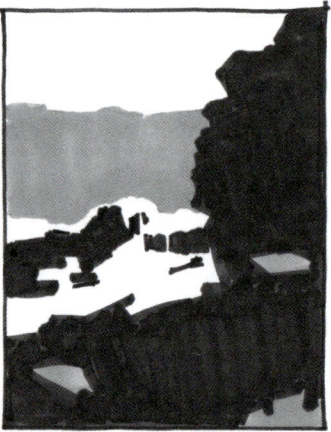

LIBERAL NOTAN: ADDING GRAY

Some subjects don't translate well into strict notan. For this, we have *liberal* notan, which adds a middle gray. Parts of the subject that can't be reconciled with white or black alone can be assigned the midtone. In this scene, the azure hills are an essential part of the overall scene. If they were made black, they would take on too much visual weight. If white, we wouldn't see them at all. The midtone defines an important part of the composition that would otherwise be lost in a strict notan.

CONSIDER: In notan design, we are not matching values, we are defining shapes. It's less important that our white, black, or gray values match reality than define the essential shapes of the composition.

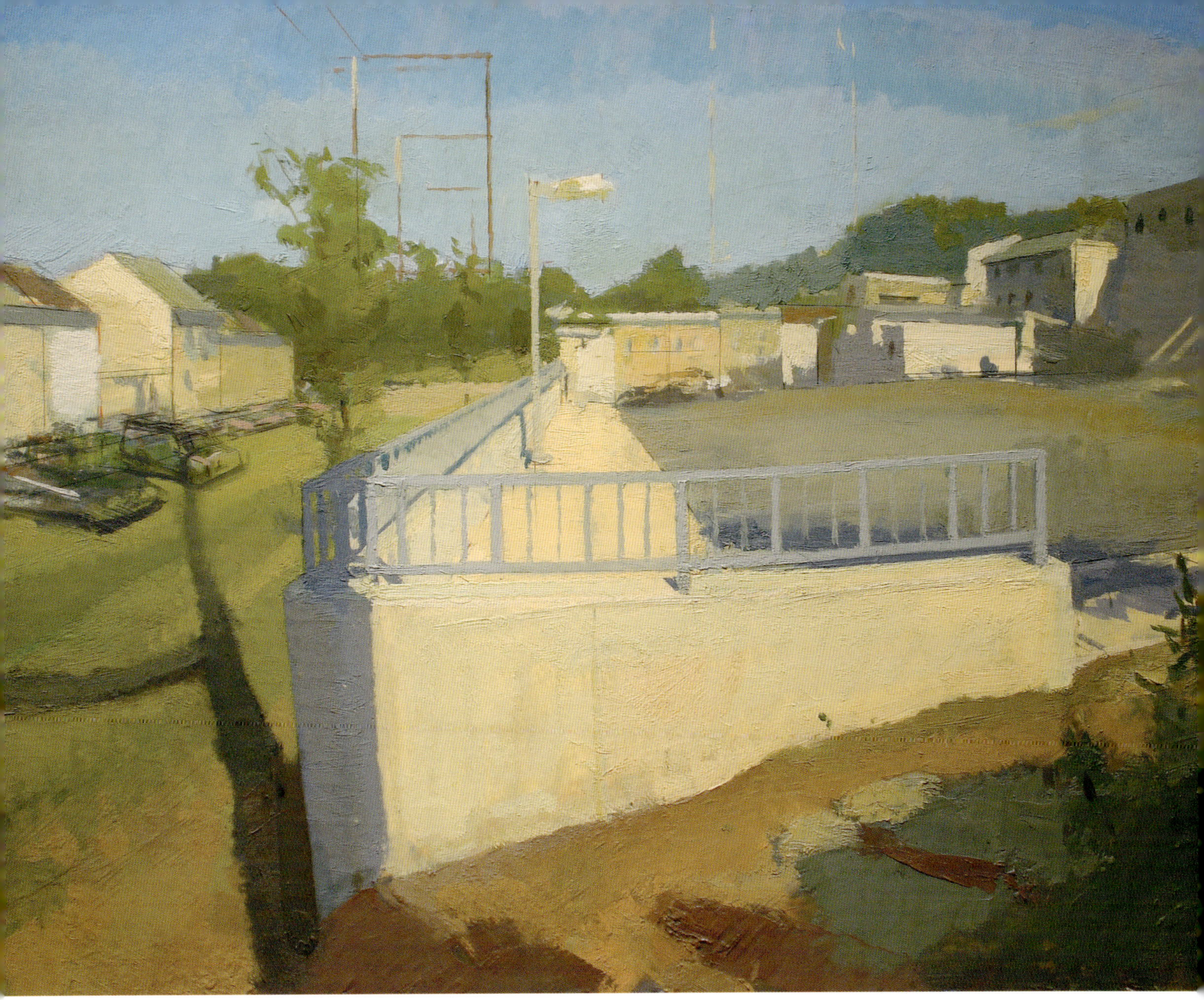

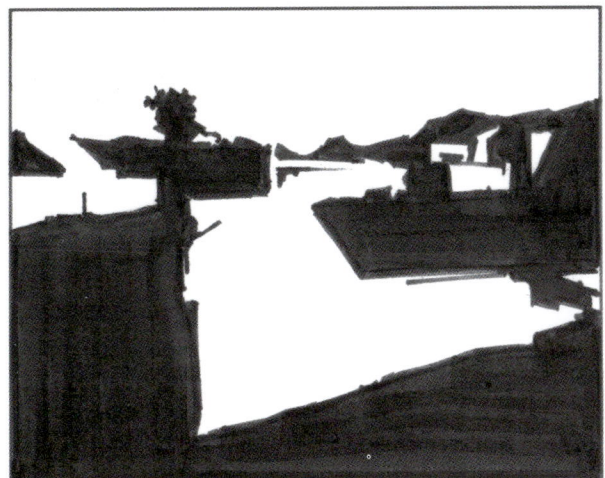

Peter Van Dyck, *Parking Lot*
Oil on rag board, 16" × 20" | 40.5 × 51 cm

Parking Lot is an excellent example of how the notan can be more about shape and pattern definition than value description. Most of the values in Van Dyck's painting are in the midrange. Thus, the notan study for a piece like this cannot simply identify patterns of light and shadow. Instead, it seeks to identify the main shapes that drive the composition. Here, the parking lot wall forms a strong shape that darts back in sharp perspective. This is captured in the notan and becomes the main event in the painting.

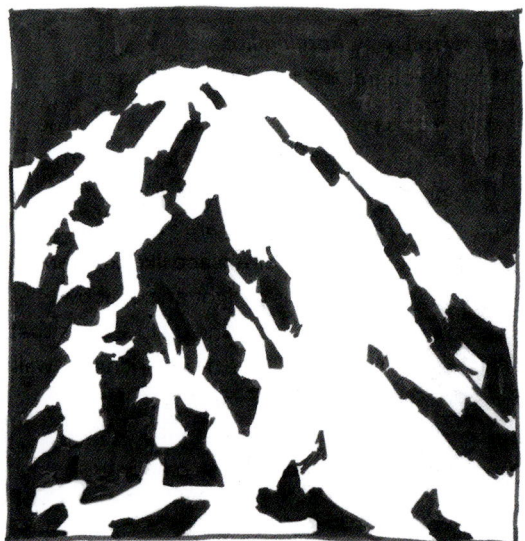

Mitchell Albala, *Mountain in Sunlight*
Oil on panel, 12" × 12" | 30.5 × 30.5 cm

Mountain in Sunlight is based almost entirely on color contrasts, with only subtle value differences. Yet, its composition is still guided by a clear notan design. The stark contrasts seen in the notan study don't get carried into the painting—but the shapes and patterns they define do. The sky in the painting is certainly not black, but in the notan, the black represents what will be an important color separation between the mountain and the sky. When we understand notan as being less about identifying values and more about shape and overall pattern, it becomes an extremely versatile compositional aid.

BUILDING A BETTER STUDY: NOTAN TECHNIQUE

In my workshops, I always ask students to do a compositional study before beginning a painting. In the absence of any previous instruction in notan or thumbnails, most will simply do a line drawing. Lines are wonderful … but they are not so effective at building masses.

Shapes are the building blocks of composition, so any type of compositional study must also be shape- and mass-oriented.

The two most important goals of a compositional study are that it adequately describes the composition in the simplest terms possible and that it is *readable*, meaning that your compositional intent is clear to anyone looking at it.

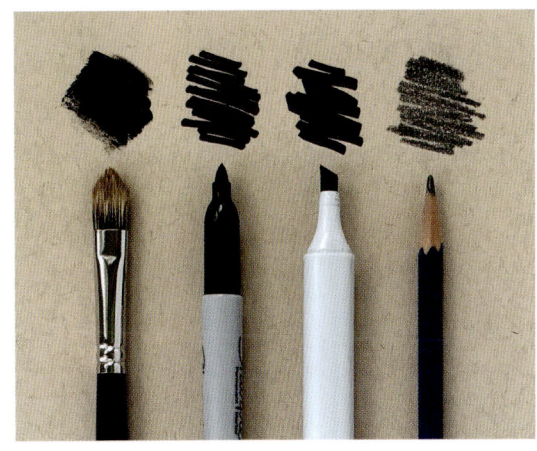

TOOLS FOR MASSING

Doing a mass-oriented compositional study requires that we shift *away* from thinking in a linear fashion. This can be encouraged by working with tools that make it easier to establish masses and broad coverage, such as soft pencils, markers, or brushes. Super fine-point markers or light pencils don't work well here. They make lines that are too thin. Pecking away at major shapes with minor tools is not allowed!

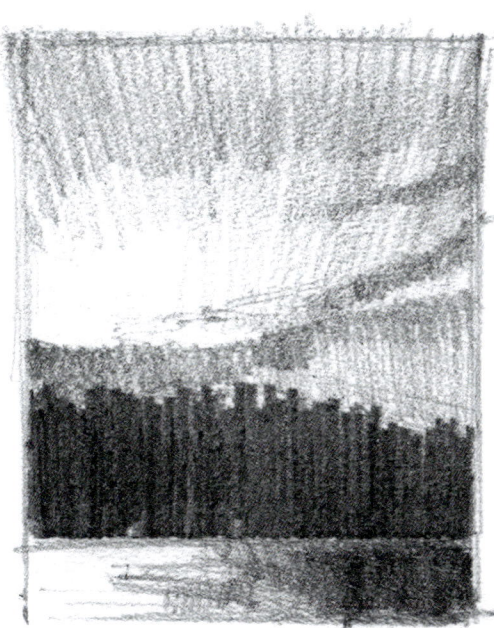

FEWER LINES, MORE SHAPES

A shape-oriented study doesn't mean we can't use lines. Lines are how we start a drawing: we measure, plot, and properly place our shapes. But outlined shapes should quickly be replaced with value masses. In this study, you can see each individual crosshatched line, but they are grouped in such a way that they form clear masses.

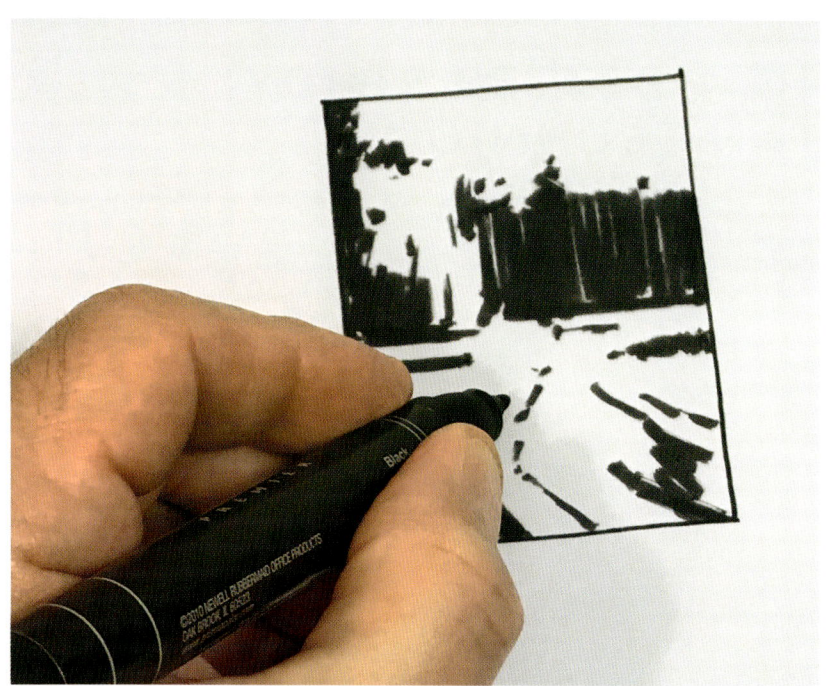

KEEP IT SMALL

Although notan studies and thumbnails are not actually the size of your thumbnail, it makes sense to keep them small, 2 to 4 inches (5 to 10 cm). Relative to the size of a small study, marks or strokes tend to be larger, bolder, and more mass-oriented. You can achieve coverage more quickly. The larger the study, the longer it will take.

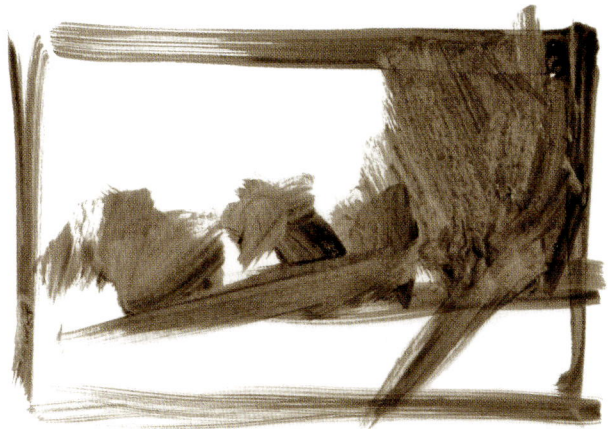

KEEP IT SIMPLE

Detail never solved a compositional problem more effectively than a better balance between lights and darks or simpler shapes. In the spirit of a shape-oriented approach, avoid detail. If you are faced with a tricky drawing problem, do a separate study to resolve those issues.

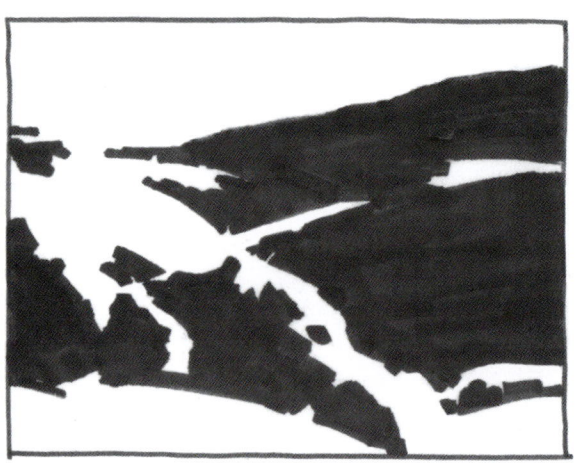

FOCUS ON THE DOMINANT SHAPES

The essence of a composition is ultimately driven by its dominant shapes. These are often the largest shapes, but more importantly the composition would lose its intent and focus without them. Minor shapes or details, on the other hand, can be eliminated without compromising the composition.

NOTAN APPS

If you like using the computer to support your creative explorations, then you'll be happy to know that most image editing apps have a feature that can "notanize" your photos. These apps are particularly handy when working in the field beacuse they allow you to easily test different notan designs on the fly.

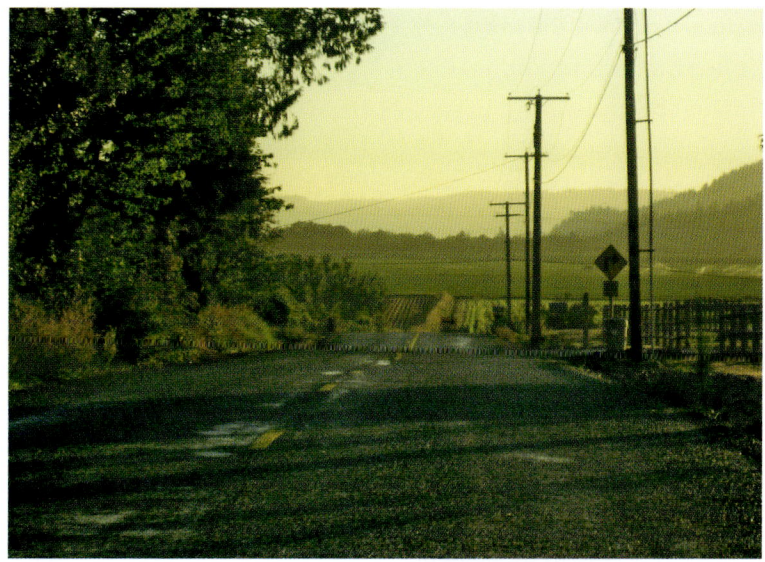

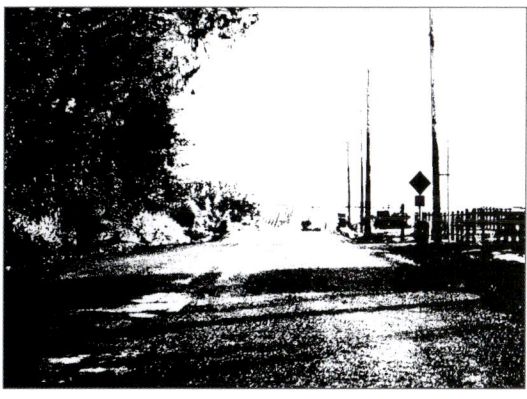
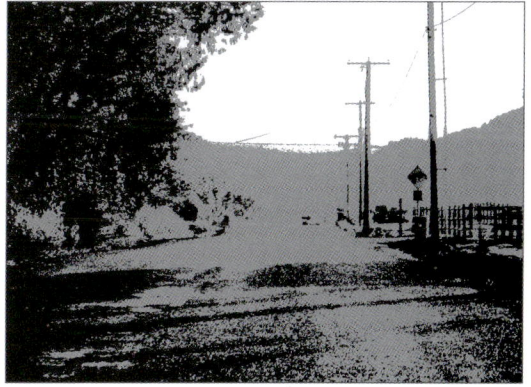

A QUESTION OF BALANCE

In image editing software such as Photoshop or Affinity Photo, the adjustment used to simulate notan is called *Threshold*. This adjustment doesn't simply convert the image to white and black, but allows you to control the *balance* between those whites and blacks. As you move the adjustment slider left or right, you can see the changing dynamics of light and dark within the notan in real time. There are also mobile apps designed specifically for the notan that go one step further and allow you to convert the image to three values. You can see whether a strict or liberal notan best conveys the essence of the composition.

REVIEW QUESTIONS: NOTAN AND THE COMPOSITIONAL STUDY

Is your notan study simple?

A notan design is never complex; it conveys the most salient aspects of the composition in the simplest terms possible.

Is your notan study readable?

Clarity and comprehension are the most essential requirements of a compositional study. Can your intent be understood in an instant? Or is the study so busy and disorganized that a viewer would have difficulty understanding what's going on?

How many shapes does the notan have?

Counting shapes is a quick way to check the simplicity of your design. Can the composition be defined with five or seven shapes? With ten? The fewer shapes there are, the more elegant the solution.

Does squinting help you see the notan design?

When you squint, midvalues tend to group with either the light or dark ends of the value range, producing a simplified light-dark view of the subject.

Are you handling the notan in a mass-oriented way?

Is your notan too linear, made up of lots of thin lines? If so, use tools that more easily establish solid masses such as a soft pencil, marker, or brush.

Are you only defining light and shadow in your notan study or shapes and patterns as well?

The lights and darks of notan *sometimes* correspond to light and shadow—but not always. The notan is ultimately a shape and pattern defining tool. Its lights and darks can correspond to any shape that is integral to the composition.

Does this subject lend itself to a "strict" black and white notan, or is the addition of a third value necessary?

In some subjects, certain areas cannot be resolved with just black and white. The introduction of a third value is necessary.

Are the lights and darks used in the same proportion?

A tenet of good design is that lights and darks should not be used in equal proportion. For greater variation and interest, there should be more of one than the other.

Are white negative spaces just as interesting as black or gray positive areas?

White spaces are an integral part of the design; never think of them as empty or blank.

Do you have a notan app loaded on your mobile device?

When working outdoors, a notan app can help you create digital notan studies on the fly.

EXERCISE: **ORIENTING TO NOTAN**

OVERVIEW: This first exercise will orient you to "thinking in notan," defining a composition with just two or three values. By tracing the patterns of light and dark, you will reverse engineer the painting to reveal the underlying notan design. There's more to this exercise than simply tracing. Most subjects (and paintings) have many intermediary values, and determining whether to assign them to white or black requires judgement. Consider doing a few different notan interpretations of the same painting. You'll see how changing the balance between light and dark or adding a midvalue affects the composition. Small changes can affect the outcome in noticeable ways.

MATERIALS: Tracing paper | Drawing tools (bold marker, soft pencil) | L-shaped cropping tool | Tape | Ruler

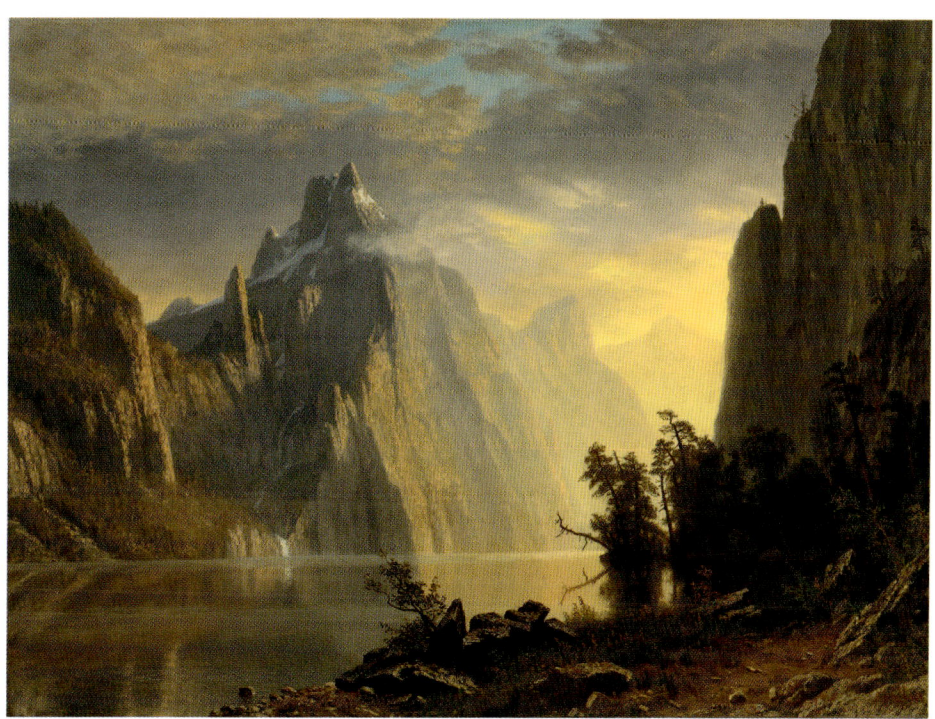

STEP 1: MASTERWORK SELECTION

Albert Bierstadt, *Lake in the Sierra Nevada*
Oil on canvas, 21⅘" × 30" | 55.5 × 76 cm. Courtesy Wikimedia Commons.

Select a painting that has clear patterns of light and dark. The more intermediary values there are, the more challenging the exercise will be. A reproduction between 4 and 6 inches wide (10 and 15 cm) is ideal. (Larger reproductions will force you to spend too much time filling in values.) Resize the reproduction if necessary. For this demonstration, I chose a work by Albert Bierstadt, a leading Hudson River Painter of the nineteenth century. The painting has a full range of values as well as intermediary values with which I will have to contend.

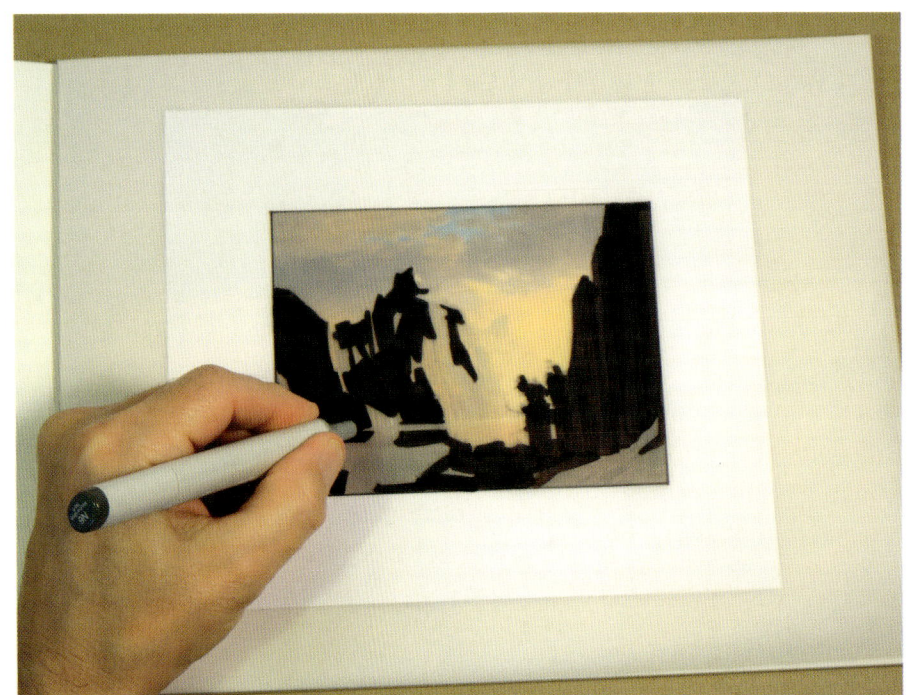

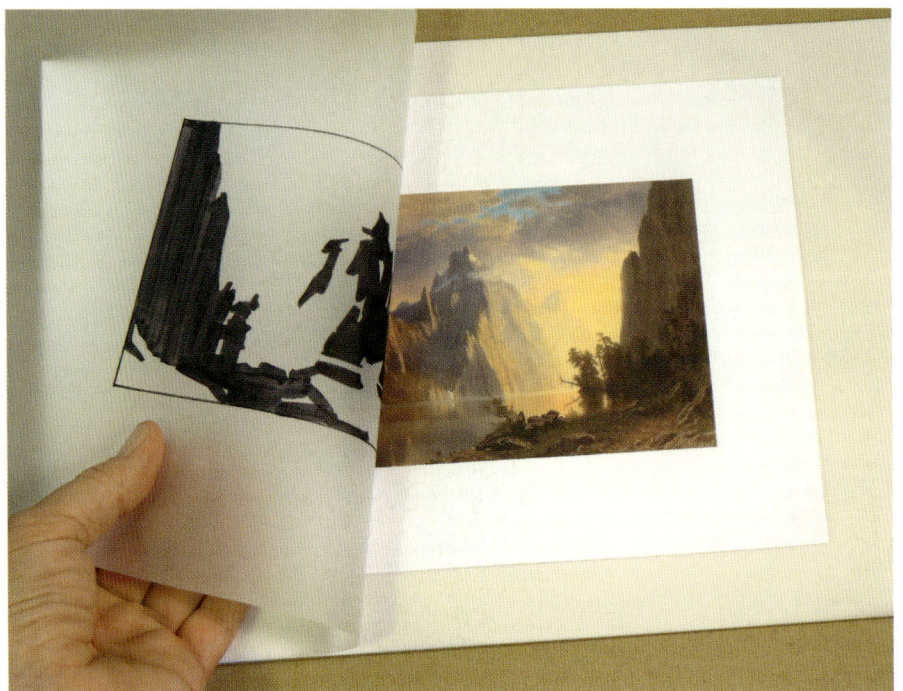

STEP 2: SHAPE- AND PATTERN-FINDING

Place a sheet of tracing paper over the reproduction. Using a marker, as shown here, or a soft pencil, begin tracing. The mountains on the left and the foreground mountains on the right are quite dark and easily interpreted as black. But the clouds and parts of the mountain closest to the sunset are midvalues. Should these passages be assigned to white or black? The goal is to find a balance that indicates the essential character of the subject. There is more than one solution. I'll do two studies in strict notan and one in liberal notan.

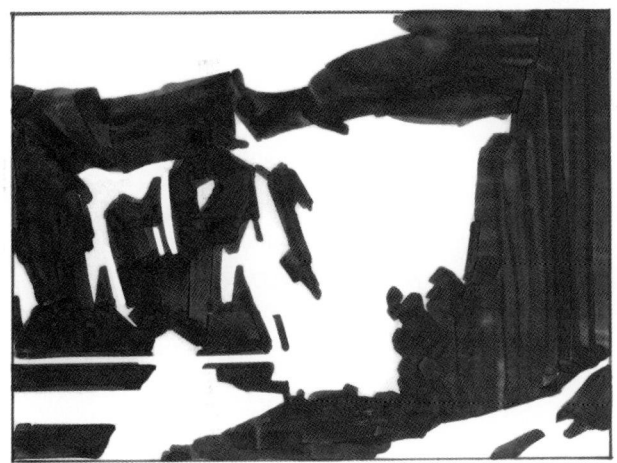

STRICT NOTAN 1

A painting with this many intermediary values is hard to pull off in strict notan. A binary interpretation, with no grays, can't capture the nuances in the clouds or in the notch between the mountains, which are essential aspects of the subject. I opt to make the clouds black and the notch between the mountains white. On the positive side, this brings out the circular composition Bierstadt employed. On the downside, the composition is overly dark. It feels too heavy and busy.

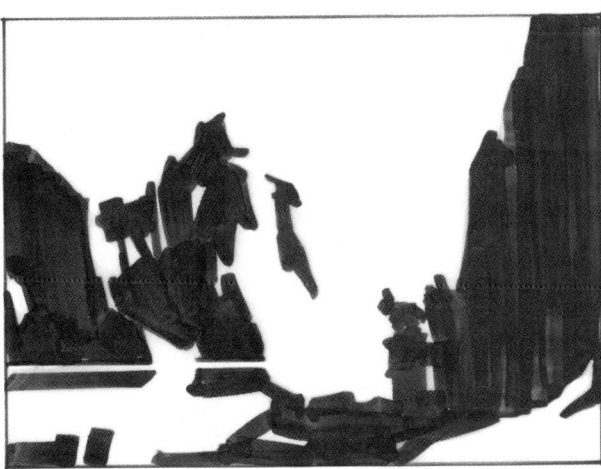

STRICT NOTAN 2

Next, I try a light-dominant composition. I lose the cloud shape which completed the circular composition, but this version feels lighter and simpler. Overall, it is more readable than the design in Strict Notan 1. It has clearer movement and a better balance between light and dark.

LIBERAL NOTAN

How does the composition change when I add a third value? It helps because the gray speaks for some of the intermediary values. It also reduces the overall heaviness seen in Strict Notan 1, while still revealing the patterns that form the circular composition.

OBSERVE: Neither the strict or liberal notans are able to convey the subtler passages of the subject—but that isn't the point. Interpreting a composition in this binary way is revealing. It exposes me to options, and exploring those options teaches me about design.

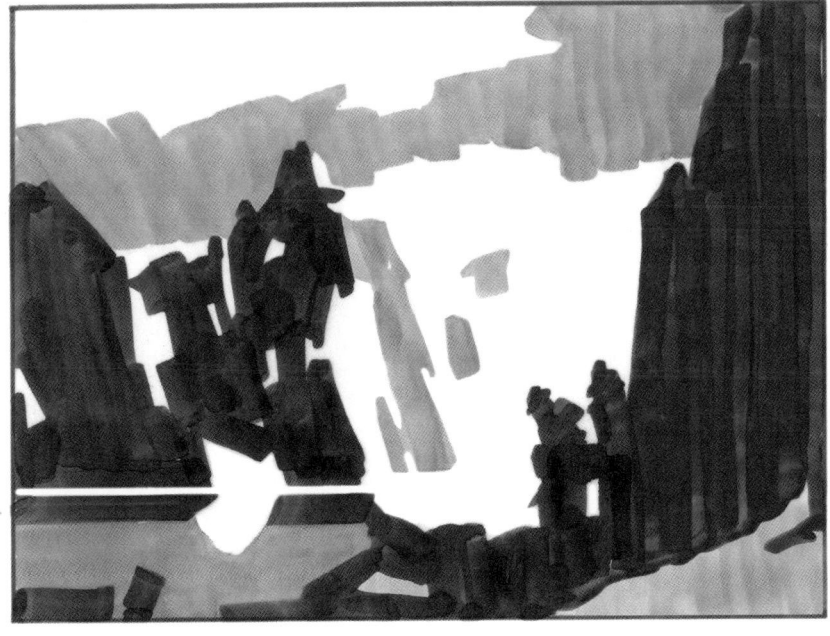

EXERCISE: **NOTAN FROM OBSERVATION**

OVERVIEW: In this exercise, you'll learn how to do notan thumbnails from direct observation, which is essential when working in the field. This is more challenging than cropping or tracing a photo because you have to draw and position the elements within an existing window in your sketchbook. To make this easier, I recommend a *placement exercise* that considers options based on where the major shapes fall within a simple grid.

MATERIALS: Sketchbook | Drawing tools (bold marker, soft pencil, or brush) | Plastic or cardboard viewfinder

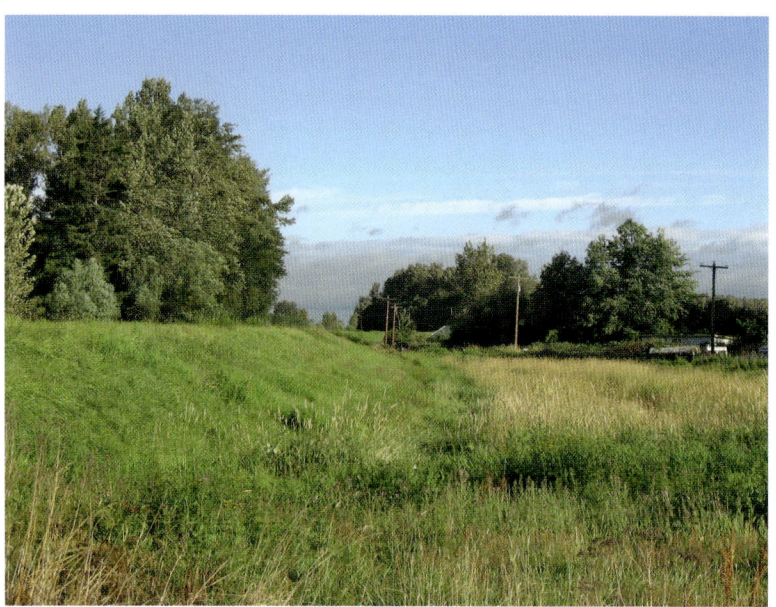

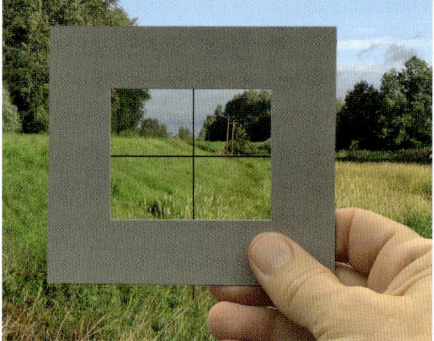

GRIDLINES

SOURCE PHOTO

Think of the main masses of your composition as blocks. Different compositions are created depending on how much space these blocks occupy within the various quadrants. In this scene, there are four blocks: two stands of trees, a large foreground that advances toward us, and the sky. Begin by looking through your viewfinder. Draw a picture window in your sketchbook and then divide the thumbnail into four quadrants by drawing light horizontal and vertical centerlines (indicated by blue lines in these studies). Consider both horizontal and vertical formats.

VIEWFINDING

You can purchase clear plastic viewfinders with grid lines already indicated. Alternatively, you can draw the gridlines on a piece of acetate and tape it to the back of your homemade cardboard viewfinder, as shown here.

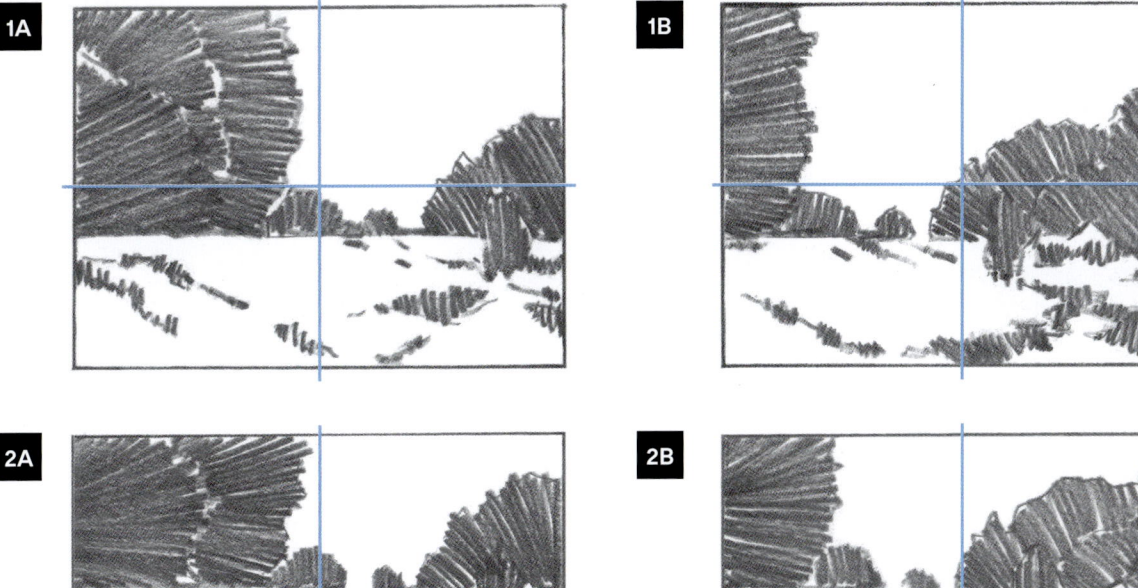

In both 1A and 1B, I have chosen a horizontal format and positioned the ground line below the midline. The foreground is shallow and the sky occupies a larger area. In 1A, the large tree on the left is dominant, and in 1B, the trees on the right become dominant.

In 2A and 2B, still using a horizontal format, the ground line now falls above the midline, so the foreground becomes larger than the sky. In 2A, the left tree is dominant, and in 2B, the trees on the right are more dominant.

OBSERVE: To assert as much variation in shape size as possible, I intentionally make one stand of trees larger than the other and make the composition either sky-dominant or land-dominant.

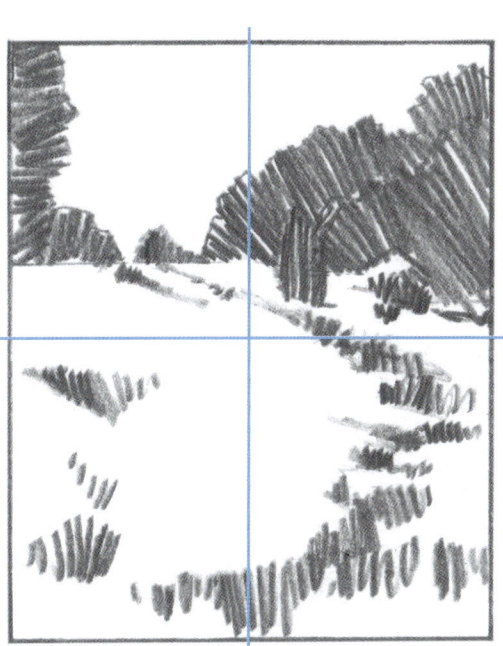

In a vertical format, the ground line sits well above the midline, creating a deep foreground with good perspective cues. This, in combination with the inward and upward action of the vertical format, gives this version the strongest suggestion of depth.

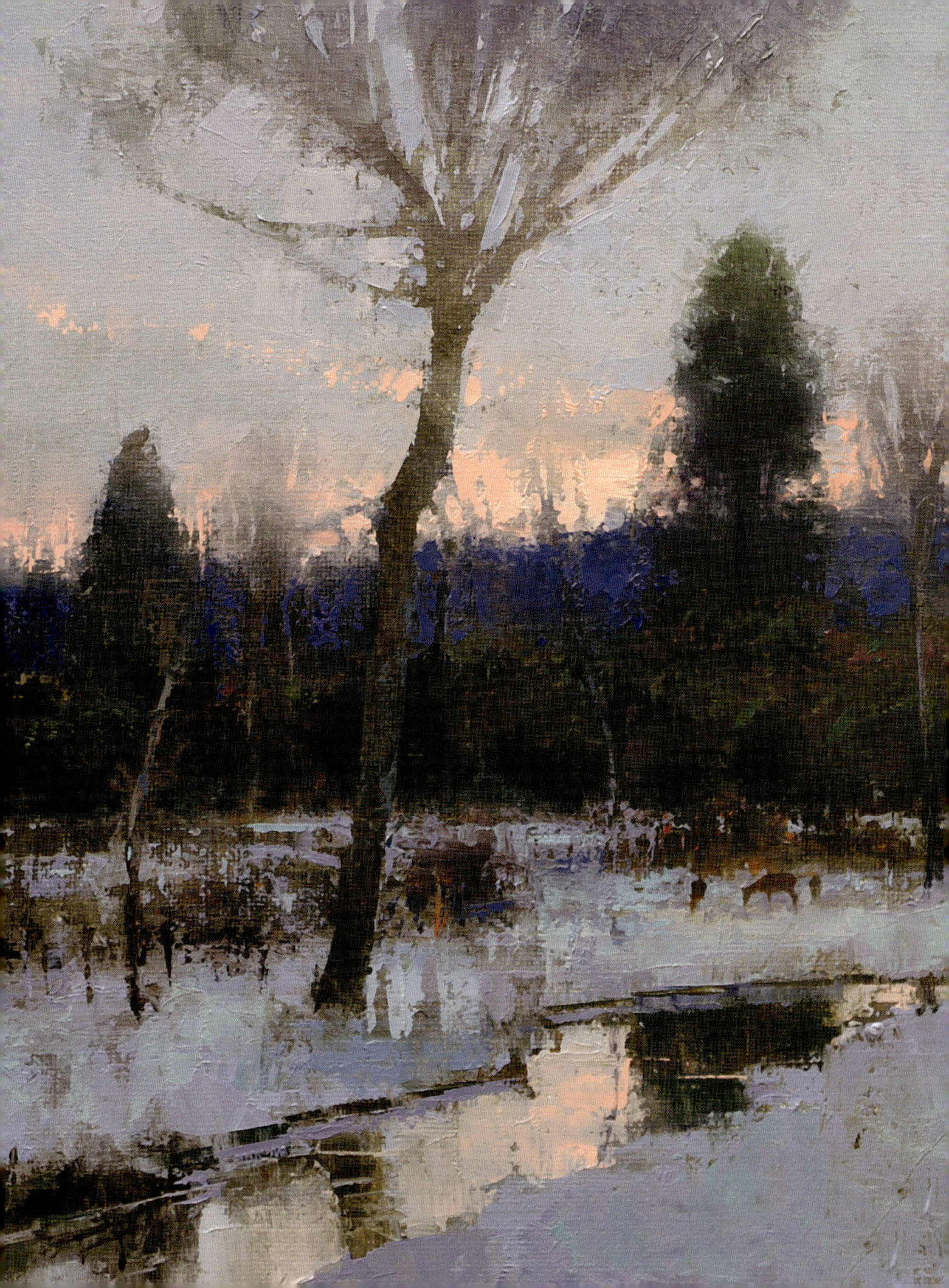

5

COLOR PRECEPTS, COLOR PARADOXES

There is no area within the landscape painter's study that is as complex and theory-rich as color. It presents the painter with many questions, not the least of which is, *How do I convert the light and color of the natural world into a painting that can impart a parallel experience to the viewer?*

The following chapters explore color from the perspective of the *color strategy*—the overarching plan that guides our color choices and helps achieve harmony. Before we begin, there are several broad truths about color that must first be acknowledged. These truths are not listed under the heading of *color theory*, but they do profoundly affect our efforts to translate light into paint.

The first precept is that pigments and painting surfaces are limited in their ability to express the brilliance of natural light. Second, a color strategy is not based solely on the colors we observe in nature; it is also the result of *informed modification*, the necessary changes we make to colors to suit the demands of the painting. And finally, color in painting is not duty bound to reality, but rather to the internal truth of the painting itself.

◄ Brent Cotton, *Winter's Calm*
Oil on linen, 10" × 8" | 25.5 × 20.5 cm

Pigments on canvas or paper cannot compete with the brilliance of natural light, but manipulating value and color in clever ways can create a parallel experience in the eyes of the beholder. Here, Cotton uses analogous harmony to achieve a deeply colored light and then adds a spark of color contrast with a warm pink accent.

RECONCILING THE DIFFERENCES BETWEEN PIGMENTS AND NATURAL LIGHT

If achieving harmony or capturing a mood or the color of the light was simply a matter of matching colors, then landscape painters would only need to cultivate one skill: mixing and matching colors exactly as they see them. Yet any painter who has ever attempted to translate the effects of light into paint has had to come to terms with the fact that this is not entirely possible. Why? Pigments are incapable of expressing the range of value and luminosity of natural light.

No matter how brilliant we make our colors or how strongly we render our value contrasts, a painting can never compete with the brilliance of sunlight.

To compensate for this disparity, painters manipulate value and color in exceedingly clever ways. So clever, in fact, they can produce color relationships that, although never matching the luminosity of natural light, can evoke the same sensations. If any of the great painters of light–J.M.W. Turner, the Impressionists, or the Hudson River painters, to name a few–were able to convince us that their light was "true," then that is a testament to how clever and skillful their use of color was.

As we will see in the next chapter, the primary vehicle for this "cleverness" is the color strategy. What particular colors, interacting in what particular ways, can produce the effects we are after?

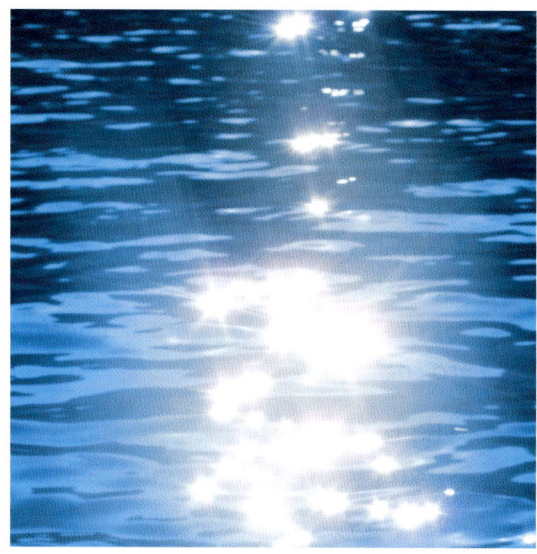

REACHING FOR THE SUN

Colored pigments on canvas or paper, as rich and saturated as they may be, can never compete with the brilliance of natural light— dappled light upon the water, a snowfield struck by direct sunlight, or the sun itself. To simulate such effects in their work, painters bend color to their will by manipulating values, color contrasts, temperature, and saturation levels.

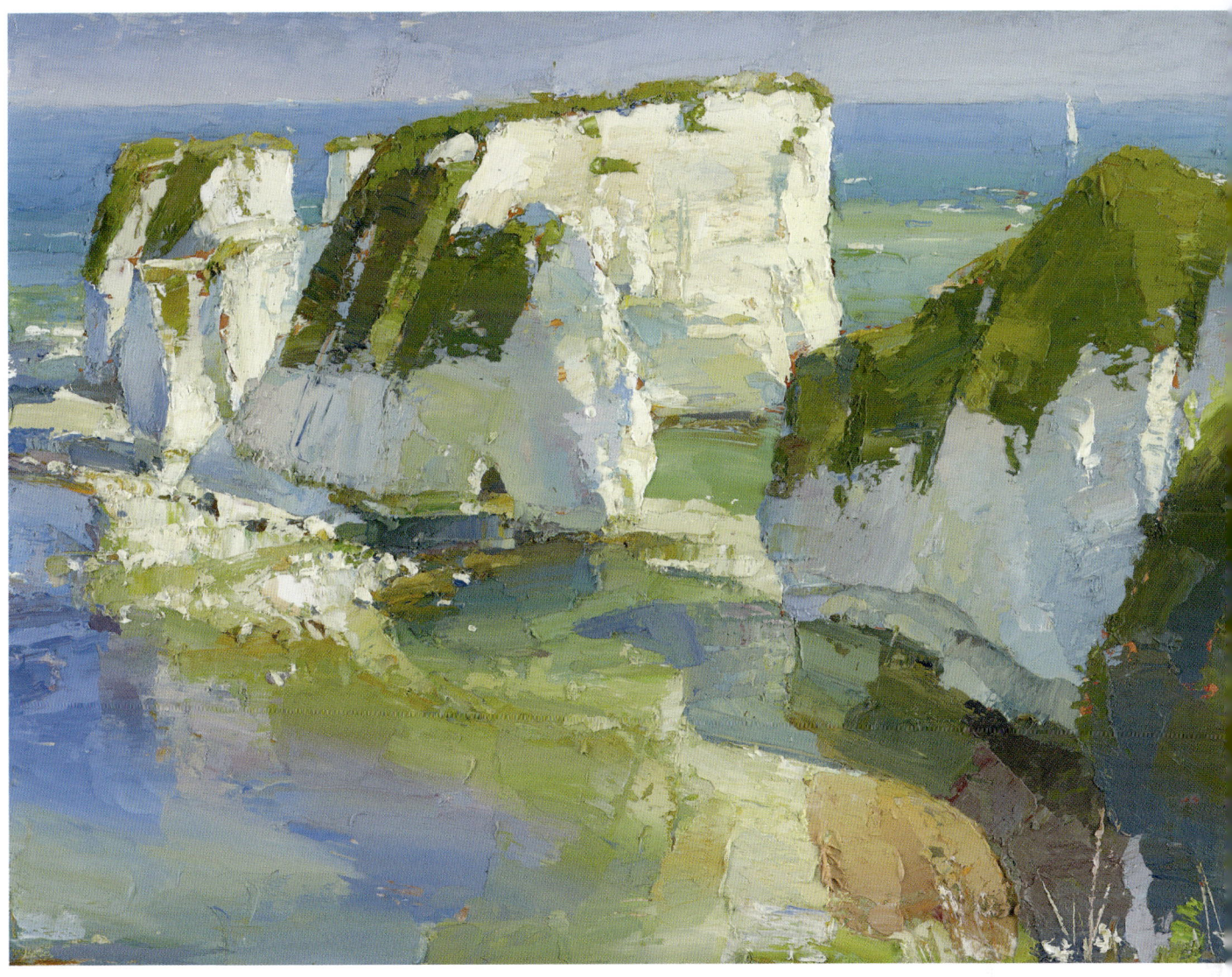

Oliver Akers Douglas, *Old Harry Rocks*
Oil on board, 18" × 24" | 46 × 61 cm

A painter's goal is not to replicate the subject, but to interpret it. He borrows from what he observes, but also alters the colors in service to the painting. To look at *Old Harry Rocks* is to experience the brilliance of the sunlight on the chalk cliffs and the richness of the azure blue sea. Yet these colors are not exactly what Akers Douglas observed. "Painted literally, the values would have been too polarized," he explains. "The whiteness of the cliffs would have looked rather bland and pale in comparison to the sea around it, so I emphasized the reflected blues, yellows, and pinks in the shadows in order to model the shapes more fully."

DIRECT OBSERVATION VS. "INFORMED MODIFICATION"

When I was in art school, one of my first landscape assignments was to paint the view out the studio window. I recall my struggle to match the color of the afternoon light that slanted across the grounds. No matter how many mixtures I tried, the color didn't seem right. When my instructor came over, he looked out the window, looked at my painting, and said, "Try adding some orange to the light areas… and make them a little darker." The color I saw outside didn't appear very orange or very dark to me. But I applied this new color anyway and much to my surprise, it worked better than any of my previous attempts. Even more surprising was that this better color was not the color I saw when I looked out the window.

Here was a paradox: a particular color, in the context of my painting, could make a more effective statement about the color of the light than when I tried to paint it exactly as I saw it.

That experience awakened me to a fundamental precept that would forever surround my efforts to paint the effects of natural light. A successful color strategy is not based solely on *direct observation*; that is, the colors we see in nature. It is also based on *informed modification*, the necessary changes we make to values and colors to achieve the desired results. The "right" color is a fluid blend between observation and interpretation.

How much does one rely on direct observation? On informed modification? It varies depending on whether we are painting outdoors or in the studio.

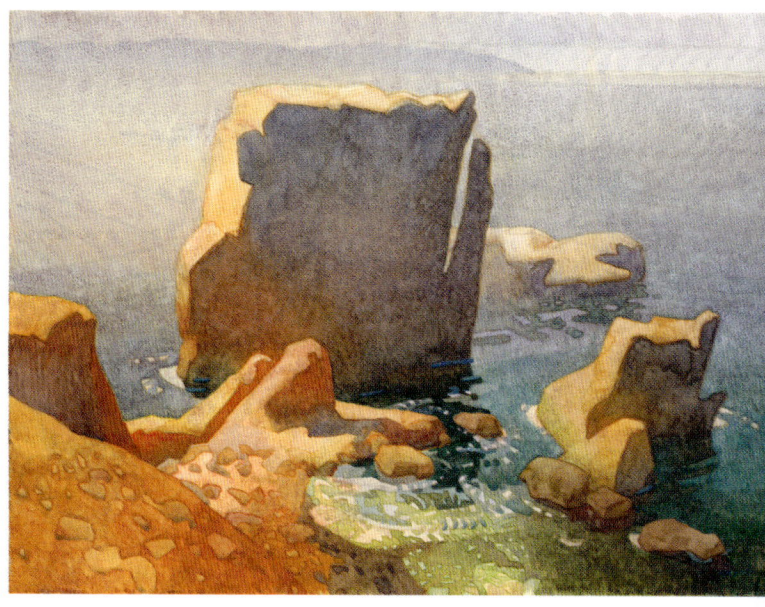

Carolyn Lord, *Shell Beach Opalescence*
Watercolor on paper, 22" × 30" | 56 × 76 cm

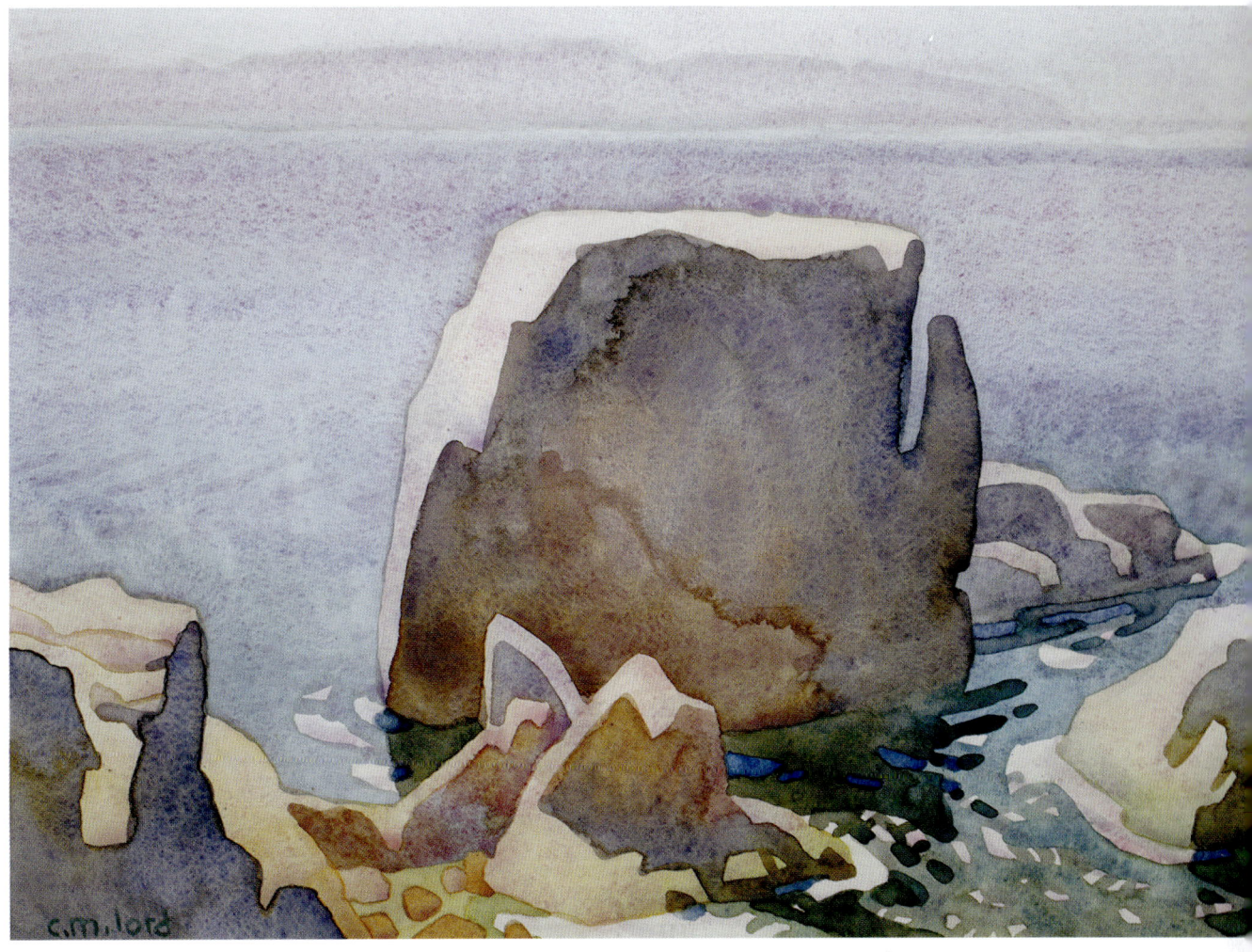

Carolyn Lord, *Opalescent Morning*
Watercolor on paper, 11" × 15" | 28 × 38 cm

When working on location, landscape painters typically lead with direct observation. They work closely with the colors they see. But even within the observational mode of plein air, a painter will need to modify the colors they see. For example, in the smaller plein air version, *Opalescent Morning* (above), Lord heightened the intensity of the bluish-purple shadows in order to bring out the difference between the light and shadow.

When working in the studio, painters rely more on informed modification: "I can take the time to consider all the elements of art, and how much of each I want to incorporate," says Lord. In her larger studio version, *Shell Beach Opalescence* (left), she brings out the temperature differences more and heightens the effects of atmosphere. She also creates greater texture. She plays into the granulating qualities of watercolor pigments, knowing they will settle into the texture of the cold press paper. This contributes to a specular effect, which in turn contributes to a sense of diffused light.

PLEIN AIR: DIRECT OBSERVATION

When we paint outdoors, nothing stands between us and the subject but the air. We can see nuances of color and value that a photo could never record. We are engaged in an intense conversation with nature, observing what is before us and trying to translate those colors as closely as we can. When surrounded by *living* color– the colors we observe when standing in nature– it is difficult to do otherwise. Plein air painters still modify colors as needed, but they primarily work from direct observation.

Monet famously described direct observation in this way: "Try to forget what objects you have before you–a tree, a house, a field, or whatever. Merely think, 'Here is a little square of blue, here an oblong of pink, here a streak of yellow,' and paint it just as it looks to you, the exact color and shape, until it gives you your own impression of the scene before you."

We know that pigments and canvas cannot compete with the brilliance of actual sunlight–but we try. Such is the dance of living color.

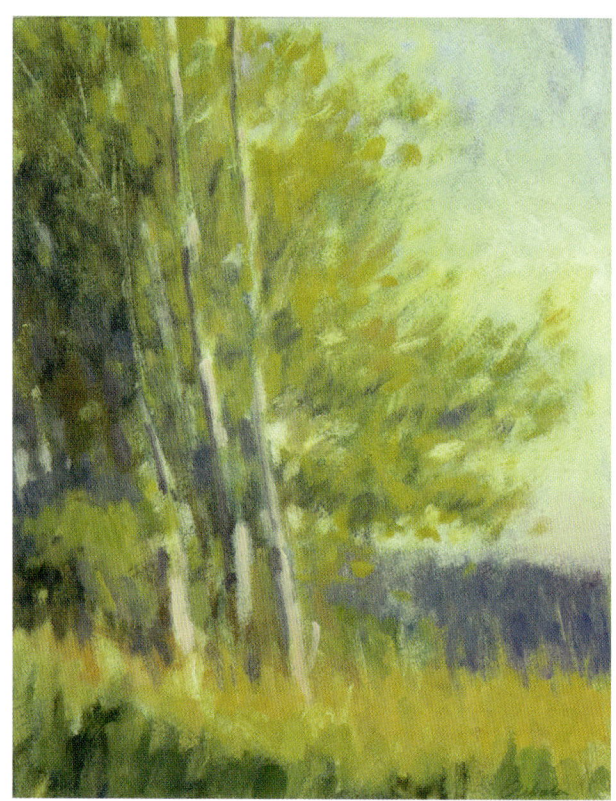

Mitchell Albala, *The Cottonwood Tree*
Oil on paper, 10½" × 8" | 27 × 20.5 cm

The joy of working outdoors comes through our response to living color. We know that skies are blue and trees are green, but when outdoors, *perceived* color is our goal—the color of an object as it appears under a particular color of light. In *Cottonwood*, the light on the horizon in the late afternoon appeared more yellow than blue, so that is the color I painted it. The shadows in the tree appeared more blue than green, so that is the color I mixed.

THE LESSONS OF LIVING COLOR

A landscape painter cannot hope to understand how the colors of natural light translate into paint if they haven't observed those colors in their natural habitat and tried to mix them. This is the *plein air* experience. When a landscape painter works in the studio, they can benefit greatly from their years of experience observing color in nature. There is no substitute for direct observation.

IN THE STUDIO: "INFORMED MODIFICATION"

In the studio, our relationship to color changes—*direct observation is no longer possible.* We are once removed from the actual subject. If we are not face to face with living color then every color choice becomes a form of informed modification. We may still "borrow" from what we have seen by means of memory, studies, and reference photos, but the color strategy is now entirely our own.

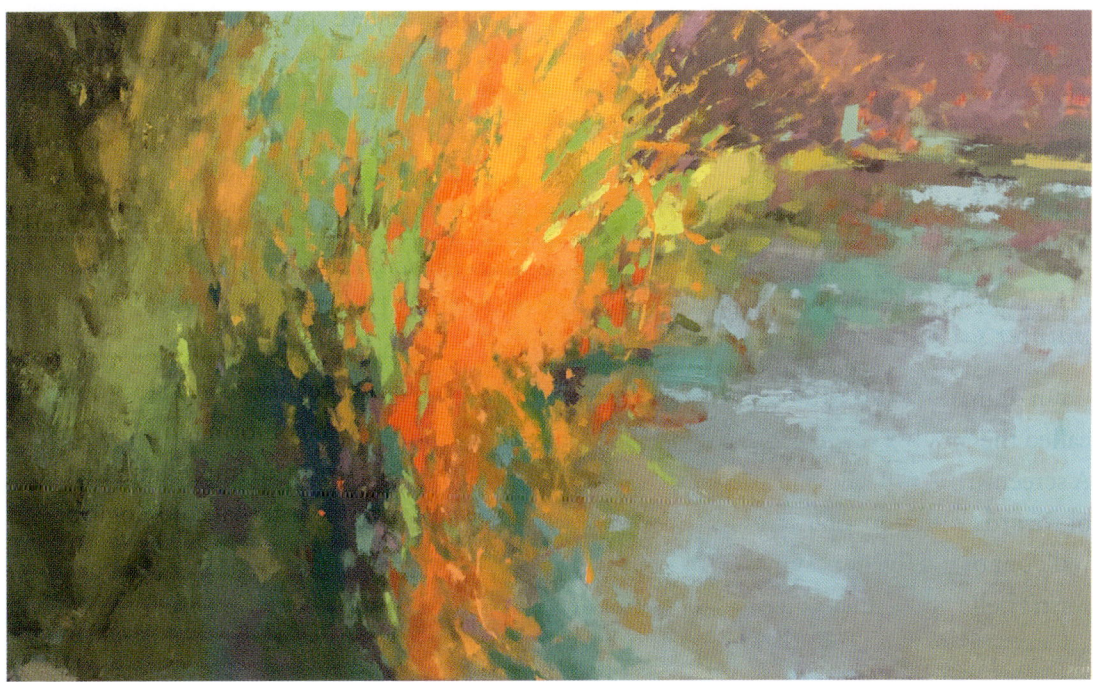

Scott Gellatly, *Waterside*
Oil on panel, 27" × 45" | 68.5 × 114.5 cm

Gellatly's *Waterside* is a significant departure from his field study, *Wetland in Autumn* (below), on which the painting is based. In the studio, Gellatly works with *informed modification*: he modifies colors based on knowledge and his own subjective interpretation. He creates a bold color tension by juxtaposing the saturated orange and greens in the center foliage against the less saturated color areas on either side.

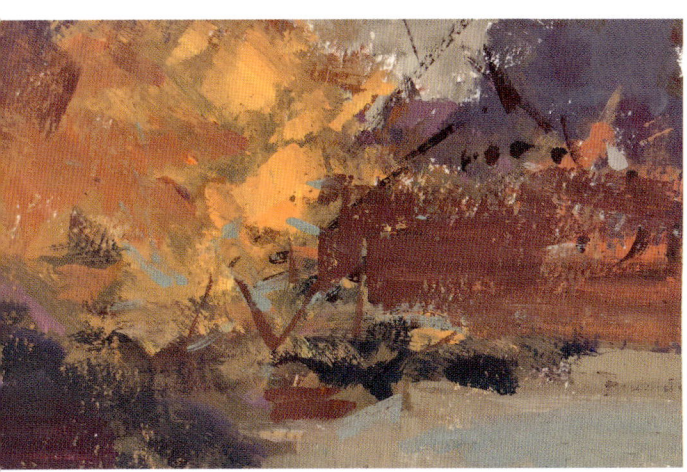

WATERSIDE FIELD STUDY

Scott Gellatly, *Wetland in Autumn*
Gouache on paper, 4" × 6½" | 10 × 16.5 cm

Gellatly's color choices in the field study are based more on direct observation. He is responding to colors he observed in the moment, taking fewer liberties with color than he does in the studio with *Waterside* (above). Gellatly says, "These studies serve as a catalog of imagery where I can find visual sparks to use as a basis for larger studio paintings."

CONVINCING COLOR, BELIEVABLE COLOR

Color grants us a wide latitude of expression. Whether we rely more on direct observation or informed modification, what matters is that the colors that end up in the final painting are *believable* in the context of that painting.

"Believable" color does not mean how accurately the colors match reality. It means that the viewer can accept the painter's reality on their own terms.

In dramatic writing, there is something called the "willing suspension of disbelief." A screenwriter can spin a fantastical tale of wizards with magical powers, but if we walk out of the theater saying, "That just wasn't believable," then the film would be considered a failure. The skilled writer knows how to weave a story in such a way that, for the brief time we spend in front of the movie screen, we *accept* it on its own terms.

The landscape painter's goal is much the same. Whether spinning a tale of color as seemingly naturalistic as a Marc Hanson's *Eclipse Day* (below) or as expressive as Mark Gould's *Glen, Canyon, Stream: Arcadian* (page 109), it must be done in a way that is believable in the context of the painting. A painting is not reality, so its colors don't necessarily have to conform to reality. But they do need to form an impression that is consistent with the internal color logic of the painting.

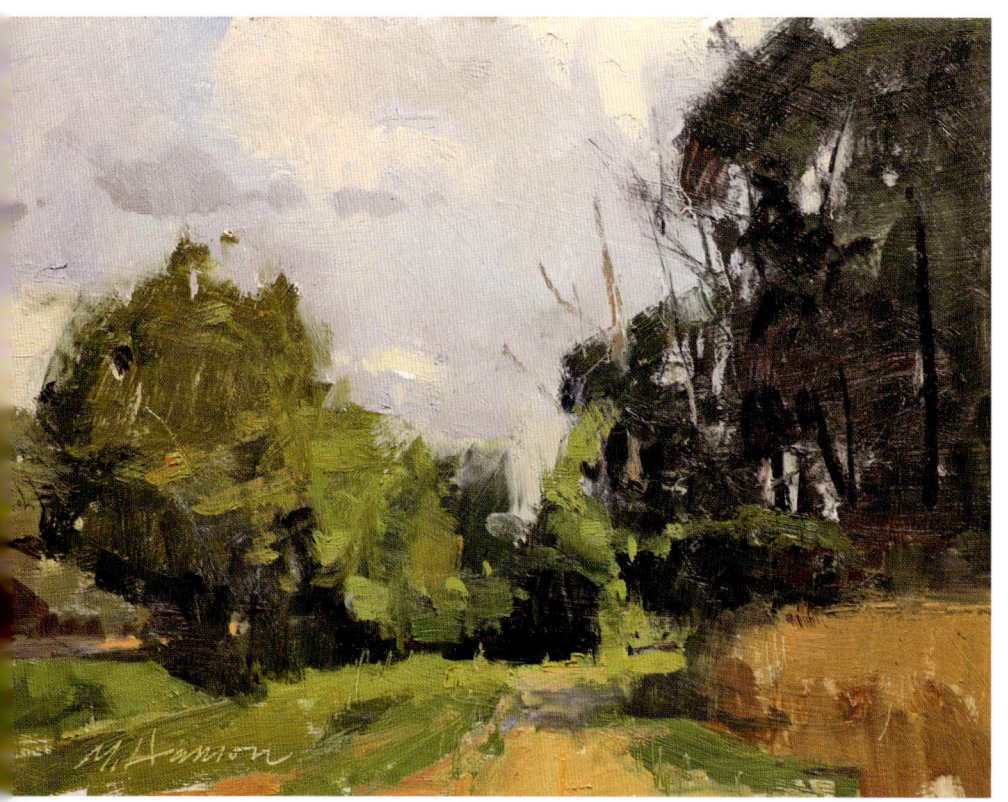

Marc Hanson, *Eclipse Day #1*
Oil on board, 9" × 12" |
23 × 30.5 cm

As much as a painter may rely on direct observation when working outdoors, some informed modification is always involved. Hanson explains, "Although the colors in *Eclipse Day* may look naturalistic (because of my own preferences and style), it is still several steps away from how it actually looked in the subject . . . I want to make color choices that are interesting as a painting, rather than only being descriptive."

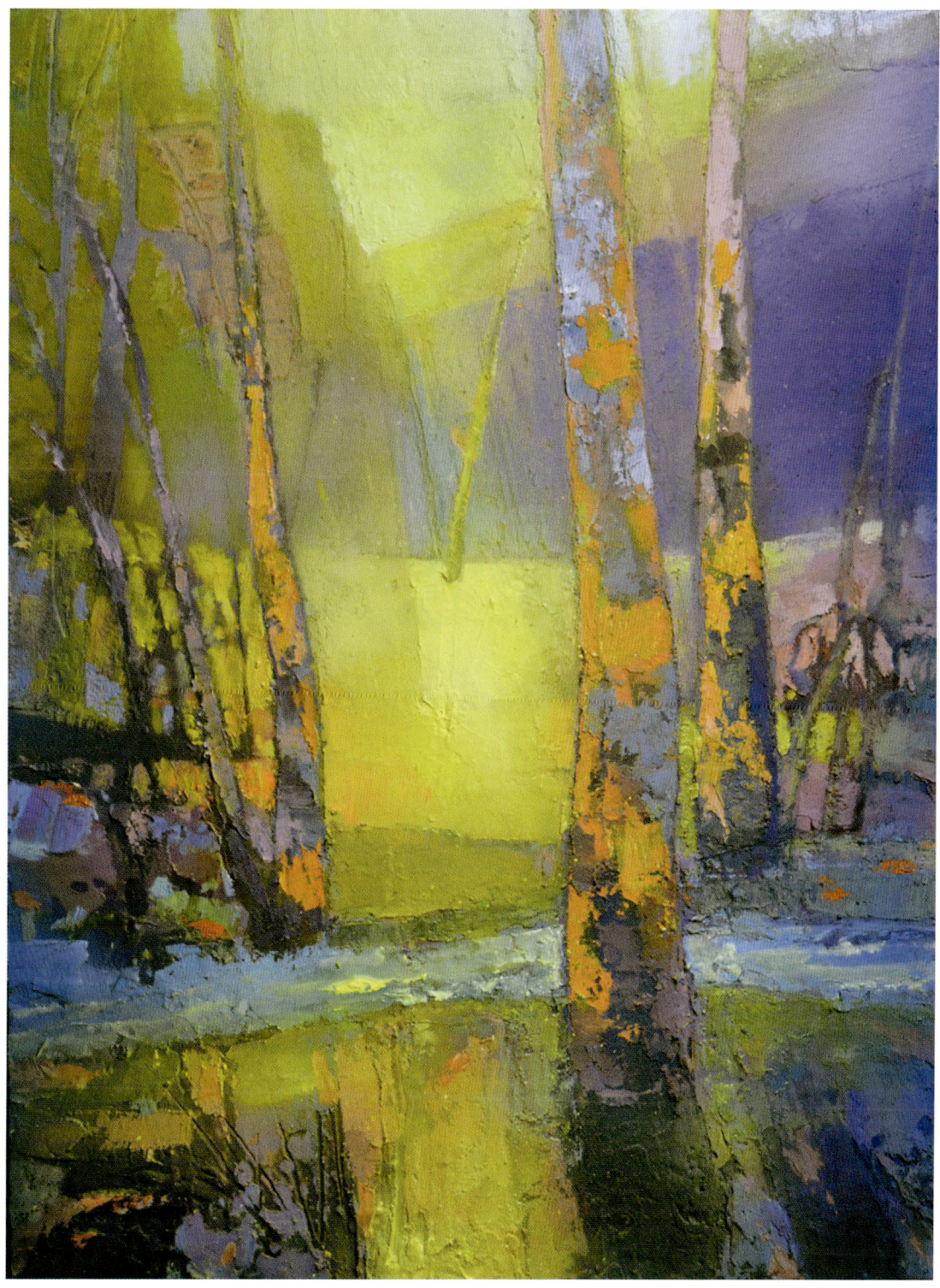

Mark Gould, *Glen, Canyon, Stream: Arcadian*
Acrylic on panel, 20" × 16" | 51 × 40.5 cm

All paintings present us with an alternate reality, but some paintings do so more than others. In comparison to Hanson's *Eclipse Day* (previous page), Gould's interpretation of color is much more expressive. His intense colors are not what we would call realistic, but in the context of painting they remind us of nature and they make sense. "One saturated color tends to lead to other saturated colors," says Gould. "Saturated colors make more sense in the context of other saturated colors."

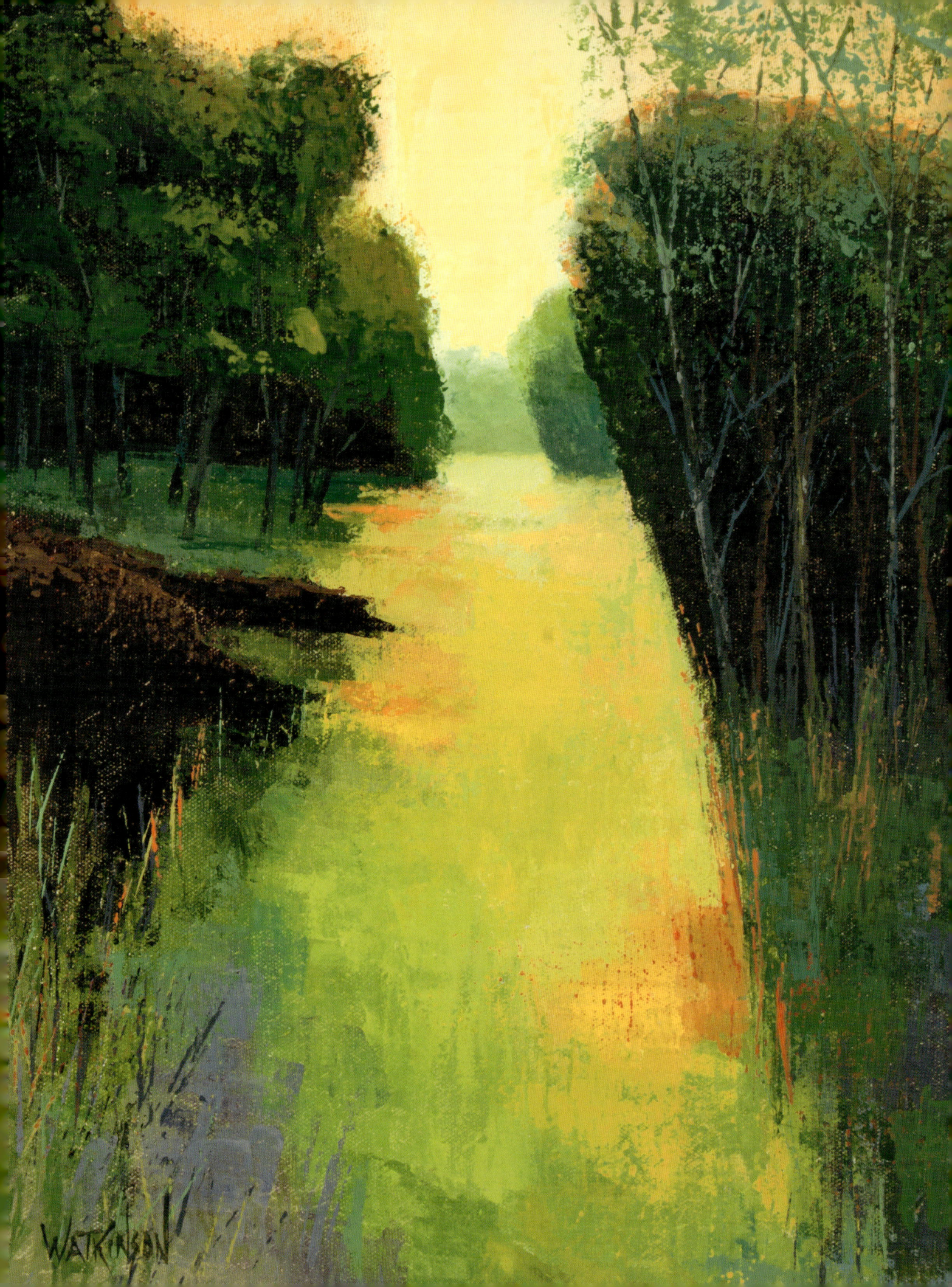

6

THE COMPLETE COLOR STRATEGY

When we observe the myriad colors of the natural world, we never think, *Those colors just don't look harmonious!* Natural light and color never fails to be convincing. But how do painters, in the synthetic world of their two-dimensional paintings, maintain that same sense of harmony and color cohesion? How can they convey a mood, an atmospheric effect, or a particular color of light?

We begin by drawing from nature's palette. We borrow her hues and value relationships, her temperatures and chromaticity. Yet, that is only a starting point. Inevitably, we discover that to achieve the effects we are after, we also have to modify colors in an informed way. We need to apply some kind of overarching plan to our color— *a color strategy*.

In this chapter, you will learn how a complete color strategy is made up of three types of color relationships: *hue interactions*, *value contrasts*, and *relative saturation*. We'll analyze several paintings to see how each of these work to produce different harmonies, colors of light, and moods.

◄ Brent Watkinson, *Evening Trees*
Oil on canvas, 30" × 24" | 76 × 61 cm

HUE INTERACTION: **SIMILARITY**, analogous with contrasting accents
VALUE CONTRAST: LOW / MEDIUM / **HIGH**
SATURATION: LOW / **MEDIUM–HIGH**

The illusion of light in painting is not achieved by mimicking nature. It is based on a color plan or strategy, which involves three types of contrast: hue interactions, values, and relative saturation. *Evening Trees* is predominantly yellow-green, but has accents of orange and blue-violet. The strong sense of sunset light is the result of strong value contrasts combined with saturated color.

DEFINING THE COLOR STRATEGY

All landscape painters strive for harmony, that unmistakable sense that all the colors in the painting cohere and work well together. Harmony is typically defined as a "pleasing arrangement of colors forming a consistent whole." The color strategy is the organizing principle through which we actually achieve "pleasing" and "harmonious."

A color strategy is a formula for color interactions, a collection of colors that relate in specific ways to produce a desired effect.

Landscape painters rely on a strategy to help guide their color choices and ensure that they form landscape-like harmonies.

A color strategy seeks to answer the landscape painter's eternal question: what particular colors, interacting in what specific ways, will be able to convey a mood, a time of day, or a particular color of light?

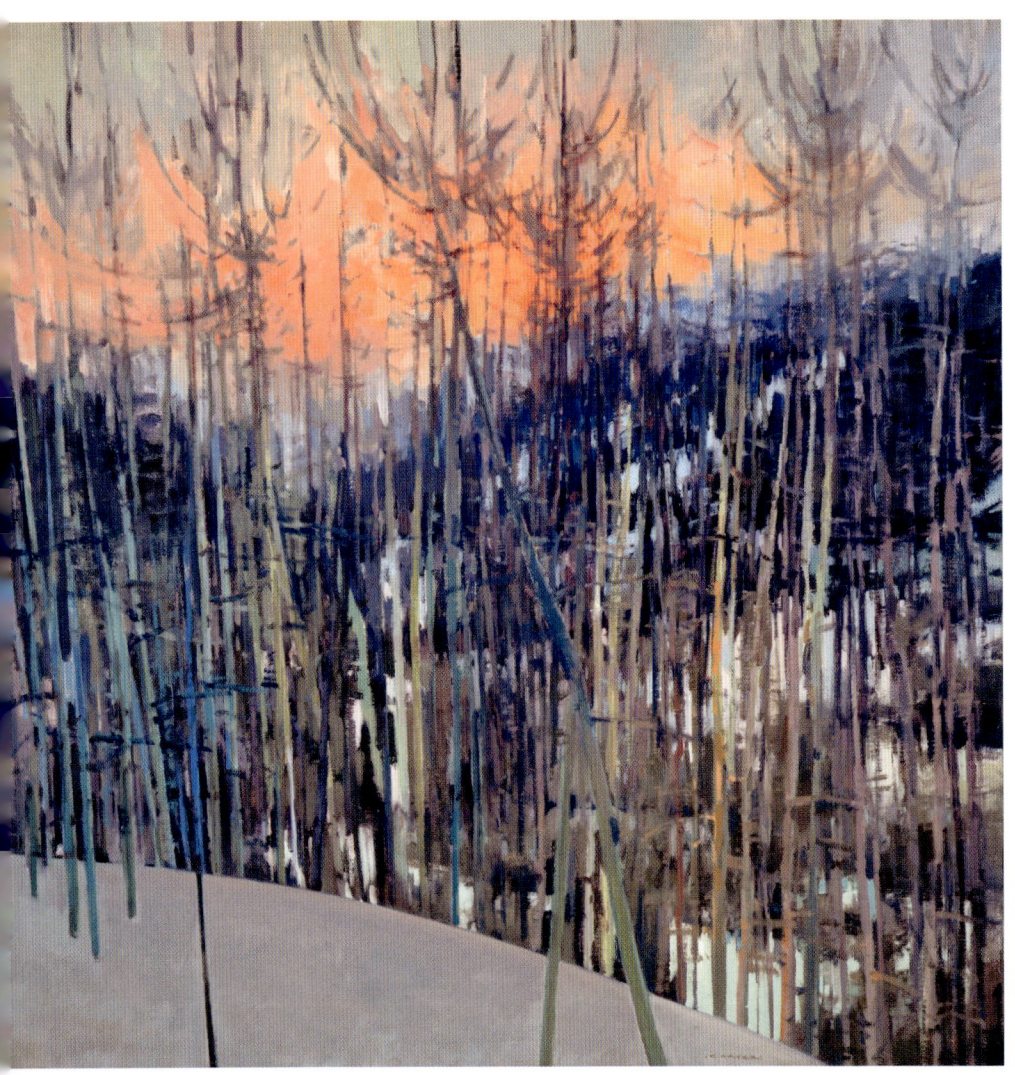

Jill Carver, *New Day*
Oil on canvas, 36" × 36" |
91.5 × 91.5 cm

HUE INTERACTION:
SIMILARITY, analogous harmony
with contrasting accent

VALUE CONTRAST:
LOW / **MEDIUM** / HIGH

SATURATION:
LOW / **MEDIUM** / HIGH

New Day beautifully captures a winter day, touched by a glimmer of warmth at sunrise. Every strategy involves hue interactions, value contrasts, and relative saturation. Here, the dominant blue-violet establishes a unifying harmony. Yet, it is the contrasting pink accent in the sky that gives the subject its special meaning.

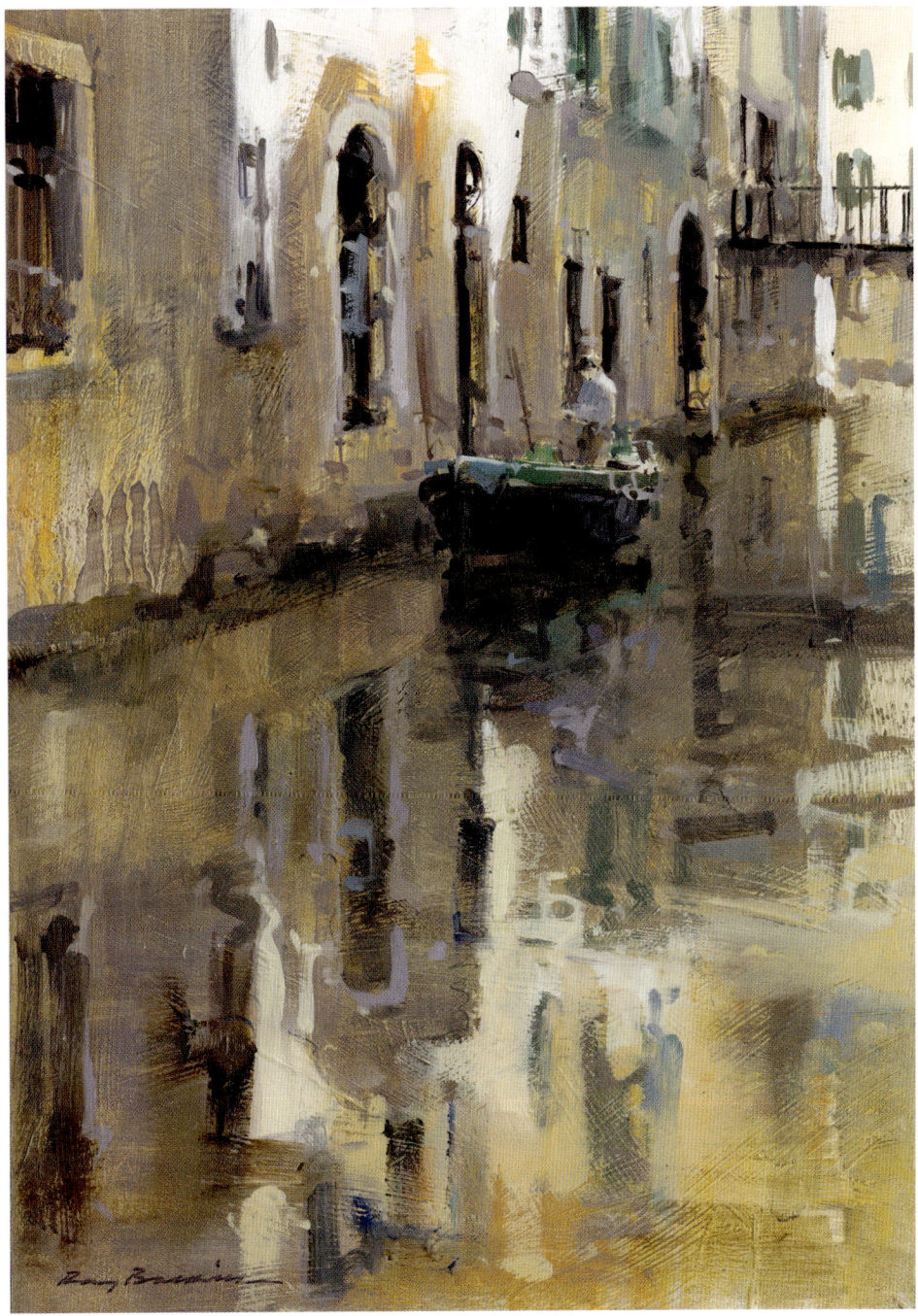

Ray Balkwill, *Venetian Reflections*
Oil on board, 10" × 14" | 25.5 × 35.5 cm

HUE INTERACTION: **DISSIMILAR**, complementary
VALUE CONTRAST: LOW / **MEDIUM** / HIGH
SATURATION: LOW / **MEDIUM** / HIGH

Venetian Reflections uses a complementary hue interaction based on yellow and violet, which corresponds to the light and shadow patterns. Complements need not be fully saturated to provide effective contrast. The values range from light to dark, but most are in the midrange, which allows the shadows to be more luminous.

CONTRAST: THE ANIMATING FORCE OF THE COLOR STRATEGY

Contrast of color—or the *differences* between colors—is the animating force of the color strategy. Whether those differences are subtle or great, they give life to our color relationships and to our paintings. Are hues similar and related or do they contrast? Are the values closely related or is the contrast strong? Are the colors saturated and intense, or are they neutral and gray-like? Or a combination of both?

In the artificial world of our paintings, contrast of color is the means at our disposal for making our colors interact in ways that simulate the effects of natural light.

DEFINING STRATEGY IN TERMS OF HUE, VALUE, AND SATURATION

When painters talk about "color strategies," they are usually referring to the color relationships found on the standard 12-step color wheel: *monochromatic, analogous, complementary, split-complementary,* and *triadic.* More precisely, these relationships refer to *hue interactions.* They define the ways different hue families interact with one another.

As vital as hue interactions are, they do not form a complete strategy on their own. A complete strategy also involves two other essential aspects of color—value contrasts and relative saturation.

These aspects of contrast act as the levers that control the overall strategy. When delicately balanced, they are responsible for every moment of color magic ever produced on paper or canvas. Controlling these relationships allows us to bend color to our will and produce the effects we are after.

HUE INTERACTIONS AND THE COLOR WHEEL

The color wheel is a handy reference for mapping the various hue interactions (e.g., analogous, complementary, etc). A complete color strategy isn't defined only by these interactions; it also considers the relative value and saturation levels of the colors. Some wheels try to indicate value differences or saturation levels, but none can describe all three aspects of color contrast in two-dimensional form. In the early twentieth century, Albert Munsell attempted to overcome this limitation with a three-dimensional color model that maps colors in terms of hue, value, and saturation. Any color mapping system, though, only shows *individual* colors. It cannot tell you how to mix a color or how that color fits into the context of your overall strategy.

Photo: The Color Wheel Company

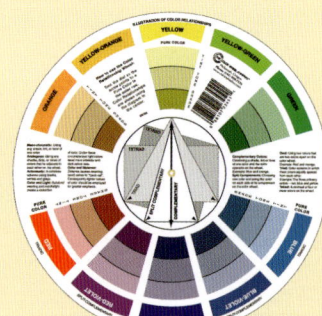

ASPECT OF COLOR CONTRAST: HUE INTERACTIONS

WHY HUE INTERACTIONS MATTER

The first aspect of color contrast is the hue interaction. These are the standard relationships we are familiar with from the color wheel. They define how different hue families interact with one another and are largely responsible for the forces of attraction and opposition we find among colors. Are the colors closely related, with tight bonds, as they are in analogous harmony? Or do the colors differ from each other as in complementary relationships?

HUE INTERACTIONS IN THE CONTEXT OF SIMILARITY OR DIFFERENCES

Painters often think of hue interactions as all there is to a color strategy, without considering any other aspects of color. They will say, *This is analogous harmony* or *This is a complementary relationship*. In fact, a painting is often a complex blend of different types of hue interactions. We see this in Brent Cotton's *When Days Are Short* (page 119). There is a strong analogous harmony at work. Yet, there is also a small complementary accent. Does this make it a complementary painting? Or is it analogous? In fact, it is both. For this reason, it is also helpful to think about hue interactions in terms of similarity or differences.

Identifying a hue interaction by name (analogous, complementary, etc.) is helpful, but not as important as recognizing whether that interaction is based on similarity or differences.

HUE INTERACTIONS BASED ON SIMILARITY		HUE INTERACTIONS BASED ON DIFFERENCES		
MONOCHROMATIC	ANALOGOUS	SPLIT-COMPLEMENTARY	COMPLEMENTARY	TRIADIC
Monochromatic and analogous are hue interactions based on similarity. Both form very cohesive and unified harmonies because their colors are so related.		Split-complementary, complementary, and triadic are interactions that rely on the differences between hues. They also create harmonies, but do so through contrast and opposition.		

THE POWER OF ONE: MONOCHROMATIC

Mitchell Albala, *Cascade Dusk*
Oil on canvas, 20" × 38" | 51 × 96.5 cm

HUE INTERACTION: **SIMILARITY**, monochromatic
VALUE CONTRAST: **LOW** / MEDIUM / HIGH
SATURATION: LOW / **MEDIUM** / HIGH

Cascade Dusk uses the simplest of all hue interactions, monochromatic. Every color in the painting is drawn from the blue family, but the blues vary in value, temperature, and saturation. Even the subtle green hints in the middle ground trees are heavily tinged with blue. The value range is compressed. On a 10-step value scale, the snowfield is about a 4 and the darkest trees about a 7. This compressed range, in combination with the monochromatic scheme, creates a sense of deep atmosphere and unified light. The snow appears especially luminous because its saturation is played against the much grayer stand of trees.

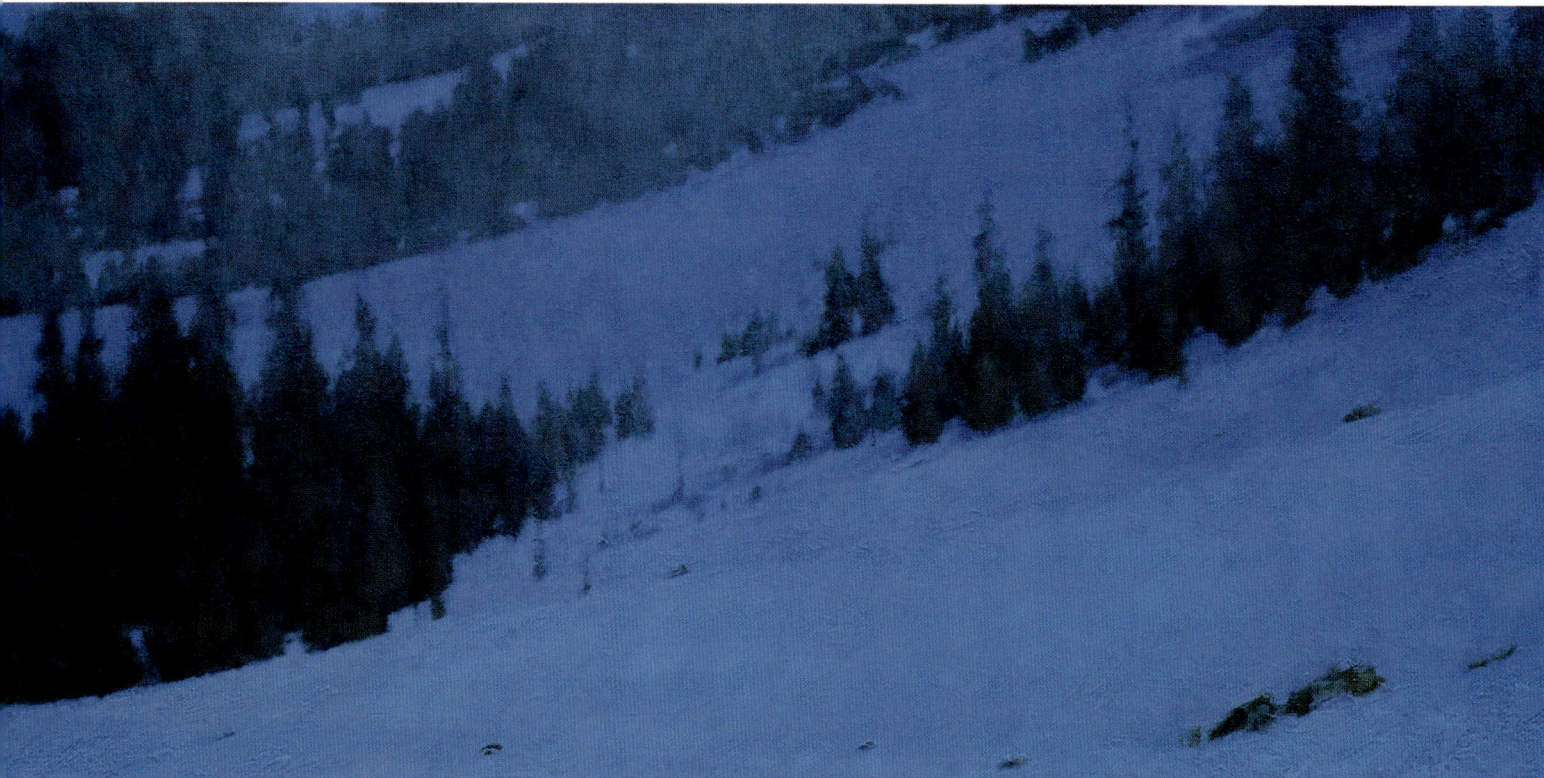

THE COLOR STRATEGY: THREE INTERRELATED PRACTICES

In the remainder of this chapter, we will review each form of contrast in turn. Keep in mind, however, that hue interactions, value contrasts, and relative saturation do not work in isolation. They are dynamically related; each one affects the other.

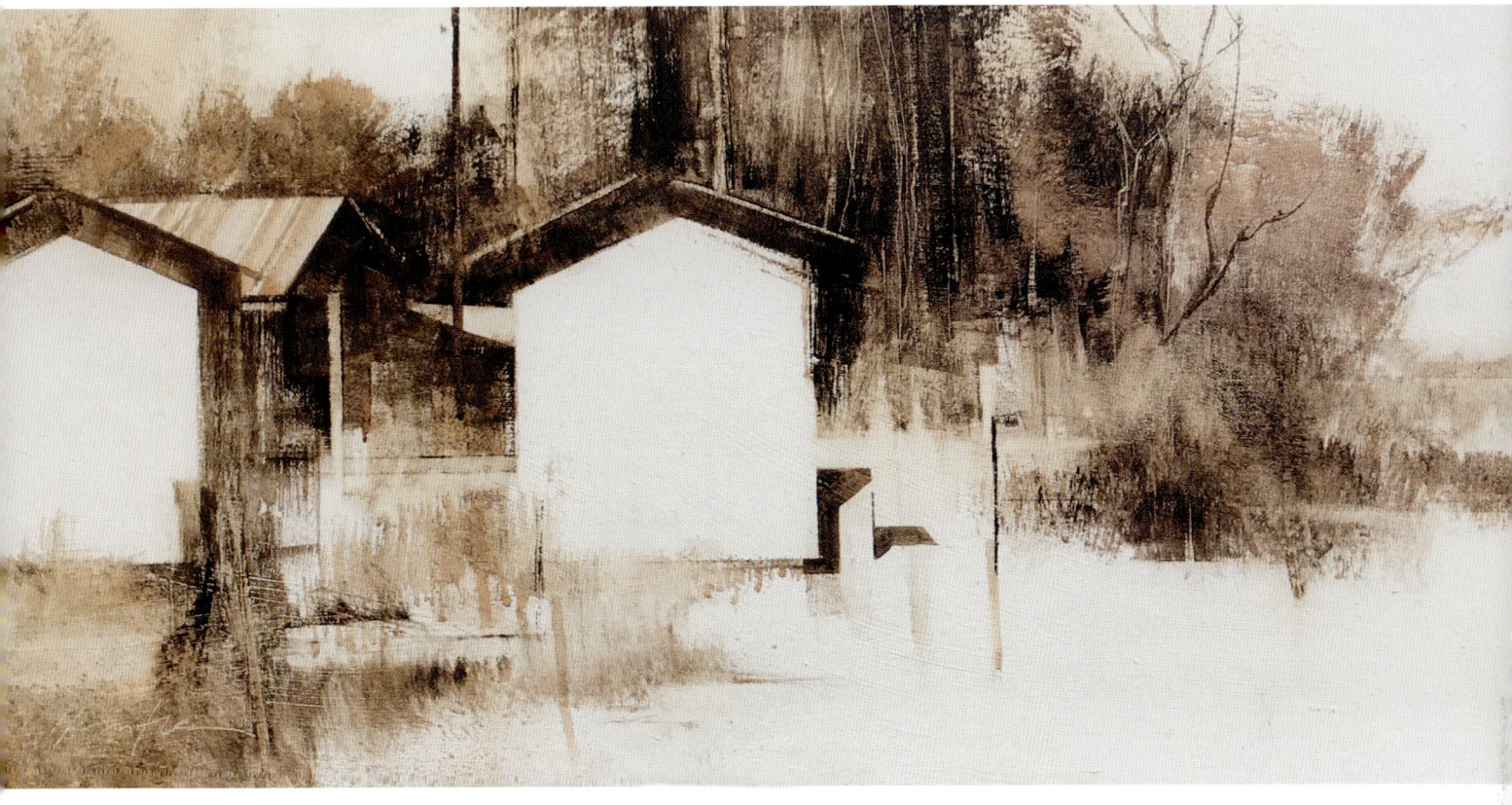

THE POWER OF LIGHT AND DARK

Charlie Hunter, *Five Five Eighteen*
Oil on panel, 12" × 24" | 30.5 × 61 cm

HUE INTERACTION: **SIMILARITY**, monochromatic
VALUE CONTRAST: LOW / MEDIUM / **HIGH**
SATURATION: **LOW** / MEDIUM / HIGH

In *Five Five Eighteen*, Hunter works monochromatically with just a single pigment, Van Dyke brown. With all the color contrast a full palette can offer, why would a painter choose this kind of strategy? The purity of light and dark alone has an inherent beauty all its own. What a painting like this may lack in color contrast, it more than makes up for with the drama of value contrasts. To achieve a range of values with the one dark pigment, Hunter uses no white. Instead, he uses the Van Dyke brown in varying degrees of opacity and transparency.

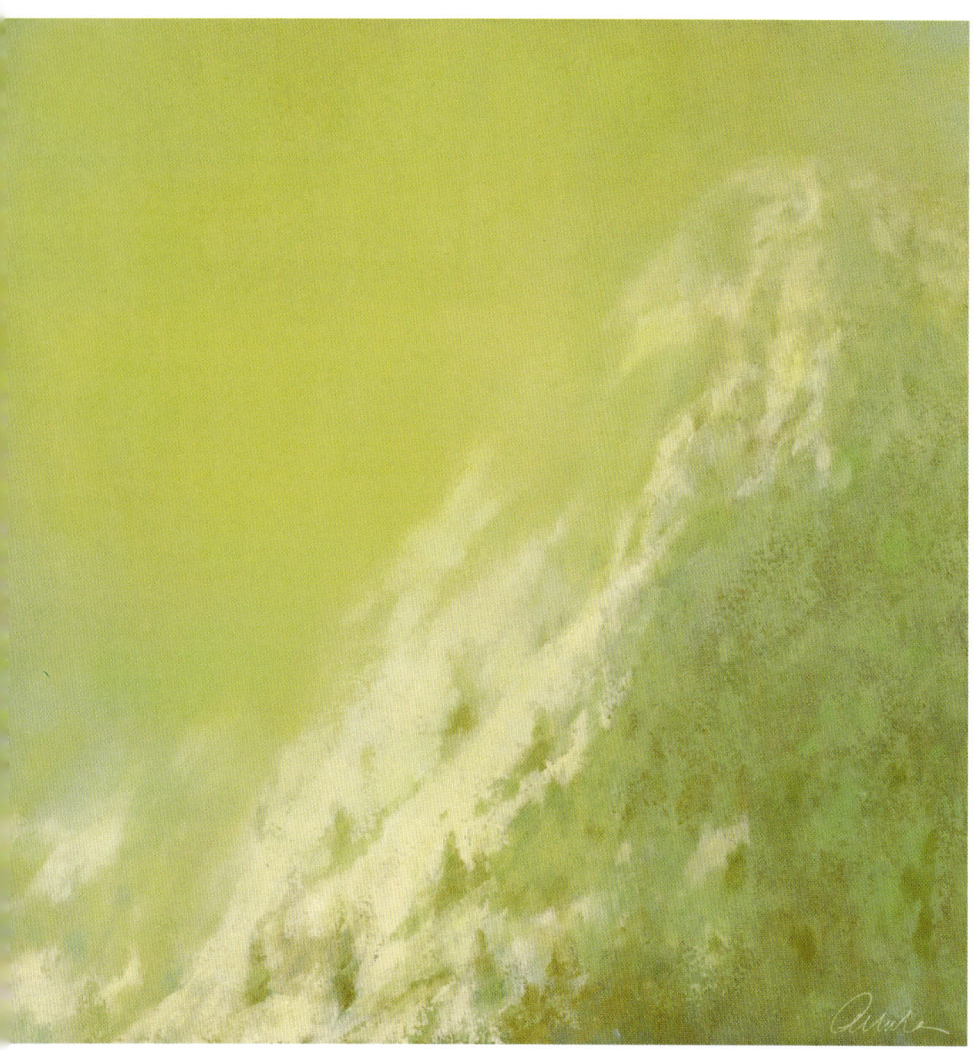

THE POWER OF KINSHIP: ANALOGOUS HARMONY

Mitchell Albala, *Snowy Ridge, Early Light*
Oil on board, 12" × 12" |
30.5 × 30.5 cm

HUE INTERACTION:
SIMILARITY, analogous

VALUE CONTRAST:
LOW / MEDIUM / HIGH

SATURATION:
LOW / **MEDIUM** / HIGH

Analogous colors are adjacent to each other on the color wheel and therefore as closely related as any two or three colors can be. The deeply colored atmosphere in *Early Light* is achieved with a three-hue analogy, ranging from yellow to yellow-green to green. Yellow is the common hue shared by all three colors in the analogy. A compressed value range also contributes to the atmospheric quality.

ATMOSPHERE AND ANALOGY

One of the magical qualities of landscape light is its ability to hold color within the atmosphere. Depending on the time of day and the amount of moisture and dust in the air, the atmosphere can reflect certain colors (as we readily see at sunset) and bathe everything it touches under a unifying veil of colored light. Analogous harmony is particularly effective at rendering this effect. The innate ability of analogous colors to create deeply harmonious relationships makes them an ideal means of simulating the illusion of colored light and atmosphere.

Photo: Obadinah Heavner

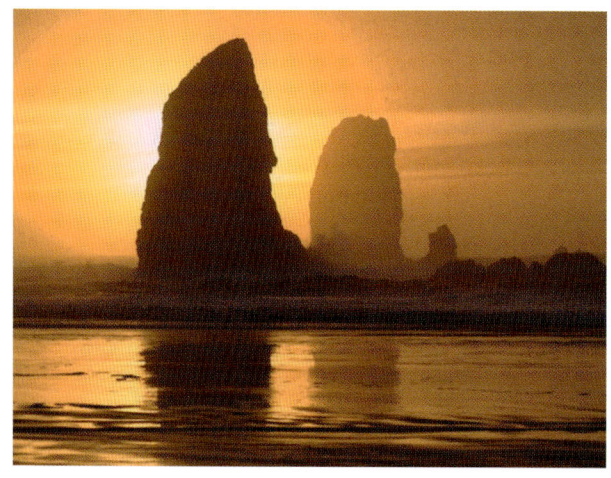

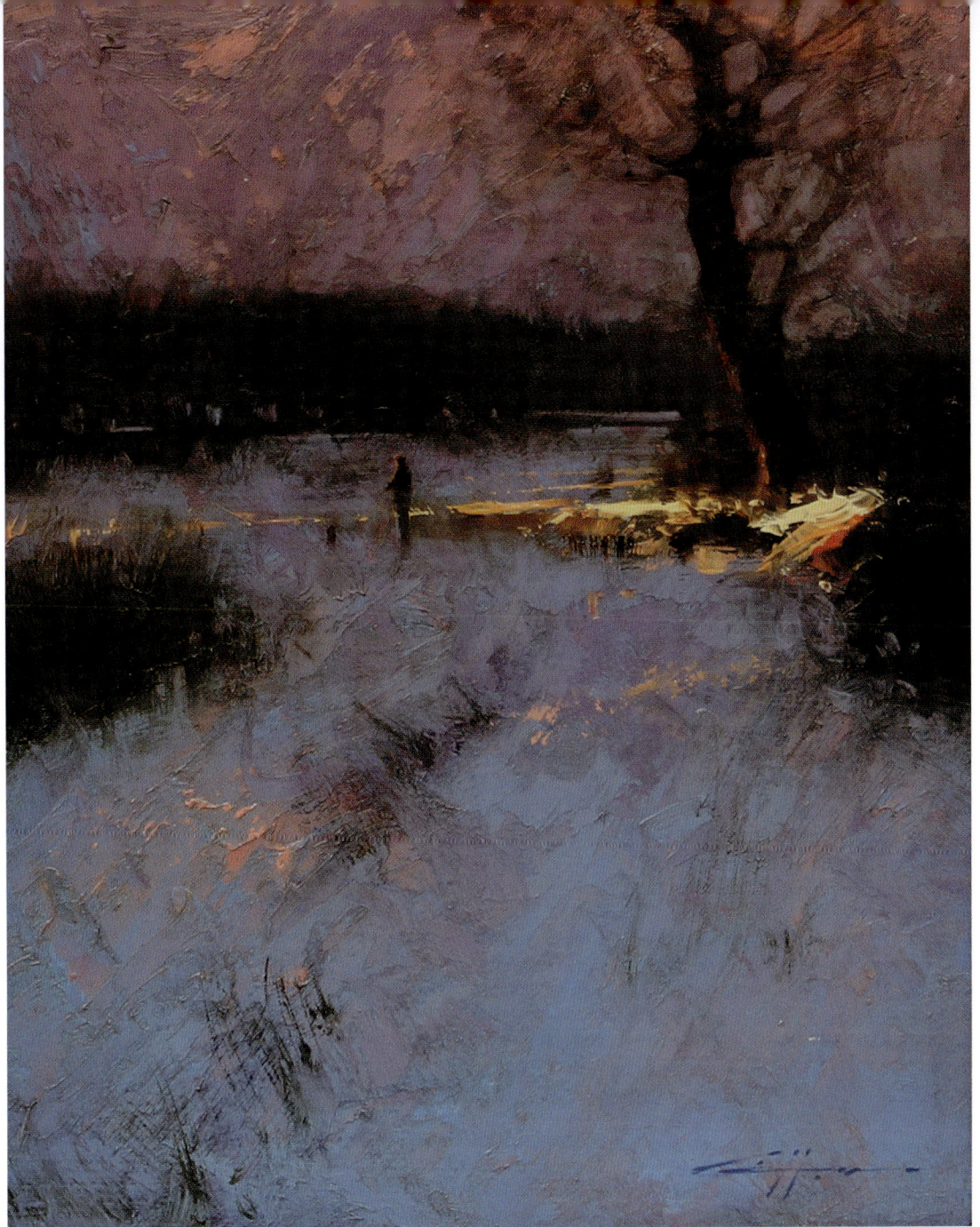

ANALOGOUS HARMONY WITH CONTRASTING ACCENT

Brent Cotton, *When Days Are Short*
Oil on linen, 10" × 8" | 25.5 × 20.5 cm

HUE INTERACTION: **SIMILARITY**, analogous harmony with contrasting accent
VALUE CONTRAST: LOW / **MEDIUM** / HIGH
SATURATION: LOW / **MEDIUM** / HIGH

If analogous harmony is so effective at suggesting unified light, why don't more painters work with it? Because it doesn't always give them the color contrast they need. In Cotton's piece, we experience all the benefits of deeply colored light through a blue-violet/red-violet analogy. Yet, he enlivens the color field with a complementary accent of yellow-orange. Cotton's use of a compressed value range also supports the illusion of a deeply colored light.

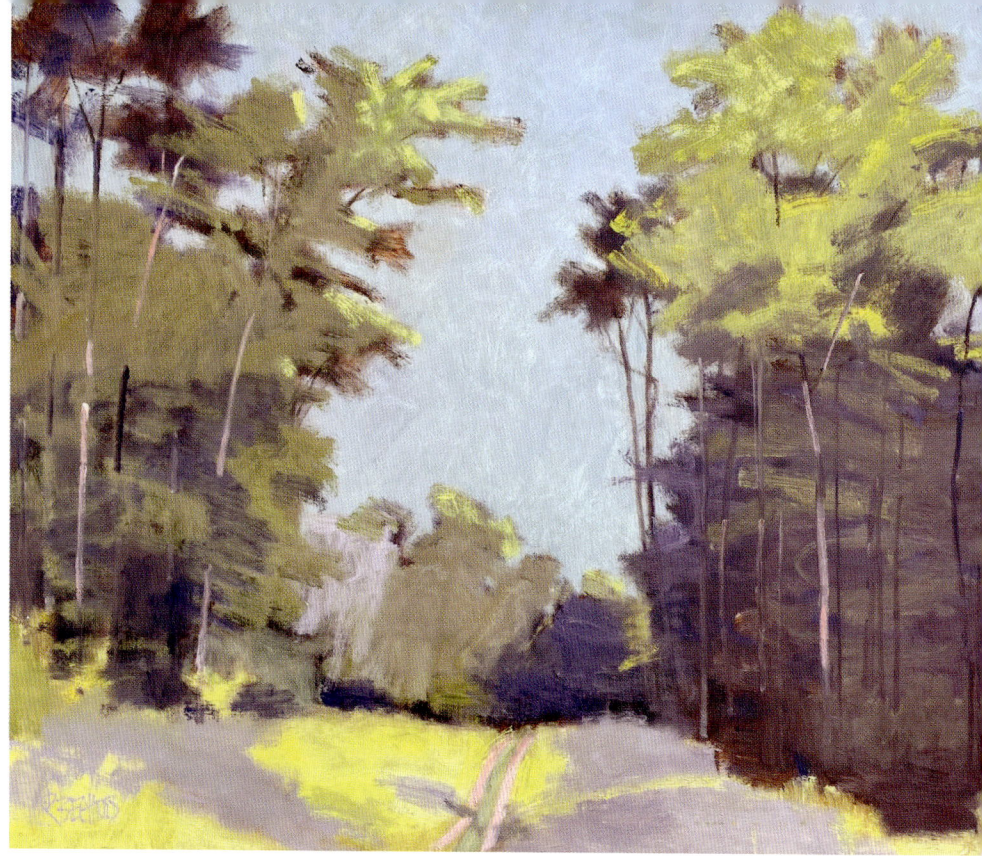

THE POWER OF OPPOSITES: COMPLEMENTS

If harmony implies an agreeable relationship among colors, then how can a pair of complements, with innate opposition and vibration, be considered harmonious? Because colors that vibrate aren't necessarily disharmonious. In fact, most painters find this type of hue interaction desirable. It creates a type of contrast that can simulate the brilliance of light through color. Complementary colors are the most potent type of hue interaction.

Rodger Bechtold, *Tall Timber*
Oil on linen, 36" × 42" | 91.5 × 107 cm

HUE INTERACTION: **DISSIMILAR**, complementary
VALUE CONTRAST: LOW / **MEDIUM** / HIGH
SATURATION: LOW / **MEDIUM–HIGH**

Tall Timber is clearly based on a complementary pairing of yellow and violet. Bechtold's handling of this radiant complementary relationship demonstrates restraint. With the exception of a few small areas, he doesn't use the yellow and violet at full saturation. That would heighten the radiant effect but look very unnatural. In most areas, the yellow and the violet are partially desaturated.

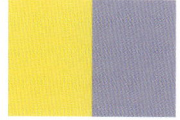 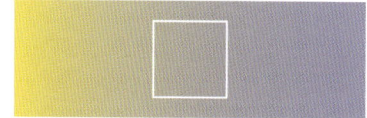

"RADIANT" AND "NEUTRALIZING" COMPLEMENTS

Complements have a dual nature. When placed side by side, they each heighten the visual intensity of the other. These are *radiant* complements. When those same colors are blended together, they have the opposite effect. They begin to cancel each other out and produce neutrals, as seen in the center of the blended swatch. These are *neutralizing* complements. Johannes Itten described it this way: "Two such colors make a strange pair. They are opposite, yet they require each other. They incite each other to maximum vividness when together and annihilate each other when mixed—like fire and water."

ASPECT OF COLOR CONTRAST: VALUE

WHY CONTRAST OF VALUE MATTERS

Value is the second form of contrast involved in the color strategy. As we saw in chapter 1, value is the relative lightness or darkness of a color. Its importance cannot be overstated. It is largely responsible for conveying a sense of light, depth, and volume. Painters often think of value as working independently of color. In fact, color and value are dynamically interrelated.

The value of a color has a direct effect on the expression of that color's chromatic identity. How light or dark a color is will affect how much we can perceive the color as actual color.

By adjusting the relative value of colors, painters are able to suggest light in different ways. Some painters rely on strong value contrasts, so much so that the hue itself plays a secondary role. This is called *value-priority*. Other painters flip the balance between color and value with a *color-priority* approach. By keeping values more in the midrange and increasing their saturation, color contrasts can do more of the work in suggesting light. Painters can also cleverly combine both approaches.

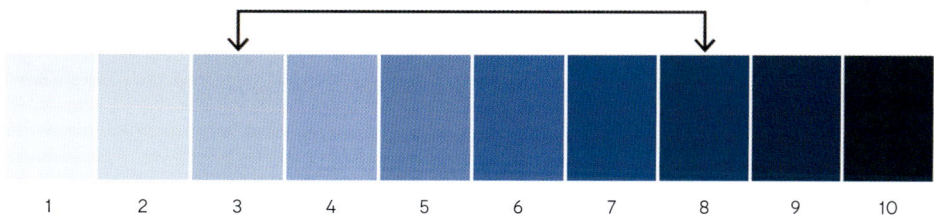

| 1 | 2 | 3 | 4 | 5 | 6 | 7 | 8 | 9 | 10 |

HOW VALUE AFFECTS COLOR IDENTITY

In this 10-step value scale for blue, *some of the blues are bluer than others*. In the midrange (3 to 8), the blues exhibit more of their characteristic "blueness." Their chromatic identity is more obvious, especially when colors are more saturated as they are in these swatches. In the values on the ends of the scale (1 to 2 and 9 to 10), the blue identity is less apparent. Extremely light- and extremely dark-valued colors hold less hue identity than colors in the midvalue range. This has important implications for painters who wish to use more saturated colors to simulate the effects of natural light.

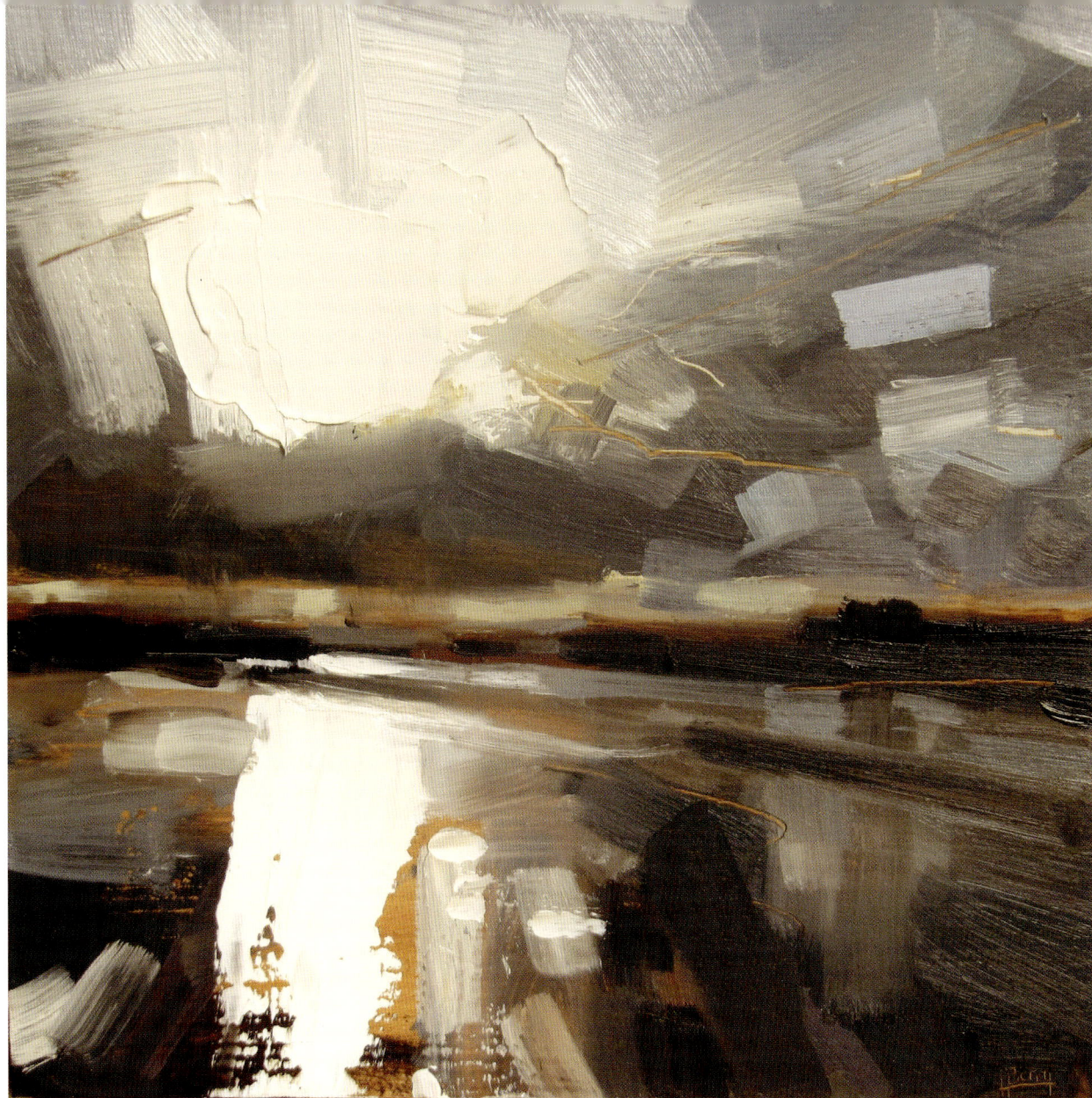

VALUE-PRIORITY

Hester Berry, *Instow*
Oil on panel, 8" × 8" | 20.5 × 20.5 cm

HUE INTERACTION: **DISSIMILAR**, subtle temperature differences
VALUE CONTRAST: LOW / MEDIUM / **HIGH**
SATURATION: **LOW** / MEDIUM / HIGH

The dramatic light in *Instow* is achieved almost entirely through strong value contrasts. In a value-priority approach, hue tends to play a lesser role. Here, there are some very subtle temperature differences between the cool gray-blues in the sky and the warmer earth tones below. But they only have a small supporting role as compared to the strong contrast between light and dark.

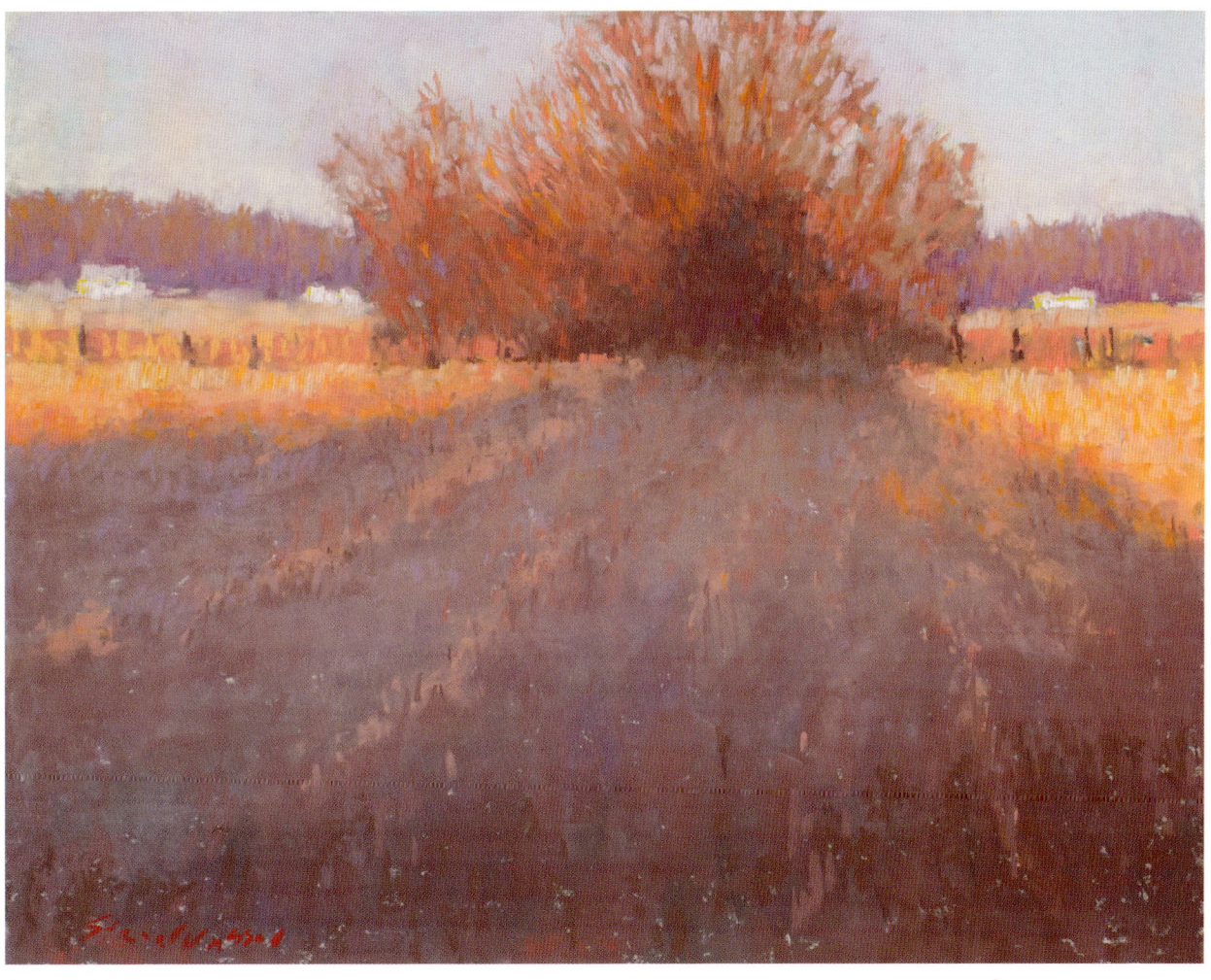

COLOR-PRIORITY

Carol Strock Wasson, *Last Light*
Pastel on paper, 16" × 20" | 40.5 × 51 cm

HUE INTERACTION: **DISSIMILAR**, complementary
VALUE CONTRAST: LOW / **MEDIUM** / HIGH
SATURATION: LOW / **MEDIUM–HIGH**

It is easy to forget that at one time a color-priority approach like this was considered scandalous. For the landscape colorist, the great legacy of nineteenth century Impressionism is this: purer color, when used in the midvalue range, can be as, if not more, effective at suggesting the qualities of light than strong value contrasts. In terms of color and value, *Last Light* is almost the opposite of what we saw in Berry's *Instow* on the previous page. Of course, there are value contrasts in *Last Light*, but they are not strong. Values are kept within the midrange where colors reveal more of their intrinsic hue identity.

ASPECT OF COLOR CONTRAST: SATURATION

WHY COLOR SATURATION MATTERS

Color saturation is the third aspect of contrast at work within the color strategy. When discussing saturation, painters are typically referring to the *overall* color saturation of the painting. For example, the colors in an Impressionist painting will have greater overall saturation than, say, a Tonalist painting, which works with less saturated colors. This is one reason why saturation plays such an important role in setting the emotional tone of a painting. An Impressionist painting, with its lighter-valued and more saturated colors, can fill us with joy; a Tonalist painting, with its darker tonalities and neutral harmonies, can invoke a contemplative mood.

Of course, individual colors within a painting may also vary in saturation. Without varying saturation levels, our color relationships would be one-dimensional. Every color would be the same pitch.

Because color has such emotional resonance with us, there is often a preference toward saturated colors. Yet, these bright colors are just one aspect of a fully balanced palette. Less saturated colors are another dimension and serve as a necessary counterpoint to saturated colors.

HIGH SATURATION ⟵⟶ LOW SATURATION

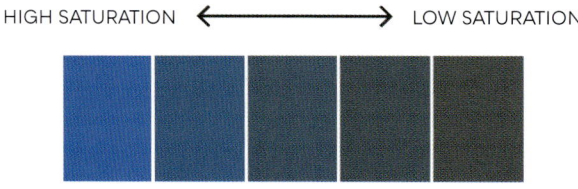

COLOR SATURATION

Like value contrast, color saturation is a relative measure. In the range of blues shown here, the values are all the same, but the saturation levels vary. The blue on the left is fully saturated (intense and colorful). As we transition right, the blues become progressively less saturated until the swatch on the right is so desaturated that it appears gray.

SEMANTICS: Saturation is also referred to as "chroma" or "intensity." Each of these words have subtle differences in meaning. Unfortunately, artists use the words interchangeably. Low saturation colors may also be called "low intensity," "neutrals," or "grays." For consistency, I refer to this aspect of color contrast as *saturation* and use the word *neutrals* to describe colors that are less than fully saturated.

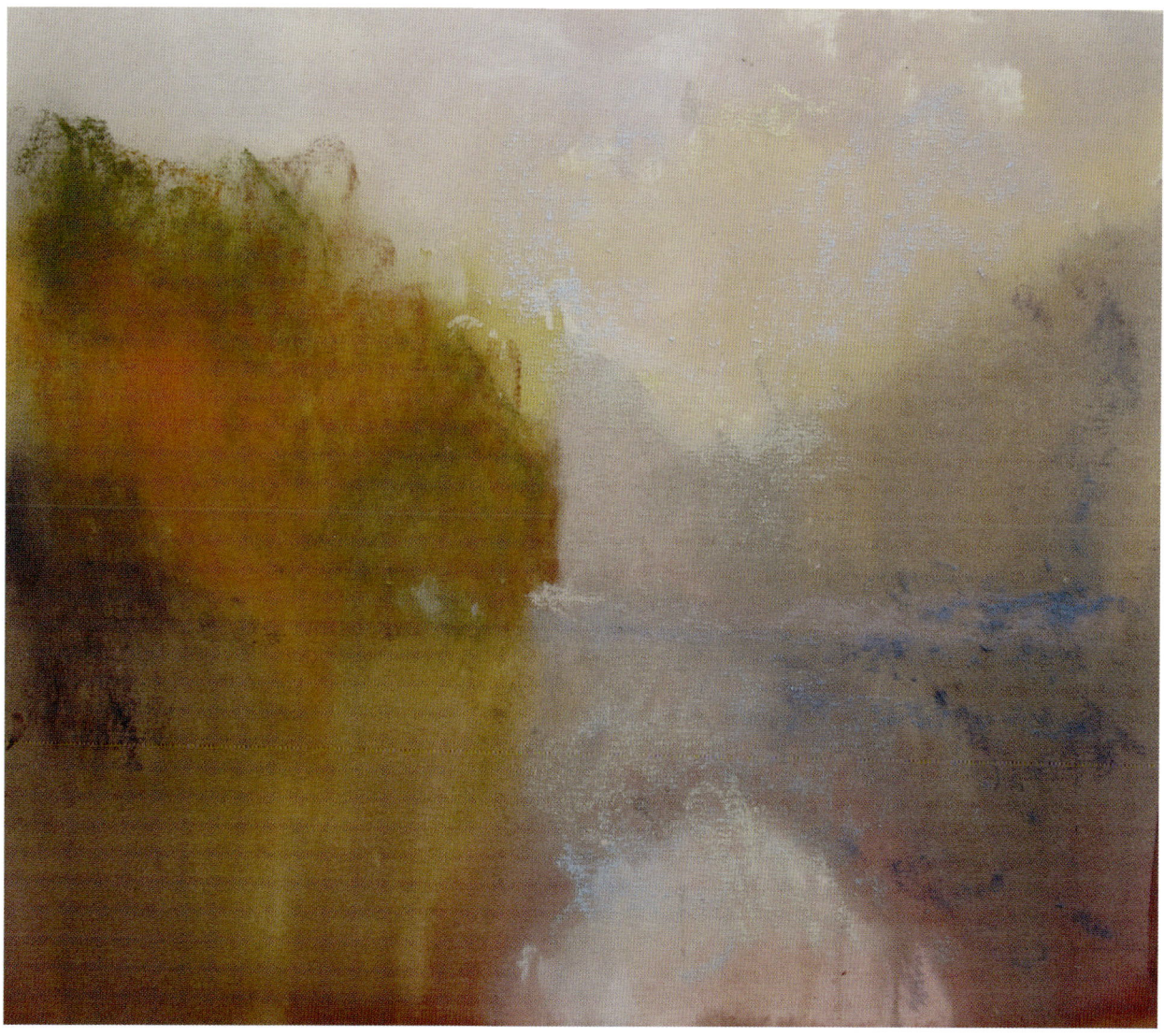

BALANCING SATURATED COLOR WITH NEUTRALS

Loriann Signori, *Subtle Grandeur*
Pastel, 9½" × 11" | 24 × 28 cm

HUE INTERACTION: **DISSIMILAR**, subtle complementary
VALUE CONTRAST: LOW / **MEDIUM** / HIGH
SATURATION: LOW / **MEDIUM** / HIGH

Saturated colors are more striking when placed alongside neutral colors, and neutral colors are more meaningful when combined with saturated colors. "I rely on the beauty of neutral colors to make the more saturated colors sing," says Signori. In *Subtle Grandeur*, we see a subtle complementary hue interaction between the orange island and the blue of the water and sky.

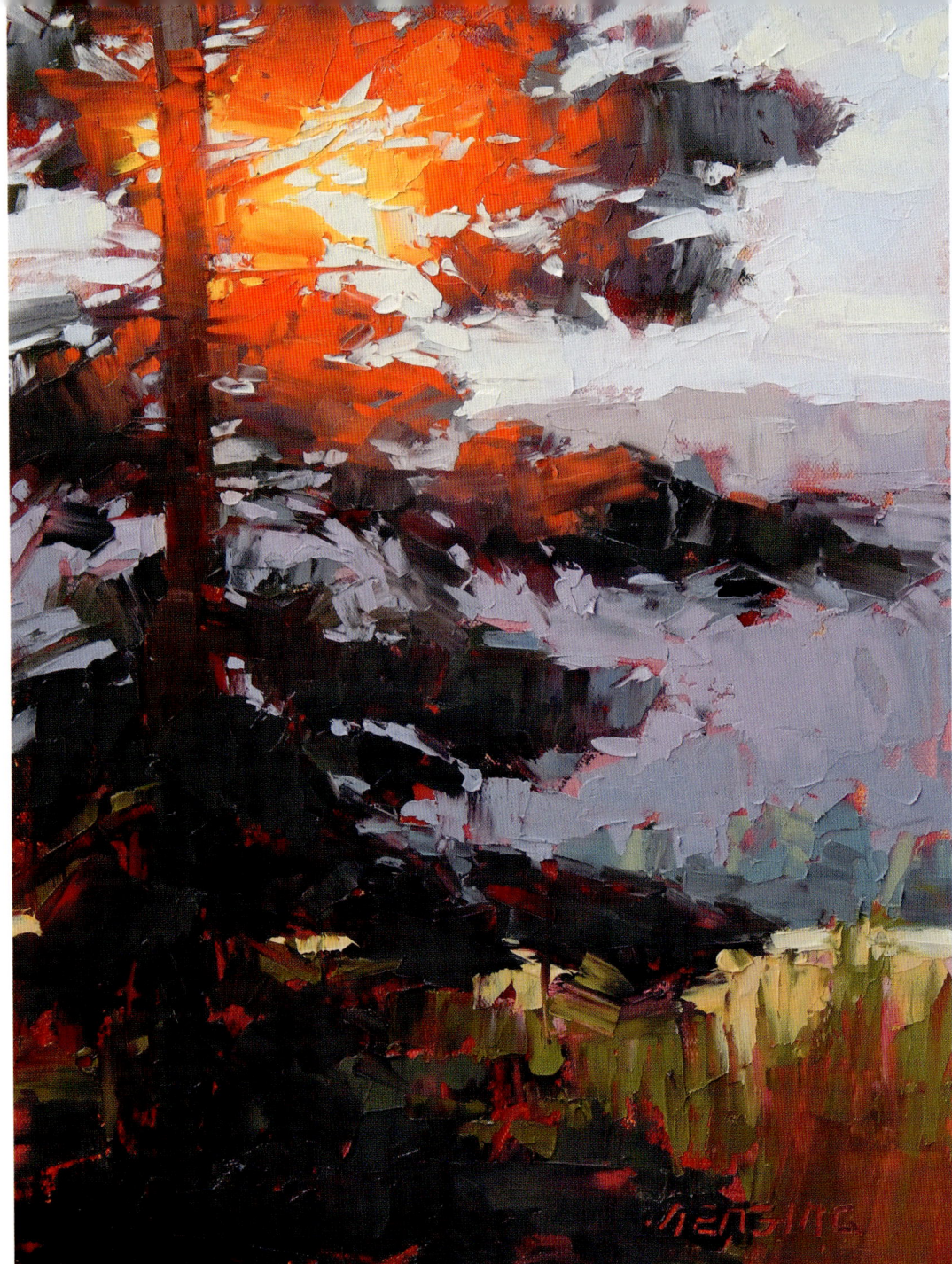

SATURATED COLOR AND RICH DARKS

David Mensing, *Excessive Moderation*
Oil on canvas, 16" × 12" | 40.5 × 30.5 cm

HUE INTERACTION: **DISSIMILAR**
VALUE CONTRAST: LOW / MEDIUM / **HIGH**
SATURATION: LOW / MEDIUM / **HIGH**

Another approach to working with saturated color is to combine the saturated colors with rich darks. This may be seen as a combination of value-priority and color-priority approaches. In Mensing's painting, saturated reds and oranges are surrounded by rich dark values which further accentuate the brilliance of those colors. This approach gives us strong lights and darks that foster an illusion of brilliant light and saturated colors to make that light sing.

THE HARMONY OF NEUTRALS

If the goal of a color strategy is to help build color unity, then low saturation or neutral palettes may be considered one of the most effective means of achieving that harmony. Neutral colors have a special power—they naturally agree with other neutral colors.

An absolute neutral would be a perfect gray, with no color bias at all. As painters make the colors in their paintings increasingly neutral, the colors begin to harmonize through a common association to neutral gray. This is beautifully implemented in David Curtis' painting on page 128.

Neutral colors cast a spell of binding. Hues that might otherwise clash in a saturated color field are calmed down when neutralized and better able to agree with each other.

CONSIDER: A neutral harmony does not mean the absence of color. Although neutrals don't shout as loudly as saturated colors do— they prefer to whisper—they are more than capable of forming harmonious relationships. As the paintings by Renato Muccillo and David Curtis in the following pages show, neutral colors are also beautiful colors.

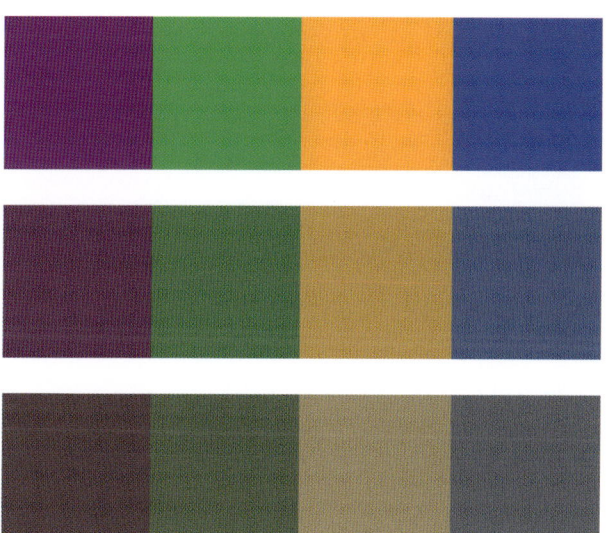

FROM DISCORD TO ACCORD

Neutral colors have an innate ability to bring disparate colors into harmony. This allows a painter to include a wider range of hues, from multiple points on the spectrum, without risking discord. In these swatches, each row has the same four hues. In the top row, the colors are fully saturated. They have little in common and are even discordant. In the middle row, the colors are partially desaturated and seem less discordant. In the bottom row, the colors are extremely desaturated, retaining only a hint of their original hue, and are considerably more harmonious and unified than in the two upper rows.

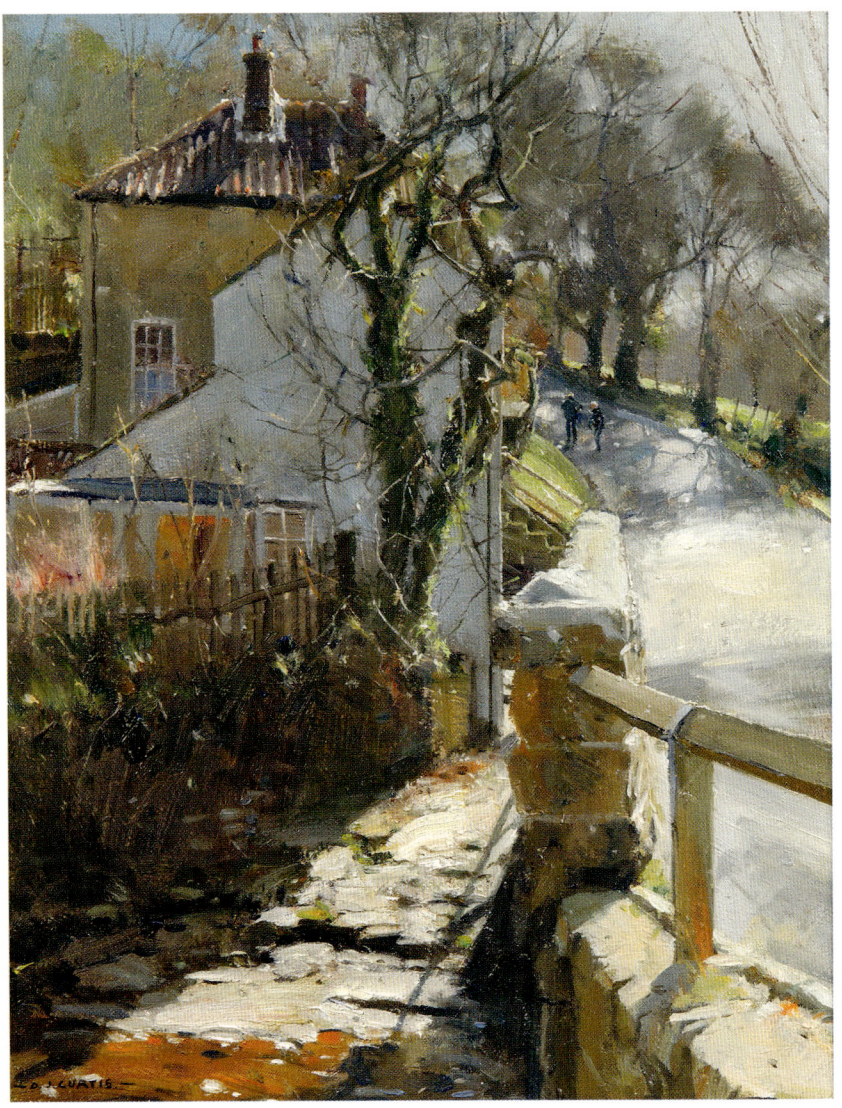

DISPARATE COLORS BROUGHT INTO HARMONY THROUGH NEUTRALS

David Curtis, *Spring Light - Beck Hole, North Yorkshire*
Oil on panel, 12" × 10" | 30.5 × 25.5 cm

HUE INTERACTION: **MULTIPLE**
VALUE CONTRAST: LOW / **MEDIUM** / HIGH
SATURATION: **LOW** / MEDIUM / HIGH

In *Spring Light*, Curtis achieves one of the most inspired feats of color harmony: he uses colors from every part of the spectrum—reds, yellows, blues, greens, oranges, and violets—yet avoids the discord we might expect with such a diversity of hues. Curtis attains this through the harmony of neutrals. Neutral colors naturally agree with other neutral colors. With the exception of the small patch of orange at the very bottom, all the hues in the painting are partially desaturated and harmonize through a common association to the neutral gray.

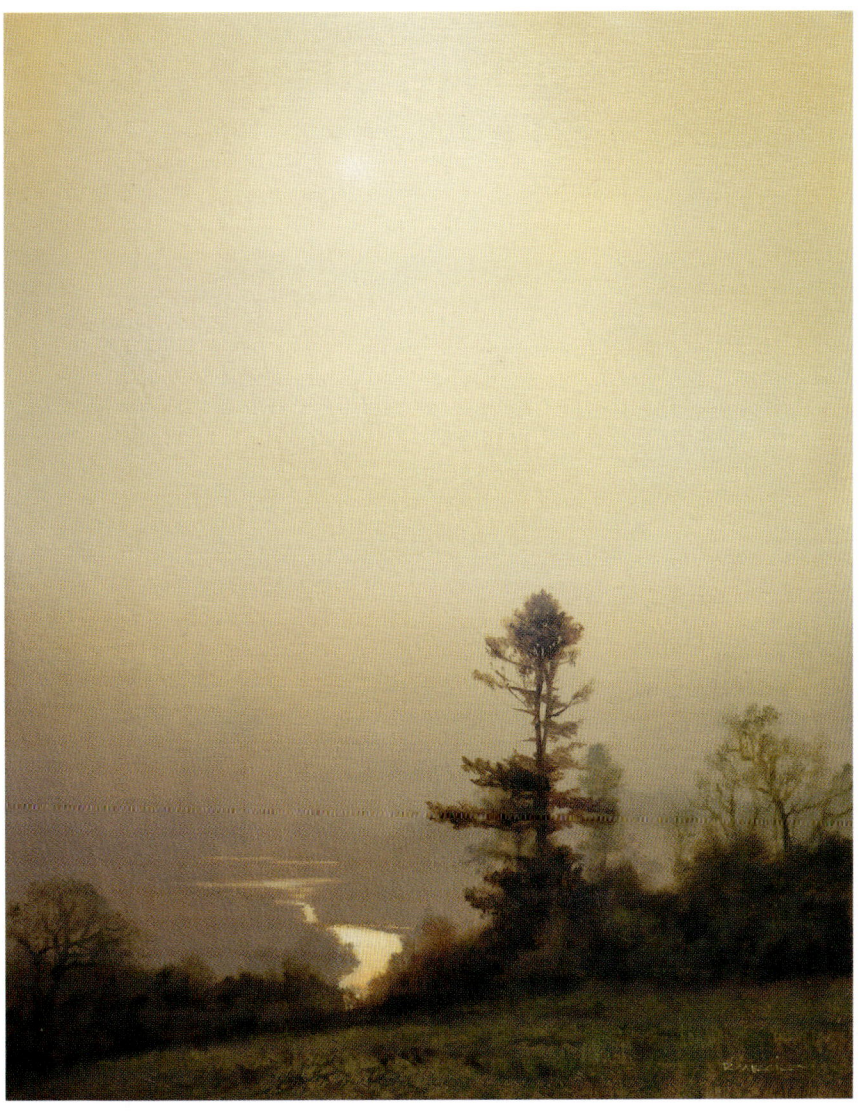

THE NEUTRAL HARMONIES OF TONALISM

Renato Muccillo, *Valley Fires II*
Oil on panel, 8" × 6" | 20.5 × 15 cm

HUE INTERACTION: **SIMILARITY**
VALUE CONTRAST: LOW / MEDIUM / **HIGH**
SATURATION: **LOW** / MEDIUM / HIGH

Renato Muccillo works in the contemporary Tonalist tradition. Tonalist painters rarely dip into saturated colors; instead, their palettes are laden with earth tones and neutral colors. When the harmony produced by neutral colors is used in combination with strong value contrasts, it's a prescription for both dramatic and unified light. Muccillo's tonalist palette includes just four colors plus white: NAPLES YELLOW, SAP GREEN, TRANSPARENT RED OXIDE, and ULTRAMARINE BLUE. The use of so few colors (a limited palette) also supports the formation of unified harmonies.

REVIEW QUESTIONS: **THE COMPLETE COLOR STRATEGY**

When developing a strategy, are you remembering that the strategy isn't only about hue interactions (e.g., complementary, analogous, etc.)?

A complete strategy also involves value contrasts and relative color saturation. How do these affect the overall color composition?

What hue interactions are at work in the subject?

Hue interactions are responsible for the forces of attraction and opposition among colors. Are the hue interactions based primarily on colors that are very related or colors that that differ widely? Or a combination of both? Is there more than one type of hue interaction at play?

Are you taking advantage of temperature differences or building all-warm or all-cool strategies?

Cool versus warm is an important aspect of color contrast. Temperature differences add variety to the color tapestry.

How do the value contrasts affect the overall color impression?

Are the value contrasts very strong? Or are the values very close? How does a color's value affect the expression of that color's chromatic identity? How light or dark a color is will affect how much we can perceive the color as actual color.

What are the saturation levels of the colors?

Are there lots of bright and saturated colors? Is the overall strategy based on neutral harmonies? Or a combination of both? How does the saturation level of the colors affect the illusion of unified light? Where might

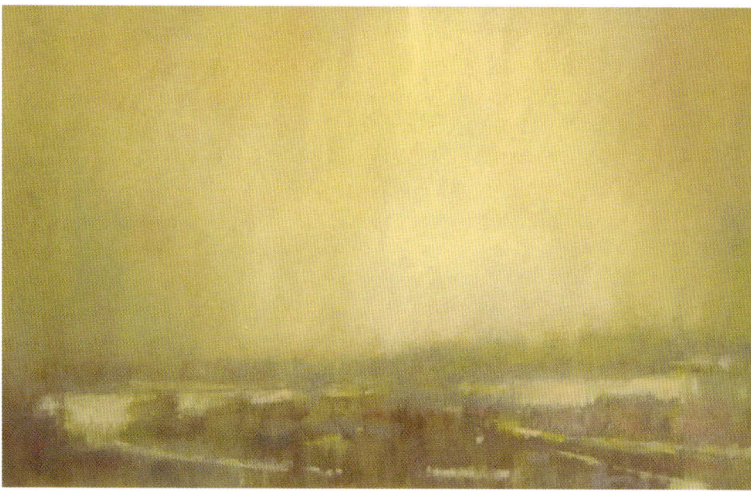

Mitchell Albala, *Ballard Bridge to Shilshole, Winter*
Pastel on paper, 5¾" × 9" | 14.5 × 23 cm

HUE INTERACTION: **DISSIMILAR**, temperature
VALUE CONTRAST: **LOW** / MEDIUM / HIGH
SATURATION: **LOW** / MEDIUM / HIGH

you need to increase or decrease the saturation?

Are you following the colors you see in the subject too closely?

The success of a color strategy is not measured by how well it matches the original scene, but by how well the painting works *as a painting*. The color you see in the subject is only a starting point. You can depart from what you see in nature (or the photo) in service to the painting.

EXERCISE: ONE SUBJECT, DIFFERENT STRATEGIES

OVERVIEW: There is no better way to experience the potential range of the color strategy than to paint the same subject using different strategies. You may not have a set of photos of the same subject with distinct color harmonies, which means you might have to be inventive with your color choices or even borrow strategies from other paintings. A color strategy is mutable and flexible; you can make almost any color scheme work as long as the color is convincing in the context of the painting. (See "Convincing Color, Believable Color" on page 108.)

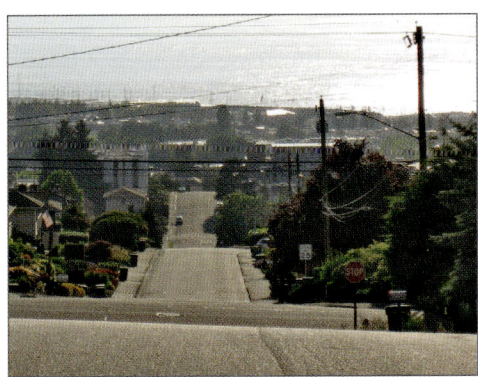

SOURCE PHOTO

The source photo has a potentially interesting composition, but it doesn't capture sunset-like colors. It will be used only as a starting point. Only one of the paintings in the series borrows the neutral harmonies found in the source photo. The strategies in all the others are largely invented. The water at the top will also be converted to a sky. In this series, each painting holds to the sunset theme, but interprets it with an entirely different palette. Each piece makes a unique statement about a particular color of light.

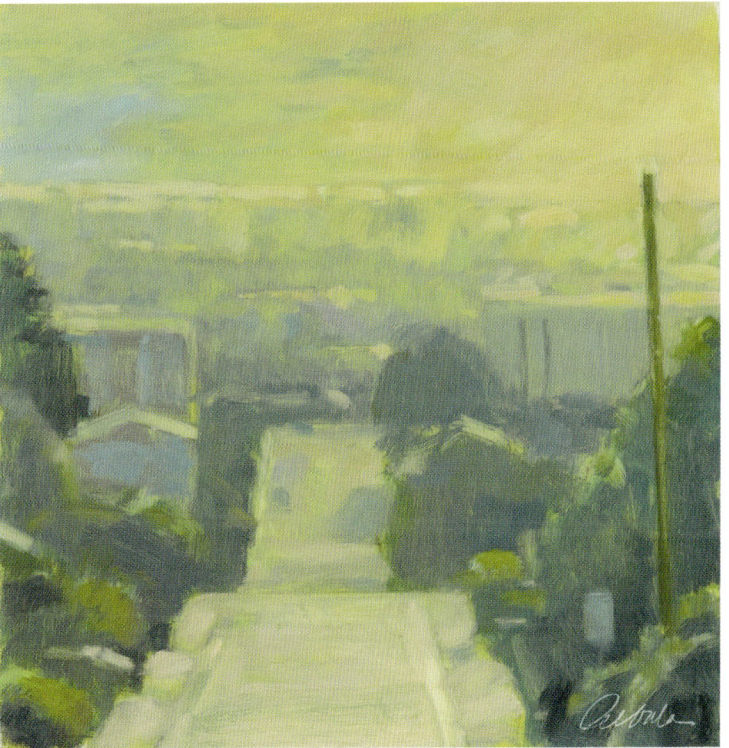

Mitchell Albala, *The Way Home, Study in Yellow and Phthalo*
Oil on paper, 8" × 8" | 20.5 × 20.5 cm

The deeply atmospheric quality in this study is achieved largely with analogous harmony—yellow/yellow-green—with hints toward blue-green. The hints of blue in the sky and the small house on the left offer gentle notes of temperature contrast. The values are in midrange, allowing the relatively saturated colors to reveal more of their chromatic identity, adding to the luminosity of the painting.

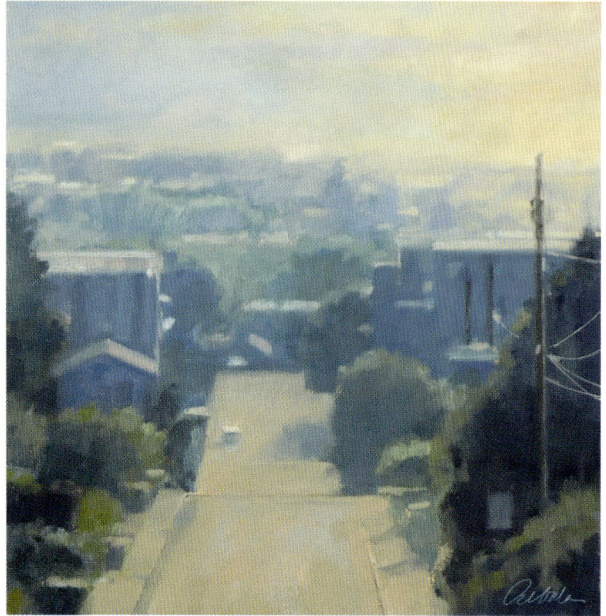 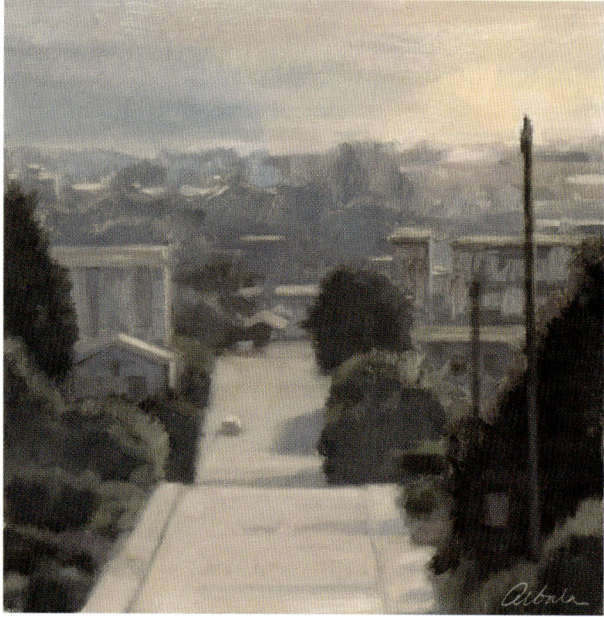

Mitchell Albala, *The Way Home,*
Study in Azure and Orange
Oil on paper, 8" × 8" | 20.5 × 20.5 cm

The hue interaction here is analogous harmony
with a contrasting hue. The pale yellow-orange
in the sky and the road is the counterpoint to
the dominant blue. Value contrasts are in the
midrange, allowing the illusion of light to be
suggested with saturated colors, as opposed
to strong value contrasts, as we see in *Study
in Grays (right).*

Mitchell Albala, *The Way Home,*
Study in Grays
Oil on paper, 8" × 8" | 20.5 × 20.5 cm

This study comes closest to the gray harmonies
found in the source photo. With a value-priority
approach, the effects of light are achieved
primarily through strong value contrasts. The
soft pinks in the sky and in the road serve as
a subtle color accent amid the predominantly
cool gray harmony.

BEYOND PHOTOGRAPHIC COLOR

Because we so readily accept photographs as a stand-in for reality, many painters make the mistake of
following the colors in the photo too closely and never consider how they might be improved. To work
with color as painters do, the "reality" of the photo must be left behind. If all we ever do is mimic the
photographic color, we deny ourselves the chance to be inventive with color, to think like colorists. Our
approach to color must be more creative than the camera. To be flexible and creative with our color
choices—as color strategies and color groups teach us—we have to be willing to depart from the color
found in the photo.

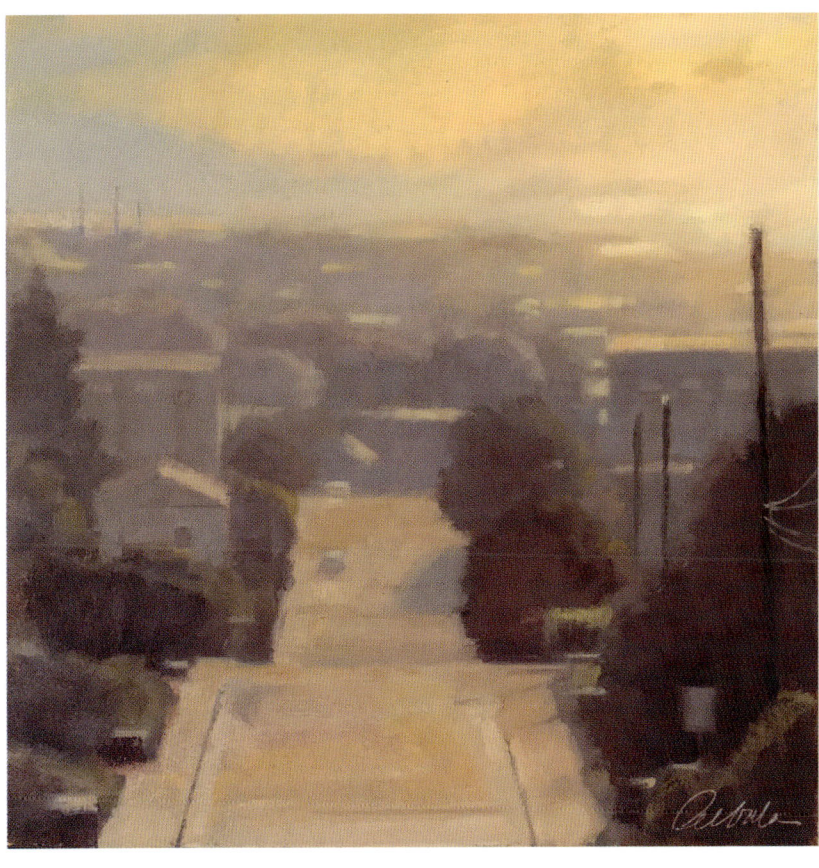

Mitchell Albala,
The Way Home, Study in Orange and Violet
Oil on paper,
8" × 8" | 20.5 × 20.5 cm

The hue interaction in this painting is complementary: yellow-orange/violet-blue. Colors within a complementary pairing need not be fully saturated to be effective. Here, the colors throughout are partially desaturated. Value contrasts are leaning toward strong, which contribute to the sense of a sunset light.

TEMPERATURE, AN ASPECT OF HUE INTERACTION

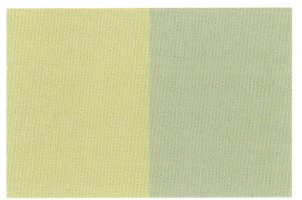 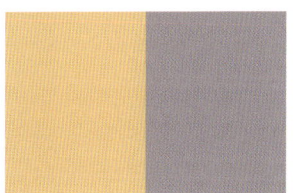

Temperature describes the "warm" or "cool" attributes of colors and is considered a form of color contrast. Temperature differences may be subtle, as they are in the yellow/green pairing, or they can be strong, as in the yellow-orange/blue-violet pairing. Temperature differences are an important way painters add variation to the color tapestry. Each of the hue interactions also reflect temperature differences.

CONSIDER: Temperature is a relative measure. A color is never cool or warm on its own. A "cool" color is only cool when placed alongside a warmer color. And a "warm" color is only warm when placed alongside a cooler color.

EXERCISE: COLOR- AND VALUE-PRIORITY, SIDE BY SIDE

OVERVIEW: One of the most essential lessons every colorist needs to learn is this: how does the value of a color affect how much we can perceive the color *as* actual color? (See "Why Contrast of Value Matters" on page 121). In this exercise, you will do two paintings of the same or a similar subject. In one, you will use a value-priority approach; in the other, a color-priority approach. This is a demanding exercise. You have to be willing to make changes to the colors you see, whether you are working from life or a photo. Kim English, a master at conveying light in the urban setting, demonstrates.

Kim English, *Entering the Narrows*
Oil on linen, 12" × 12" | 30.5 × 30.5 cm

The sense of light in *Entering the Narrows* is achieved primarily through strong value contrasts. The yellow light on the street appears more vibrant when played against the near-black colors that surround it, but value contrasts still do most of the work. In the dark shadows, colors are still visible, but they hold much less of their hue identity.

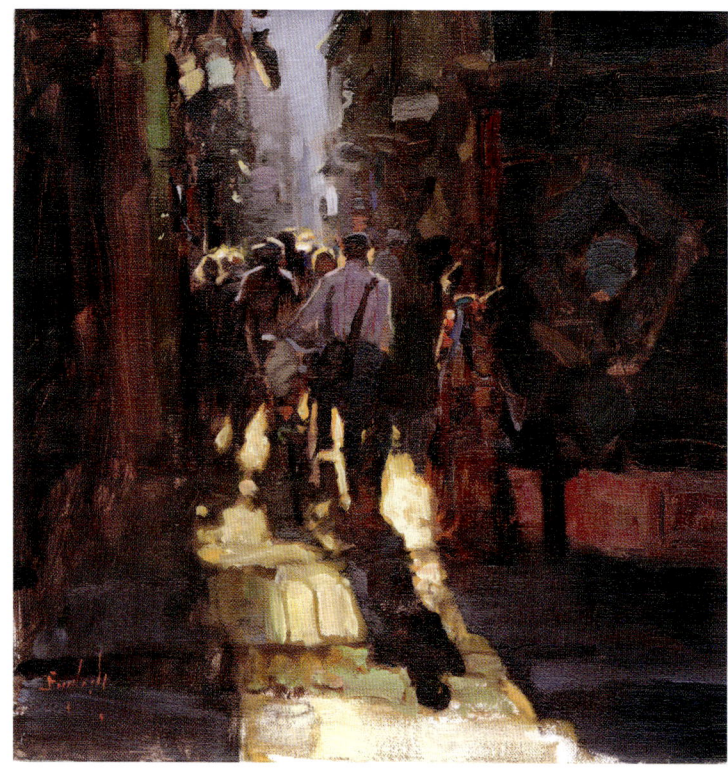

In a value-priority approach, the painter uses the full range of values available to them, from very light (1) to very dark (10). Strong value contrasts are a tried-and-true means of creating an illusion of light. In a color-priority approach, the painter forgoes extremes of value and instead keeps the values in the midrange (approximately 3 to 8). By holding values to this range and making those colors more saturated, the innate hue identity of those colors is more apparent and color can do more of the work of suggesting light.

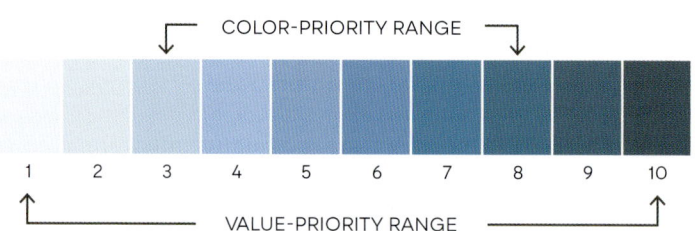

COLOR-PRIORITY RANGE

1 2 3 4 5 6 7 8 9 10

VALUE-PRIORITY RANGE

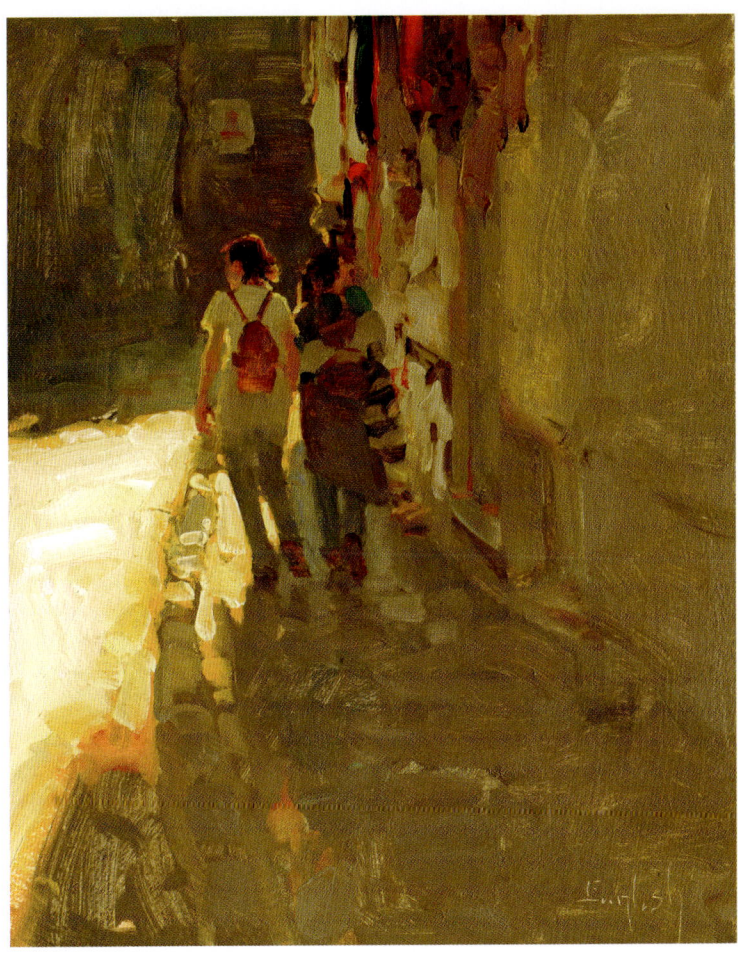

Kim English,
Walk Through Granada
Oil on panel, 14" × 11" | 35.5 × 28 cm

In *Walk Through Granada*, light is suggested in an entirely different way. There are still distinct value differences between light and shadow, but because the shadows are *much* lighter, color takes on a greater role in suggesting light. When values are kept in the midrange, the hue identity of the color is more apparent; the colors sing and the shadows become luminous.

TIPS

- **Select an appropriate source photo.** The key to both versions is how you modify the values, so pick a source photo that has clear patterns of light and shadow.

- **Keep it simple.** Your goal is not to create a *tour de force* masterpiece, but to experience the difference between these two approaches to rendering light. There's no need to choose a complex or detailed subject.

- **Refer to the 10-step value scale.**

- **Value-priority version.** Use the full range of value, from 1 or 2 to 9 or 10. Color may play a role, but the contrast between light and dark will do most of the work.

- **Color-priority version.** Stay away from very light colors (1 or 2) or very dark colors (9 or 10), as they hold little of their intrinsic hue identity. Keeping the values in the midrange, between 3 and 7, and increasing the saturation level of the color, is the key to the color-priority approach.

- **Inspiration.** Color-priority is the approach used by Impressionists. Look to contemporary and classic examples for inspiration. See Strock Wasson's *Last Light* on page 123 and Albala's *Mountain in Sunlight* on page 90. For value-priority, see Berry's work on page 122 and Albala's *Study in Gray* on page 132.

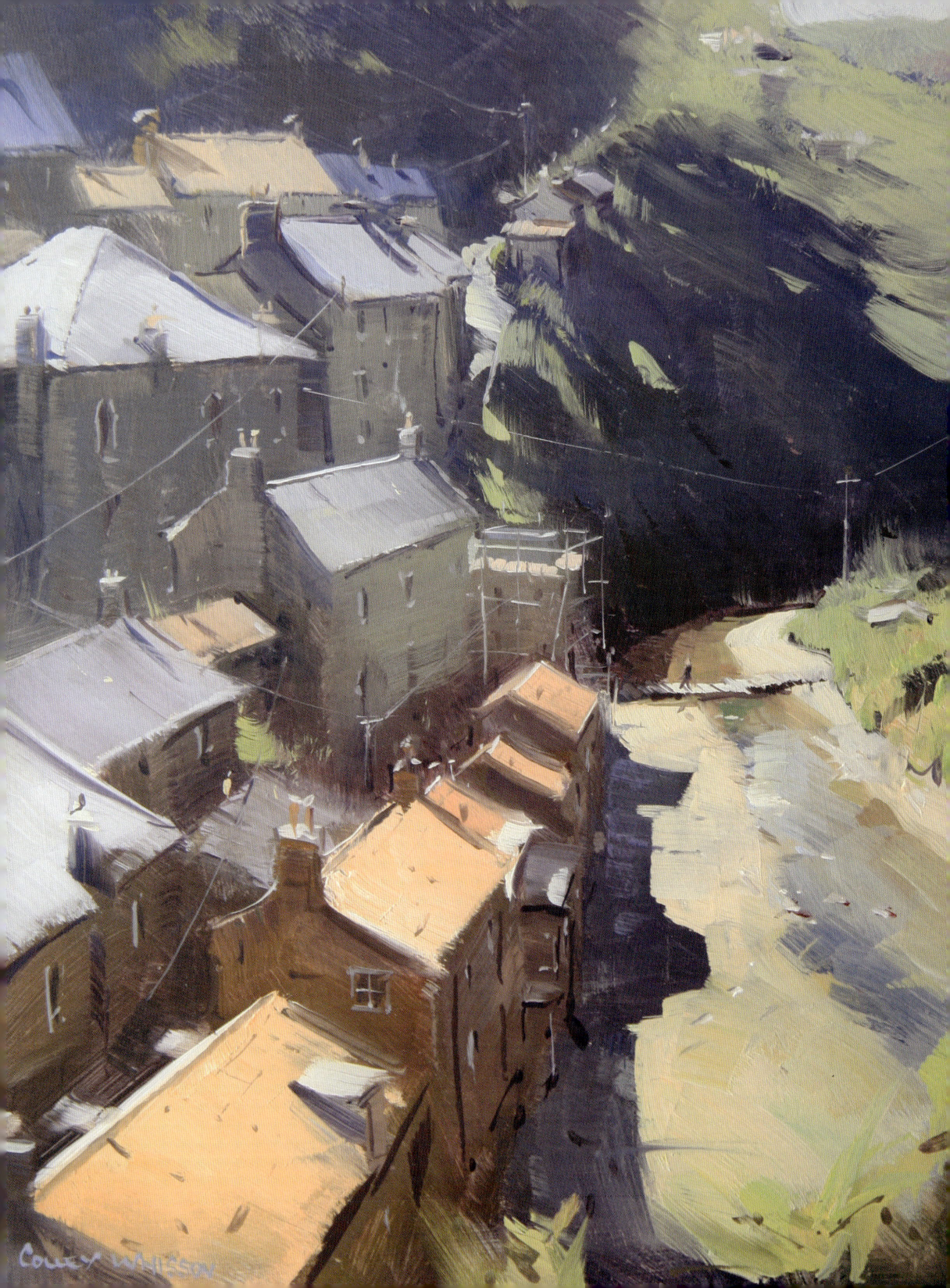

7

COLOR GROUPING

Landscape painters are explorers, especially in the realm of color where options are nearly infinite. One of the paradoxes of the artistic practice, however, is that narrowing our options often leads to better results. We use *limited* values to simplify value relationships and differentiate shapes. We build stronger compositions by using a *limited* focus that eliminates extraneous information. Limits are also helpful when working with color.

Because color can be so seductive, painters can be tempted to infuse their work with a range of hues from every part of the spectrum. But even a novice will recognize that harmony isn't achieved by using *every* color. As Sir Kenneth Clark said, "All color is no color." In fact, our paintings will have more landscape-like harmonies if instead of drawing from too many color families, we work within a limited number of *color groups*.

In this chapter, we will learn how color groups work by analyzing them in several paintings. We will also do an exercise that will help you identify color groups in your own work.

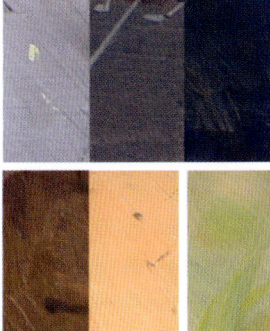

◀ Colley Whisson, *English Rooftops, Staithes, England*
Oil on panel, 12" × 9" | 30.5 × 23 cm

Color grouping is a way of achieving harmony by organizing colors into a limited number of families. All the colors in Whisson's painting fall into three groups, as shown in the swatches: the dominant blue group (in the upper houses and hillside shadow); orange (in the lower houses); and a light warm yellow-green group.

DEFINING THE COLOR GROUP

When we examine color strategies in the most successful paintings—those with unified color and landscape-like harmonies—we usually find that all the colors fall into a limited number of color families. One family is often dominant. Painters sometimes refer to this as the color "key" or color "chord" of the painting. There may be a single chord (as in a monochromatic painting), but more commonly, there is a dominant chord and a few minor chords. These are the color groups.

The idea behind color grouping is this: a painting made with fewer groups has a better chance of producing unified harmonies than one made with a large number of divergent colors and groups.

Grouping imposes no limits on the many individual colors there may be in a painting, but it does ask that those colors fall into a small number of color groups.

Grouping doesn't inhibit coloristic expression. Rather, it allows us to *focus* on that expression and allows it to better simulate the way color behaves in the natural world. Once you begin looking at landscape paintings through the lens of color grouping, you will see that color groups are used *all* the time. In fact, every painting in this book uses color grouping.

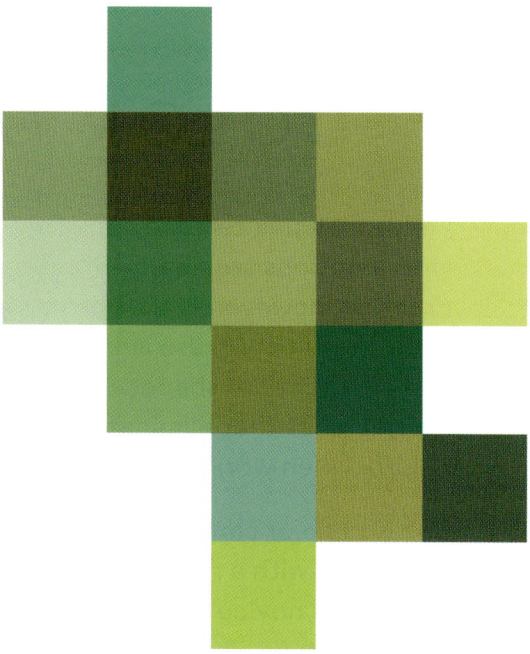

Like a musical chord, in which related notes combine to form a unified sound, a color group contains individual "notes" of color, related in hue, that collectively form a unified and harmonious impression. The greens in this group are different values, temperatures, and saturation levels, yet all belong to a single green group.

COLOR GROUPING BY NATURE

Color grouping may sound like a specialized theory or practice, but it is simply a way of taking what occurs naturally in the landscape and carrying it into our paintings. The natural world routinely groups its colors. Certain types of scenes, such as gardens or urban landscapes, may be an exception. They can present a variety of colors from every part of the spectrum. In such cases, a painter must be prepared to impose color groups by organizing all the colors into fewer groups.

When a subject is blurred, small differences of color melt into their component groups, leaving only the *average* of all the colors. Blurring like this is similar to the squinting we do when reading values and looking for simplified masses, except here, we are trying to reduce all the colors to their component groups.

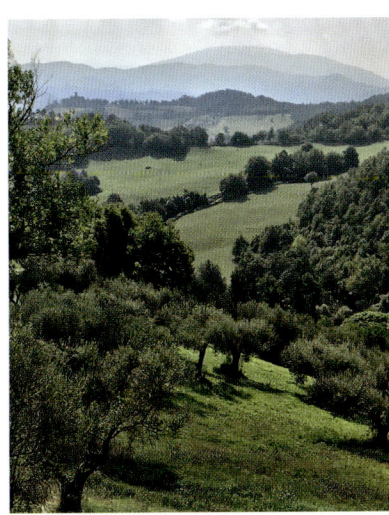
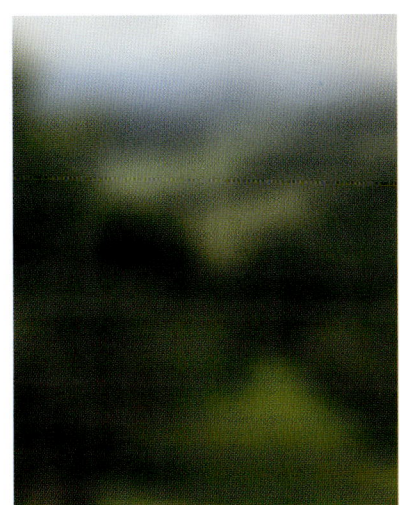

Many subjects consist of a single color group, as in this verdant Italian scene. When color groups are this closely related (especially when they are green), the painter makes an effort to insert more color variety than they may actually see. Here, they might add more yellow to the sunlit portions or bring out the blues and violets within the shadows.

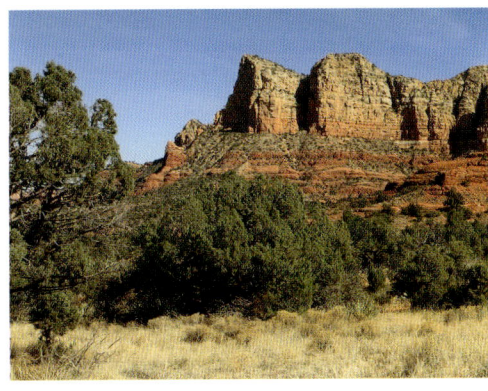
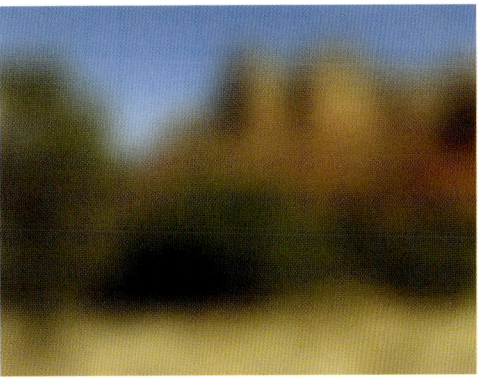

This scene has several color groups: the light ochre in the foreground grasses, the green foliage, the blue sky, and the red rocks. The foreground grass and the ochre color in the distant rocks, though separate elements of the landscape, are related colors and so form a single group.

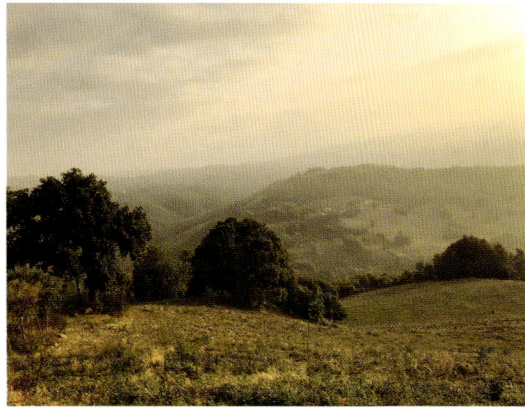 

The most lyrical type of color grouping occurs when the color of the light itself casts a unifying veil across the entire scene. Here, each color family—yellows, greens, blues—are all tinged with the warmth of the morning light. We often find this kind of grouping at sunrise and sunset or in scenes with deep atmospheric perspective.

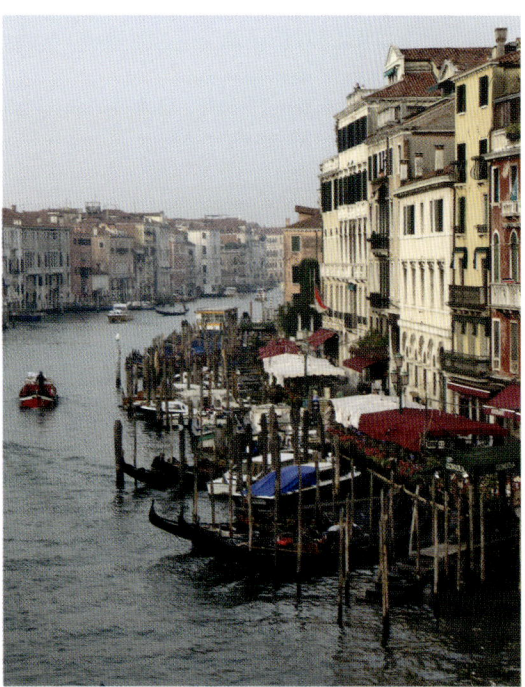 

This scene has a wider variety of color, yet still appears well-grouped. This is because the colors are unified through a common association to the gray tonality that runs through the entire scene. Neutral colors naturally harmonize with other neutral colors. (Also see "The Harmony of Neutrals" on page 127.)

COLOR GROUPING IN ACTION

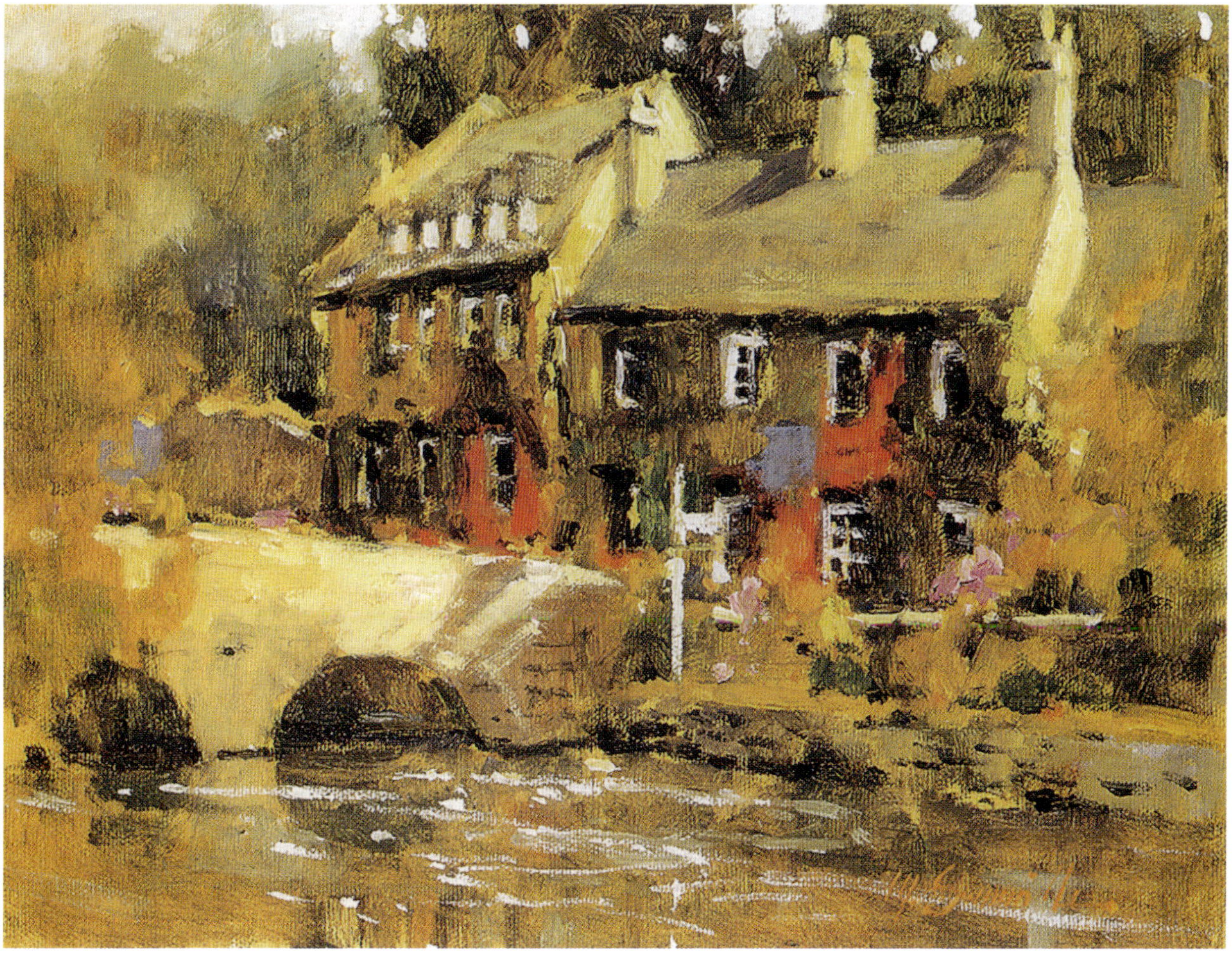

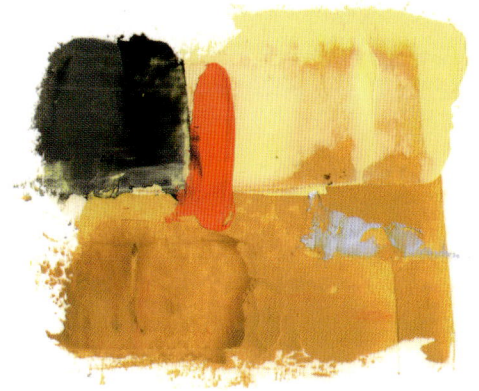

Marilyn Simandle, *Swan Hotel, England*
Oil on canvas, 9" × 12" | 23 × 30.5 cm

A single color group often dominates the color composition. In Simandle's *Swan Hotel*, yellow ochre is clearly the ruling hue. A second dark, black-green color group is found in the front of the hotel, behind it, and under the bridge. The red strokes in the middle add a lively accent. Ordinarily, such a small amount of color would not qualify as a group, but in this case, it plays such a key role in spicing up the color composition that it can be considered a group in its own right.

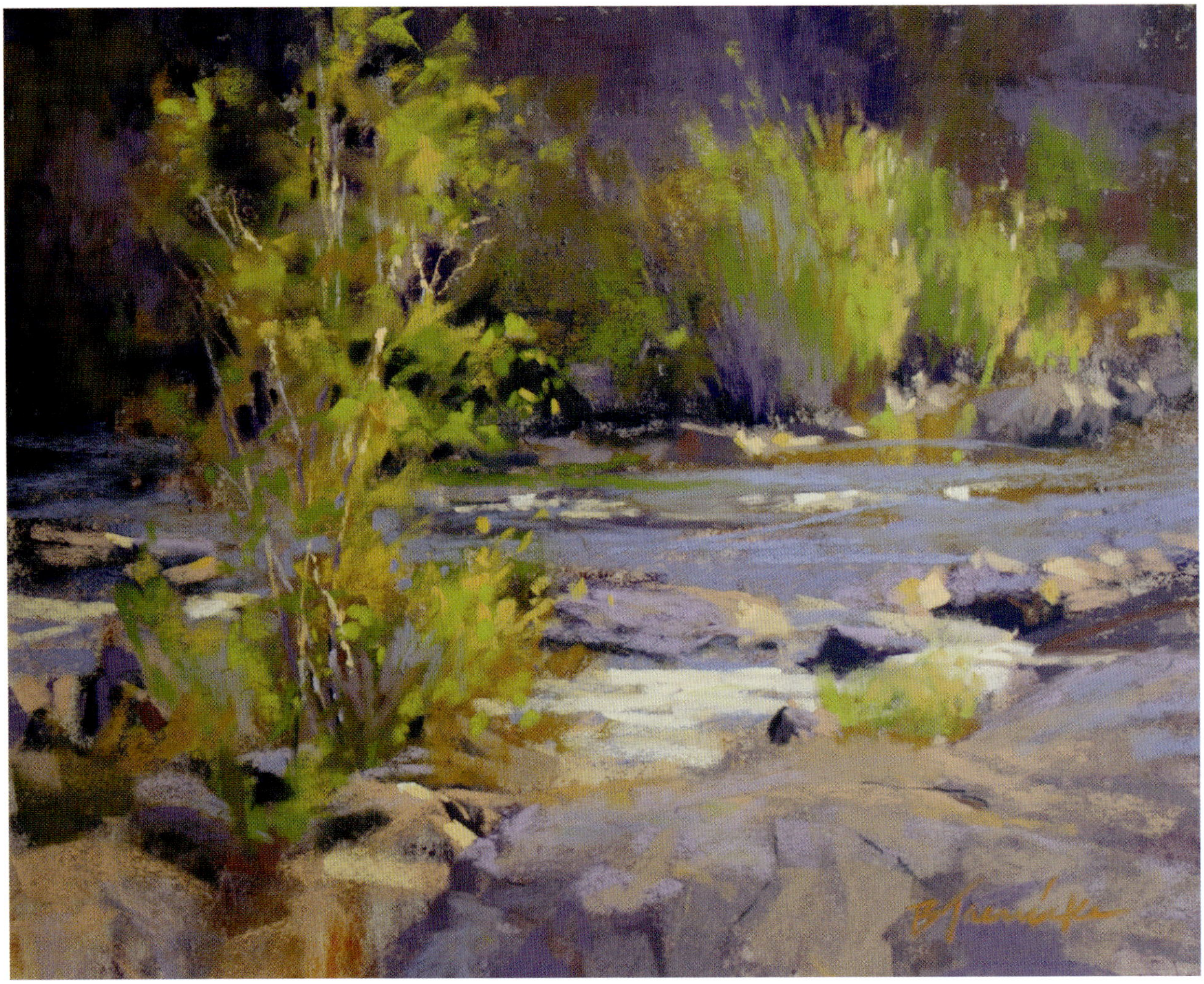

Barbara Jaenicke, *Remembering Spring*
Pastel on mounted paper
8" × 10" | 20.5 × 25.5 cm

There are three main color groups in *Remembering Spring*. Blue-violet is the dominant hue. The yellow-green in the trees and the pale orange in the foreground rocks are secondary groups. The painting has many small strokes of broken color, each one a particular temperature, value, and saturation level. If you look carefully, you can see that all the individual colors fall comfortably into one of the three main color groups. (Also see Jaenicke's color groups in *Golden Light of Winter Day's End* on page 157.)

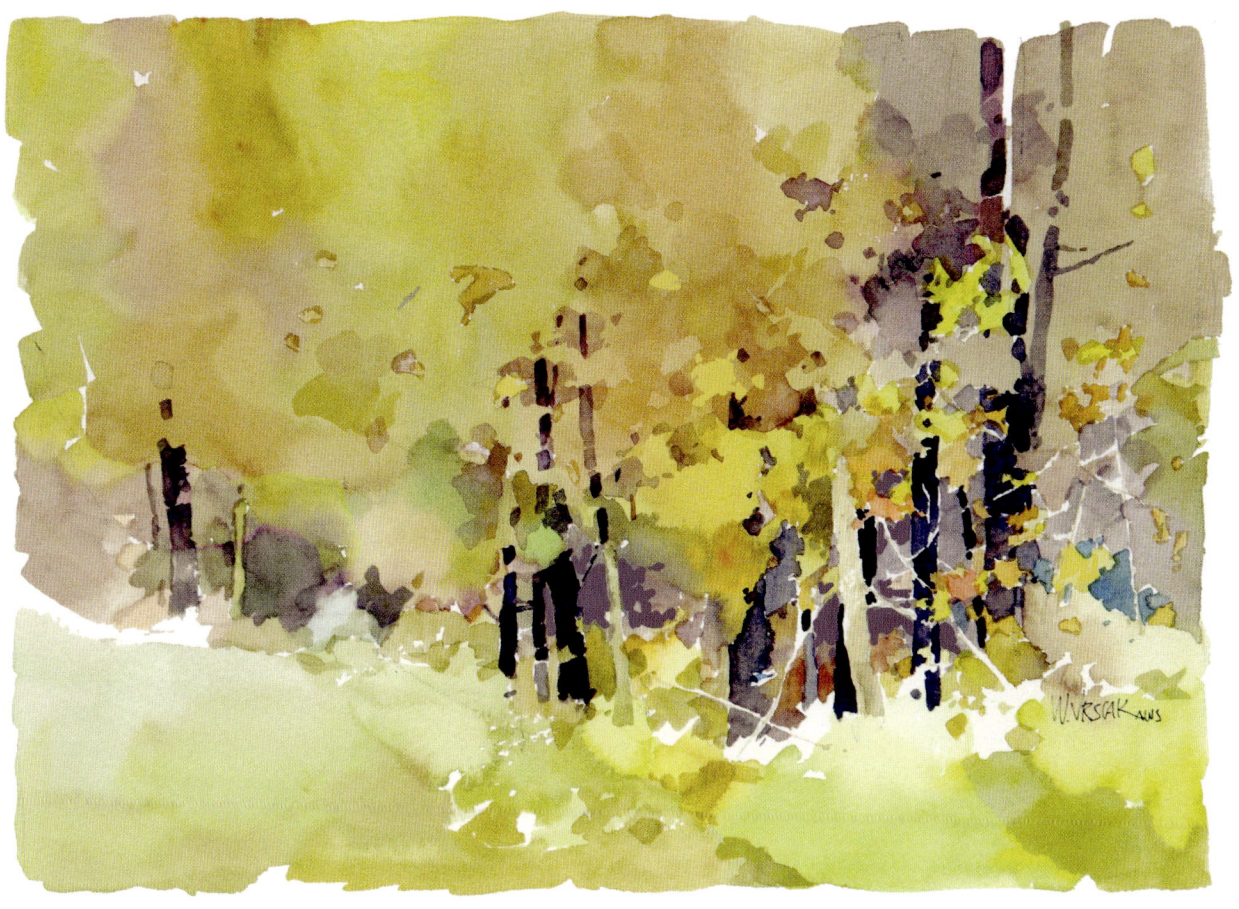

Bill Vrscak, *Woodland Autumn*
Watercolor, 17" × 23" | 43 × 58.5 cm

Woodland Autumn is a semi-abstract tapestry of many different hues, all of which fall into three main groups. The large tree in the upper left forms the dominant group, yellow. There are subtle hue and temperature shifts within the main body of the yellow, but all are closely related to the yellow. A smaller but related group is the dominant yellow-green foreground. Separating those two groups is an area of pale violet that arcs across the entire picture. Its violet hues complement the yellow within the other two groups. Tiny red and turquoise accents in the lower right add sparks of interest, but are used judiciously, so as not to overpower the main groups.

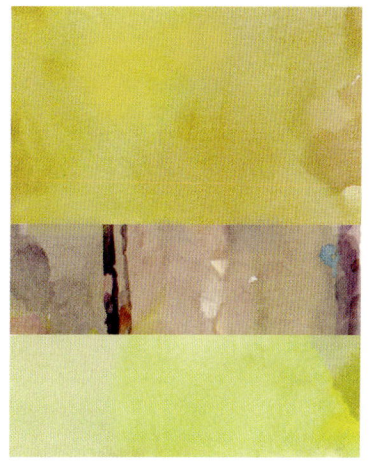

THE COLOR STUDY: TESTING COLOR GROUPS AND THE STRATEGY

As we develop a painting, we will naturally fine-tune color relationships, but the better idea we have of our color direction at the start, the better chance we have of hitting our color target. Whether painting outdoors or in the studio, there's no better way to pretest our color plan than with a simple color study. Which colors and mixtures form the strategy and the color groups?

Color studies are practical *and* fun. They are also a low-pressure exercise. You are less likely to be invested in a quick "disposable" study than you would be with a larger "precious" painting. The color study is a safe avenue to explore (and get lost) without a large commitment of time or attachment to the outcome. Of course, color studies sometimes come out very well and can stand as small gems in their own right.

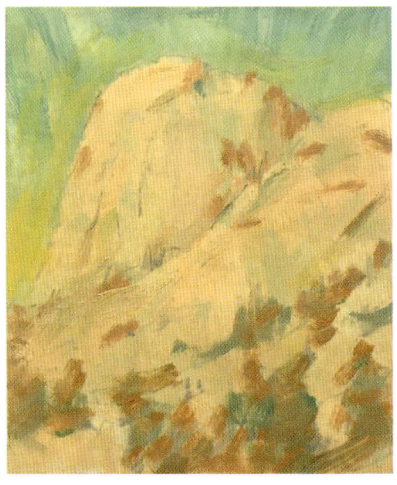

Mitchell Albala, *Peak Study, Orange*
Oil on paper, 4" × 3½" | 10 × 9 cm

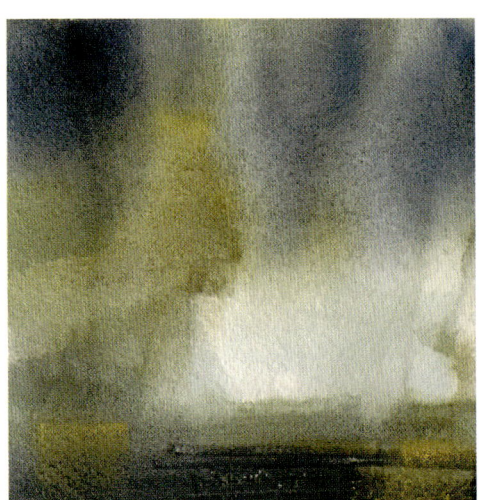

THE PAINTED THUMBNAIL
Mitchell Albala, *Study, Copper Morning*
Watercolor, 3½" × 3½" | 9 × 9 cm

A color study is like a painted thumbnail. It doesn't have to be tight or polished to tell whether or not the colors are working well together.

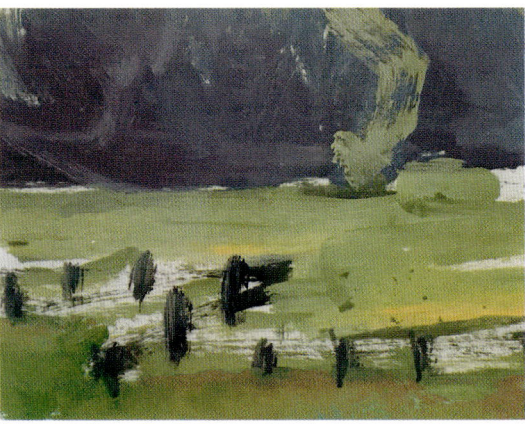

IN SUPPORT OF PAINTERLINESS
Mitchell Albala, *Study, Camano Farm*
Oil on paper, 3" × 4" | 7.5 × 10 cm

The smaller the study, the more *painterly* and gestural it often is, as seen in each of the studies shown here. Many painters strive for expressive mark-making, but find it difficult to translate into larger pieces. A gestural, painterly study like this can serve as an inspiration, a reminder of the more expressive strokes they aspire to in larger work.

COLOR GROUP SWATCHES AS A STUDY

Color groups are the most basic expression of a color strategy. This makes color group swatches, like those we've seen throughout this chapter, small but powerful color studies in their own right. A color study typically depicts the subject—but it doesn't have to. Sometimes, a simple arrangement of colors is all that's needed to assess the color relationships.

EXPLORING YOUR OPTIONS: EXPANDING YOUR RANGE

We are so used to trying to paint the colors we see (especially when referencing photos) that it's easy to become restricted in our ability to be experimental with color. By doing a series of studies like those below, you'll discover more color options than you ever thought possible. Don't tell yourself that you shouldn't try certain color combinations. Try each of the hue interactions. Explore neutral palettes. What colors will turn day into night? If you run out of ideas, find a color strategy in another's painting and apply it to your own study. (Also see the exercise "One Subject, Different Strategies" on page 131.)

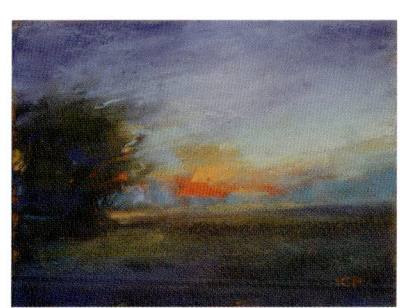
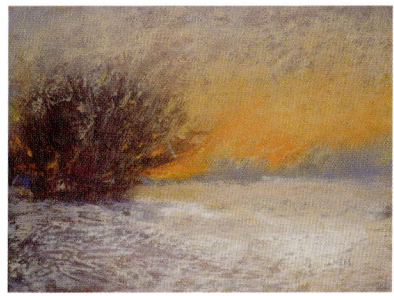
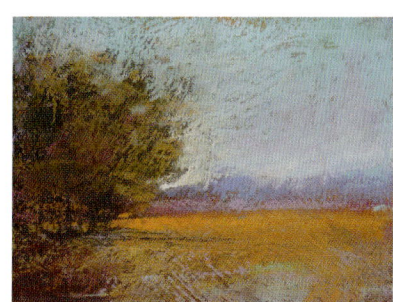
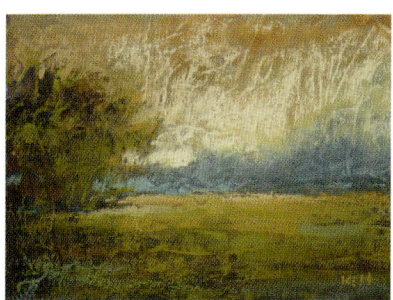
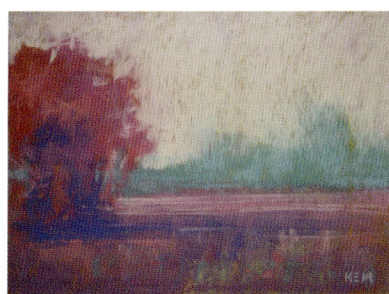
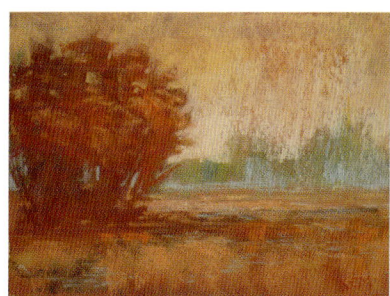

Karen Margulis, *Landscape Variations*
Pastels on paper, 3½" × 5" | 9 × 13 cm

These six studies are from over one hundred Margulis did of this motif. Each one suggests light at a different time of day or under different atmospheric conditions. "In this series, I wanted to explore how many ways I could interpret a simple landscape," says Margulis. "I pushed myself to go beyond local color to discover how color changed the emotional tone of the painting."

REVIEW QUESTIONS:
COLOR GROUPING

Are there naturally occurring color groups in the subject?

With few exceptions, the natural world routinely groups its colors. Can you identify the groups in the scene? What are the colors of each group?

How many color groups are there in the subject?

The fewer groups there are, the greater the chance that the strategy will convey landscape-like and unified harmonies.

How do the color groups in the painting relate?

How the color groups relate is an expression of the color strategy in its most basic form. Are there hue interactions at play? Are the groups similar in hue or do they contrast? How strong are the value differences? How saturated are the colors? Does the arrangement of colors form the impression you are after?

Are the color groups used in differing proportions?

A color strategy works best when the color groups are not used in equal proportion. There is often a dominant group and a few smaller groups. Which group is dominant, and which ones play a lesser role?

Are you distinguishing between individual colors and groups?

A painting can have dozens or even hundreds of individual colors. This is never discouraged. However, you should always ask, *How can the many colors be organized into a small number of groups?*

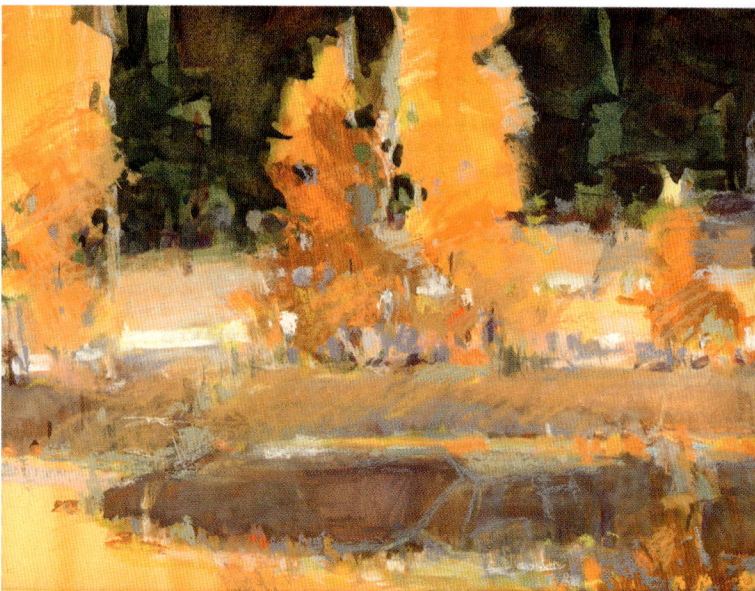

Catherine Gill, *Lake Cle Elum Road*
Watercolor and pastel on paper,
11" × 15" | 28 × 38 cm

Have you done a color study or swatch test to evaluate the groups?

A color study is a reliable way to test the efficacy of your color groups and, in turn, the color strategy. It's also a way to determine which pigment colors and mixtures will form the groups.

EXERCISE: IDENTIFYING COLOR GROUPS

OVERVIEW: There's no better way to get a firm grasp of color groups than to analyze them in the works of others. In this exercise, you will create a set of color swatches that represent the color groups in an existing painting. There is more to this exercise than simply matching colors. A painting may consist of dozens or even hundreds of individual colors. Identifying a color group often means finding the average of several related colors.

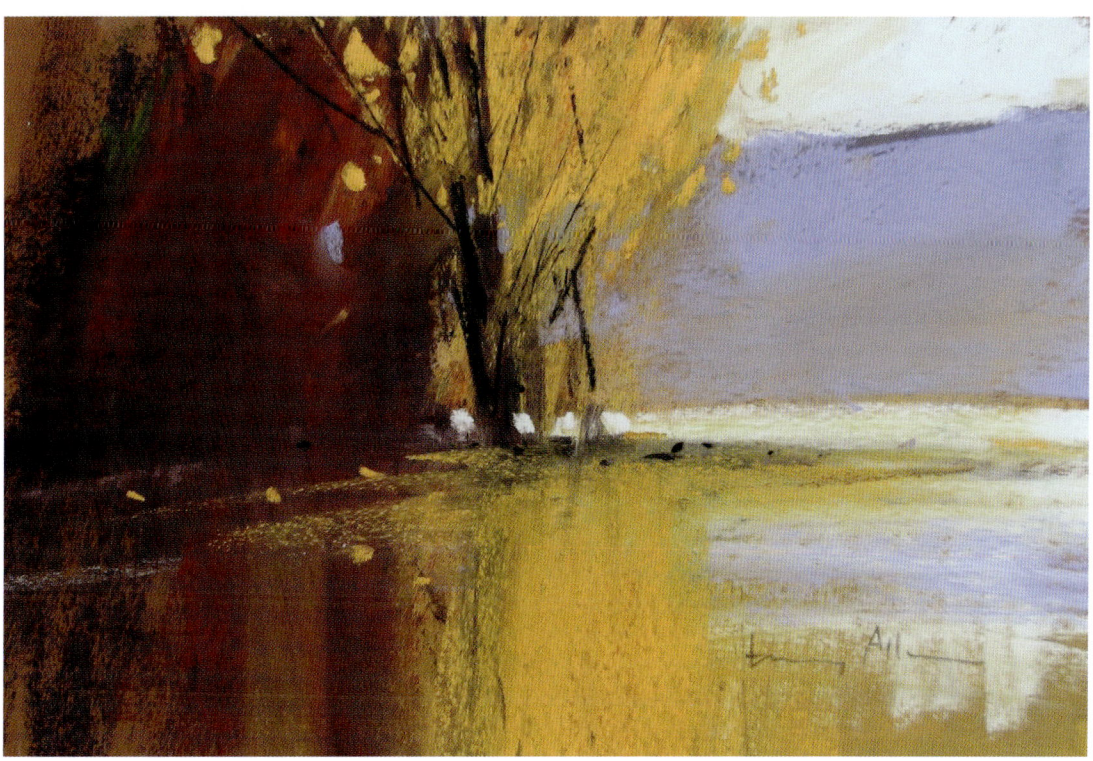

Tony Allain, *Autumn*
Pastel on sanded paper, 10" × 12" | 25.5 × 30.5 cm

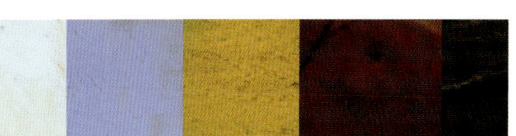

The color groups in some paintings are very easy to identify. Allain's bold, decisive shapes each correspond to their own color group: dark magenta, golden yellow, blue, and a small amount of black. Doing the exercise with a painting like this is very straightforward. It is much more challenging when the painting has many colors woven together in a complex tapestry.

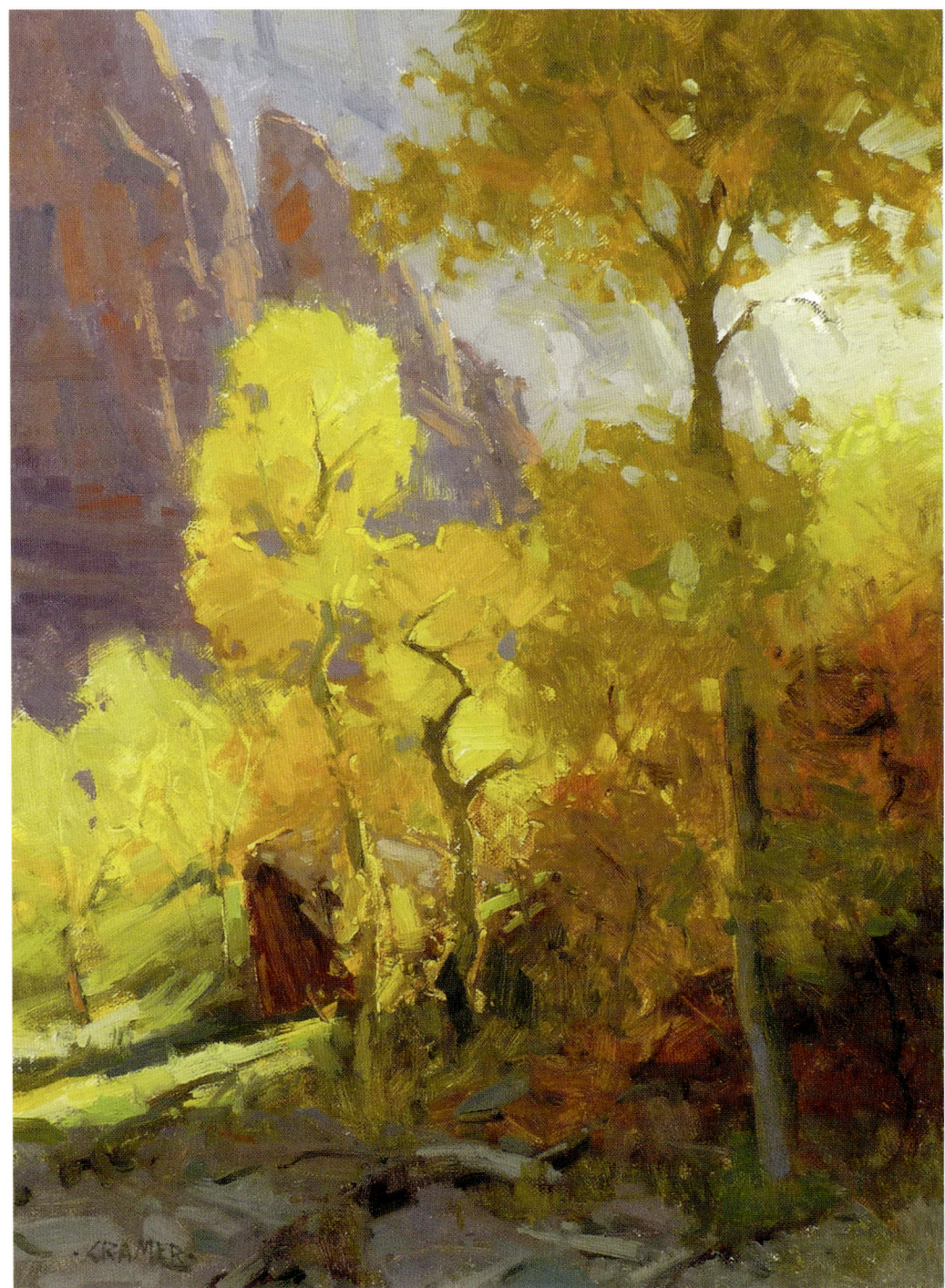

Bill Cramer, *Moment in the Sun*
Oil on linen, 16" × 12" | 40.5 × 30.5 cm

STEP 1: SELECT A PAINTING WITH GOOD COLOR GROUPING

You can find many good examples of color grouping throughout this book. In this painting, I see three major groups. The dominant group is formed by the autumn yellows and golds in the trees. A smaller but important group is the violet mountain, which complements the yellow. The third group is a set of blue-grays, found in the sky and in the shadows at the very bottom of the painting. There are certainly more than three colors in the painting, but they all fit into one of these three groups.

STEP 2: SELECT COLORS AND CREATE GROUPS

The next step is to select the colors that will best form the color groups found in the painting. Selecting colors according to how they fit the strategy is called *targeting* and is discussed fully in the next chapter. With just four pigments (plus white), I have a limited palette, which will help keep color mixtures more cohesive.

LEMON YELLOW + YELLOW OCHRE: The yellows in this painting range from full saturation (in the sunlit areas) to neutral (in the shadows), so I select two yellows that reflect this. They are also very close to the colors seen in the painting.

ALIZARIN is a magenta-like red that, when mixed with ULTRAMARINE, will create the violet in the mountain. It is also used for the red accents in the mountain and in the shadows of the trees.

ULTRAMARINE, when mixed with red and yellow in the right proportions, will create the blue-gray color in the sky. ULTRAMARINE is a much better fit for the color harmony in the painting than a warm blue like PHTHALO, CERULEAN, or MANGANESE.

OBSERVE: There are more *individual* colors in this painting than color groups. Although you are matching colors to some degree, a single color group is often formed by the *average* of several related colors. On this palette, there are three yellow mixes that vary in temperature, saturation, and value, but they all form one yellow-gold group.

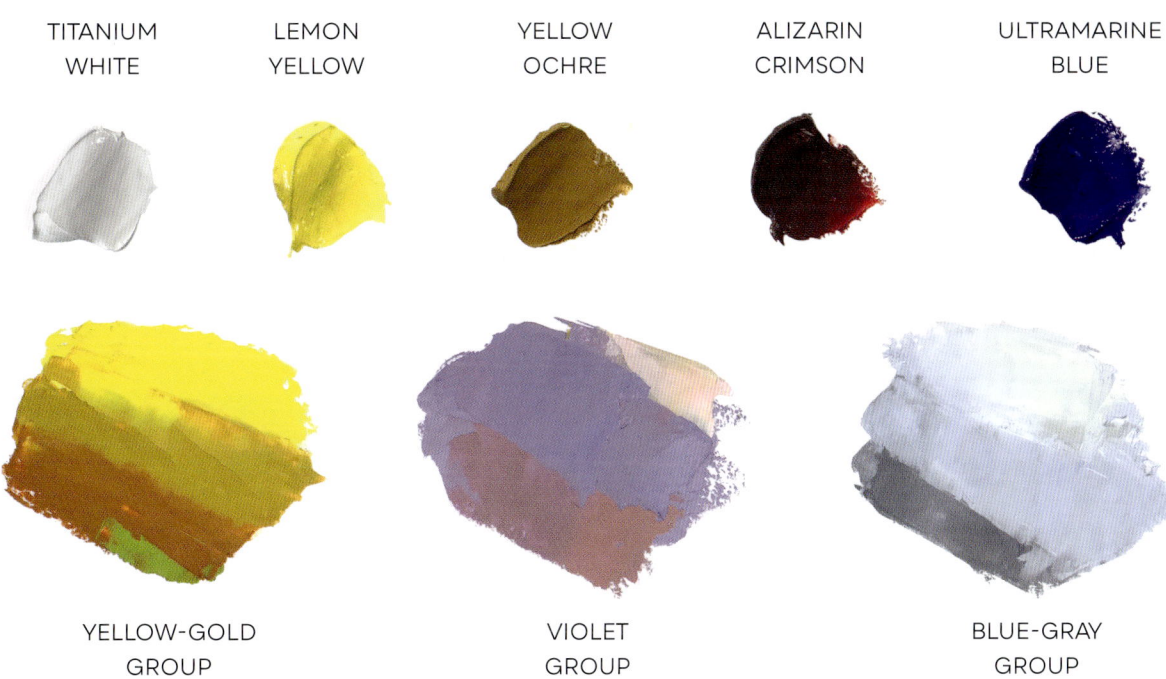

TITANIUM WHITE   LEMON YELLOW   YELLOW OCHRE   ALIZARIN CRIMSON   ULTRAMARINE BLUE

YELLOW-GOLD GROUP   VIOLET GROUP   BLUE-GRAY GROUP

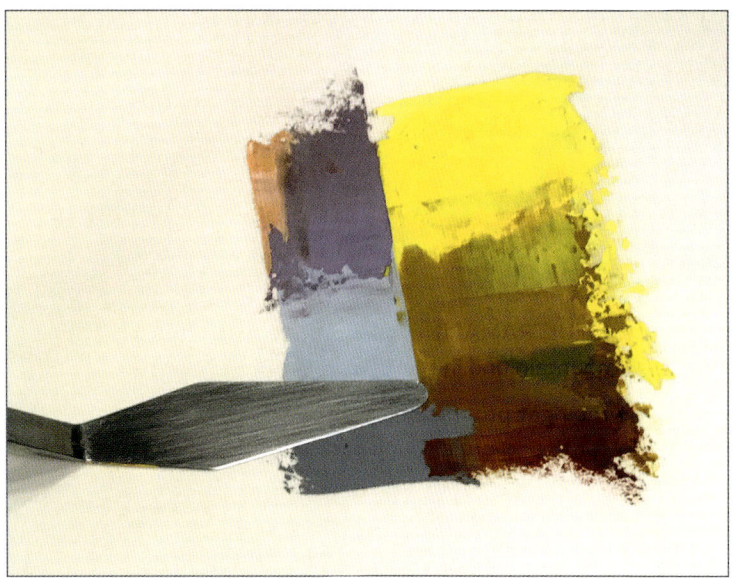

STEP 3: CREATE YOUR SWATCHES

Once your groups are mixed, begin building the swatch set. Place each color down on your surface with a palette knife. (A quality painting surface is not necessary; paper from your sketchbook is adequate.) If a color doesn't appear correct when you place it alongside another color, adjust the mixture on the palette and reapply the swatch. (This is why you use the palette knife; it allows you to easily reapply colors.) You may indicate small accent colors—as I did here with the light orange accent in the violet and the green accent in the golds—but the main color groups are the priority.

IMPROPER SWATCHING

A common mistake in creating swatches is to sample the individual colors from the painting, creating nine, ten, or more swatches. The goal is to create swatches that roughly correspond to the few color groups in the painting.

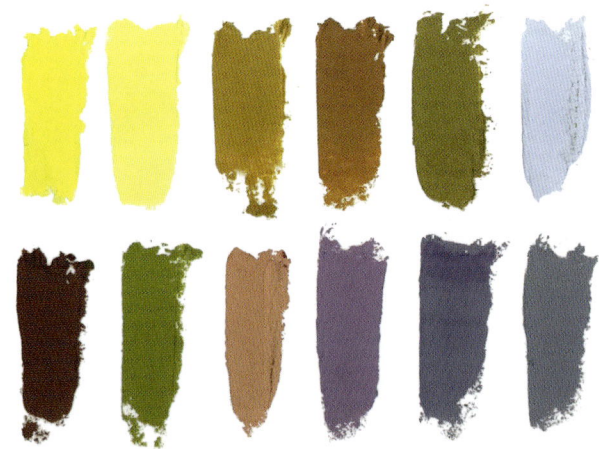

STEP 4: FINAL COLOR SWATCH

The final swatch set should have the same color "flavor" as the painting and be unmistakably recognizable as belonging to that painting.

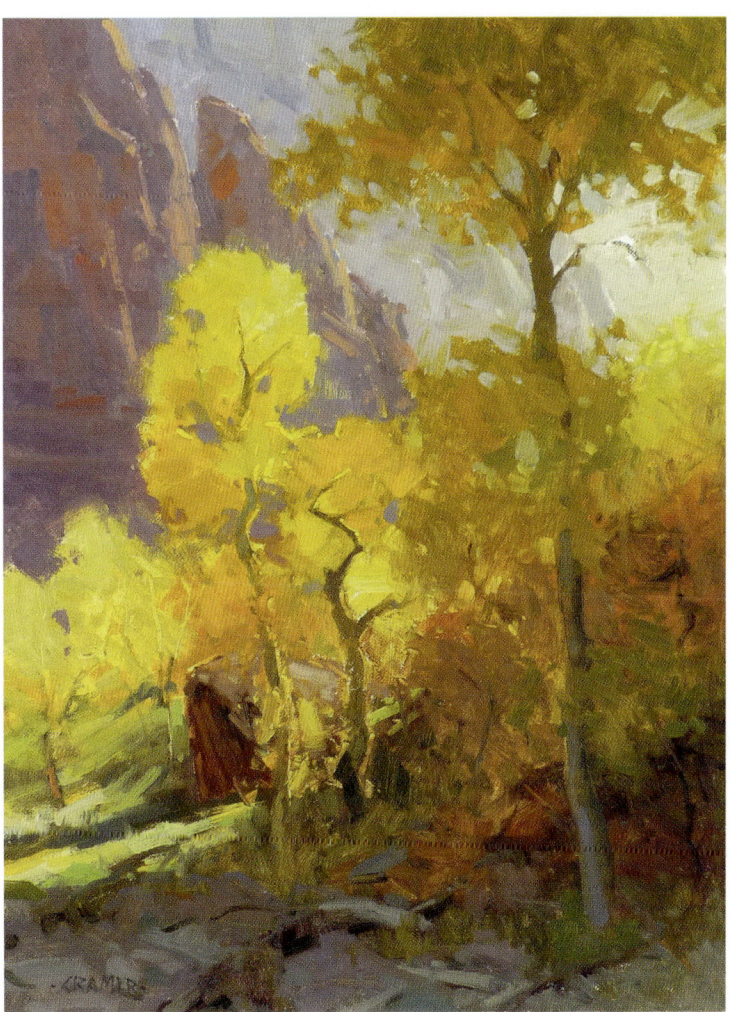

WORKING WITH COLOR GROUPS IN YOUR OWN PAINTING

Learning to identify color groups in the works of others is a first step toward understanding how color groups work. When developing the color groups in your own painting, you'll use the same procedure as you did in the preceding exercise. Whether working en plein air or from a photo, always begin with a swatch or color study. This is especially important when working from photos. We often make the mistake of following the colors in the photo too closely and don't consider how they might be improved. (See "Beyond Photographic Color" on page 132.)

PRACTICE: Do a study and then *evaluate*. How do the groups relate? What is the dominant group? The minor groups? Are the colors too saturated or too neutral? Is an accent color needed? Most importantly, does the arrangement of colors form the impression you are after? Then, do a *second* study that incorporates the changes you think are necessary and use *that* study as your color reference.

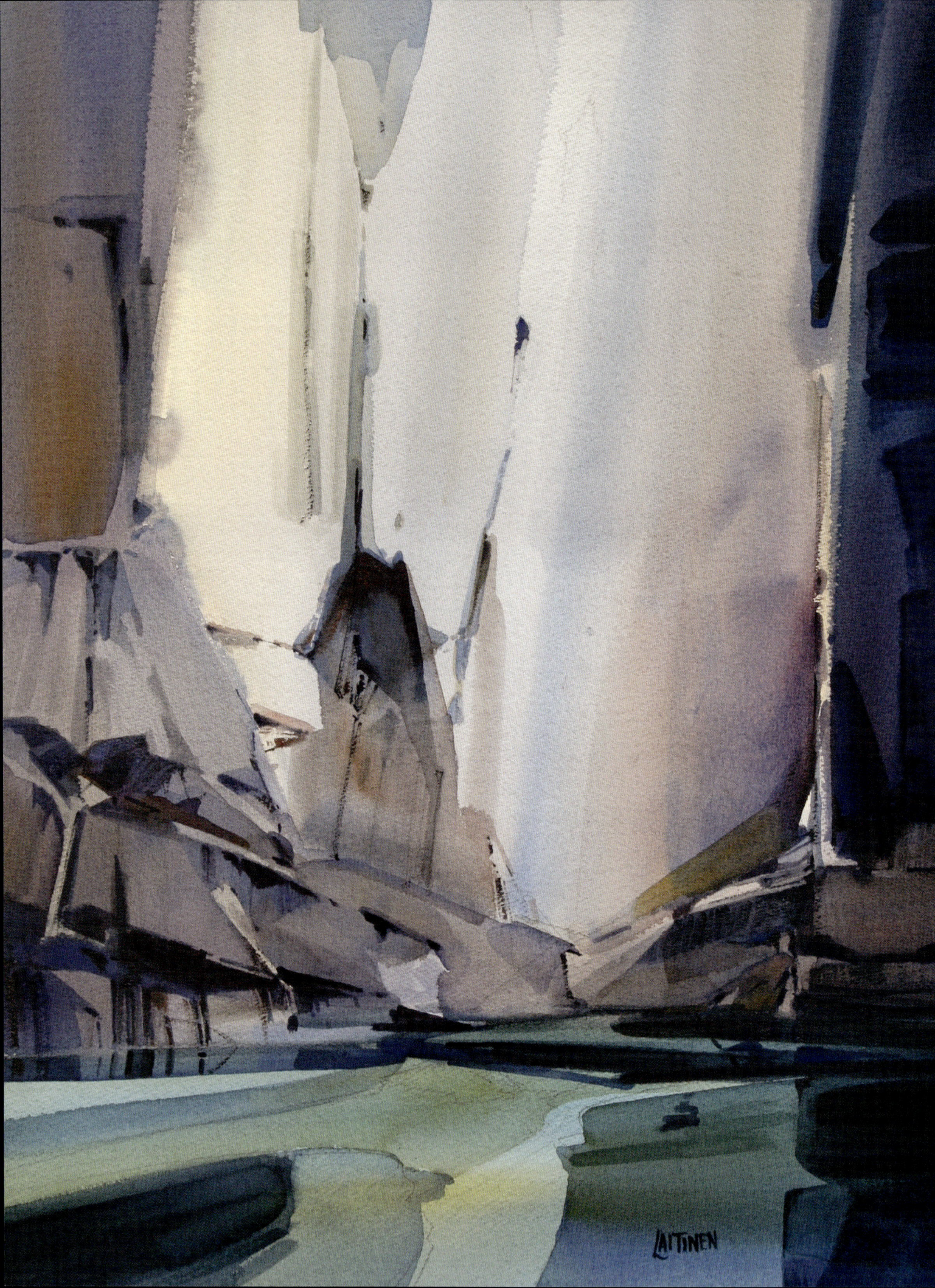

8

PALETTE STRATEGIES

Working with color strategies and color grouping reinforces our understanding that color choices are never arbitrary. Every choice is driven by our color goals for that painting. So, it stands to reason that the particular colors we choose for our palette will not be arbitrary either. Like ingredients in a recipe, the particular pigments we use in a painting will direct the kind of harmonies or "flavors" that can be achieved. Our palette and color strategy have a reciprocal relationship: the strategy determines which colors we will include on our palette and the palette supports the strategy.

We will review two essential practices in the palette strategy: the limited palette, which simplifies color mixing and helps build more cohesive harmonies, and *targeting*, in which we choose the colors that best conform to the color strategy. We will also review the split primary palette, a popular all-purpose palette for oil, acrylic, or watercolor painters.

◂ Dale Laitinen, *Night Quarry*
Watercolor on paper, 30" × 22" | 76 × 56 cm

Laitinen's palette includes eight colors, plus a neutral tint. Each color has a different hue, temperature, and saturation level. This gives him a wide latitude in developing the various harmonies he needs for different paintings. A painter's palette directly supports their color strategy.

THE LIMITED PALETTE

There are so many pigment options–dozens in oil, acrylic, and watercolor and *hundreds* in pastel–that we couldn't possibly use them all. Nor would we want to. *Every palette must have limits.*

In a genre that relies on color richness and diversity, restricting the number of pigments might seem contradictory to our mission. As with so many aspects of the painter's practice, however, limiting options doesn't actually limit us. It leads to better, more focused results. There are several advantages to working with a limited palette:

- A limited palette is practical and efficient. It simplifies color mixing because it doesn't load up with every conceivable color, only those appropriate to the task at hand. What are the fewest colors you can use to achieve your intended harmony?
- Fewer colors produce mixtures that are more cohesive, which leads to more unified harmonies.

ULTRA-LIMITED VS. LIMITED PALETTES

Some palettes are ultra-limited, with just red, yellow, and blue, plus white. Using so few colors forces painters to do more mixing, which in turn, helps them discover how colors can be mixed from the three primaries. For this reason, the ultra-limited palette is often prescribed to fledgling painters (although seasoned painters find benefit in working with it as well).

Most painters prefer to work with a slightly expanded, but still limited, palette, which might include eight, ten, or twelve colors. The additional pigments allow them to mix any color they want, but are still few enough to make the palette manageable.

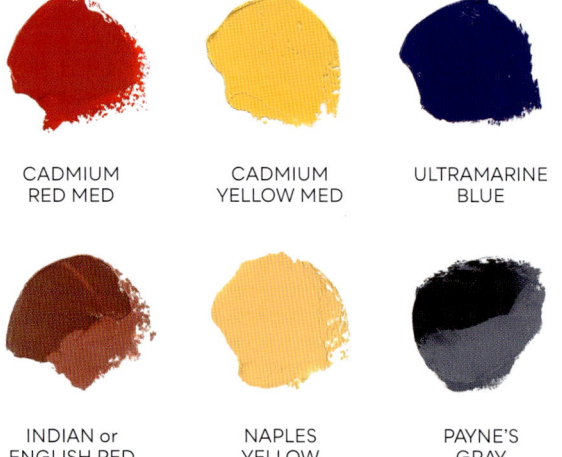

| CADMIUM RED MED | CADMIUM YELLOW MED | ULTRAMARINE BLUE |

INDIAN or ENGLISH RED   NAPLES YELLOW   PAYNE'S GRAY

THE THREE-PRIMARY PALETTE

Painters are taught that they can mix any color the want from the three primaries (plus white). This is not entirely accurate. A three-primary palette can steer color mixtures in a particular direction and not allow the painter to mix any color they want. There are so many different types of reds, yellows, and blues, that depending on which primary is used, you will get different results. The TOP PRIMARY SET includes only saturated pigments. With these you could create both saturated mixes and (by mixing complements together) neutral mixes. The BOTTOM PRIMARY SET includes neutral versions of the primaries. These also allow you to mix a wide range of colors, but because these pigments are inherently neutral, the mixes would also be neutral. You would never be able to mix saturated colors.

THE TARGETED PALETTE

For convenience, a painter might keep their most frequently used colors on their palette at the ready—*but they won't use all of them in every painting.* When a painter considers a pigment's properties—its value, its temperature, and its saturation level—and chooses it according to how it best fits the color strategy, they are *targeting* their palette.

For example, if the yellows in the painting need to be bright and saturated, then you would naturally select a yellow that is also bright and saturated, such as those from the CADMIUM or HANSA families. If the painting has more neutral harmonies, you might pick a more neutral yellow such as NAPLES YELLOW or YELLOW OCHRE.

Targeting is an essential part of the palette strategy. It directly supports the practice of color strategies and color grouping.

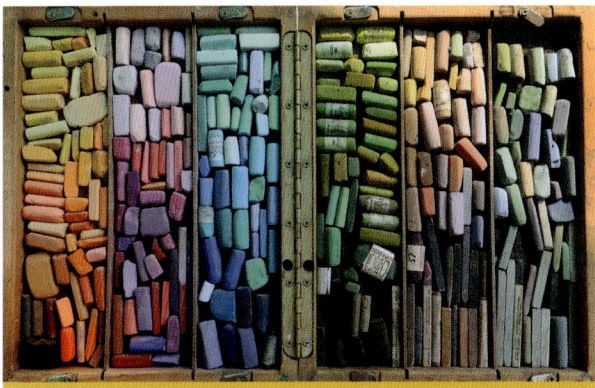

COLOR MIXING: WET MEDIA VS. PASTEL

There are clear differences in the way wet-media and dry-media (pastel) palettes are formed—but the goals are the same. Oil and water-media painters might have a few dozen pigments in their collection. They use a select few for each painting and mix them together to create countless instances of new colors. Pastel painters, on the other hand, don't mix on a palette. They can mix two or more colors on the surface of the painting, but for the most part, they rely on having a wide variety of pastels of every imaginable hue, value, and saturation level.

Photo: Loriann Signori

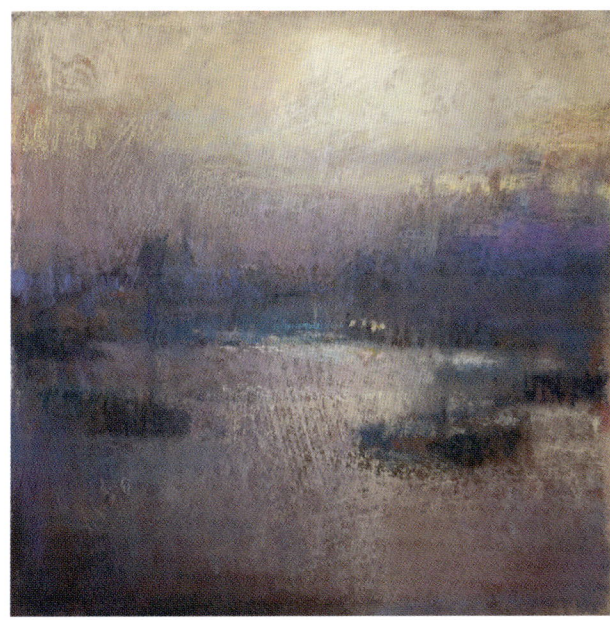

Loriann Signori, *From Silence to Symphony*
Pastel on paper, 8" × 8" | 20.5 × 20.5 cm

From the hundreds of sticks a pastel painter has, they pull out a smaller group that fits the color plan of the painting. For the pastel artist, this is their version of a targeted palette.

WHY WE TARGET: DIFFERENT PROPERTIES, DIFFERENT RESULTS

Why does choosing a particular blue or particular red matter so much? *Because all colors are not created equal.* Within any given color family there are many different pigment varieties, all of which have different properties. For instance, there are many varieties of blue, each with a different value, temperature, and saturation level. By understanding these properties, we can choose the pigments that best target the strategy. Below is a small sampling of the different properties of pigments within the same hue family. The top row shows colors in oil, the middle row displays an equivalent pigment in pastel, and the bottom row is watercolor.

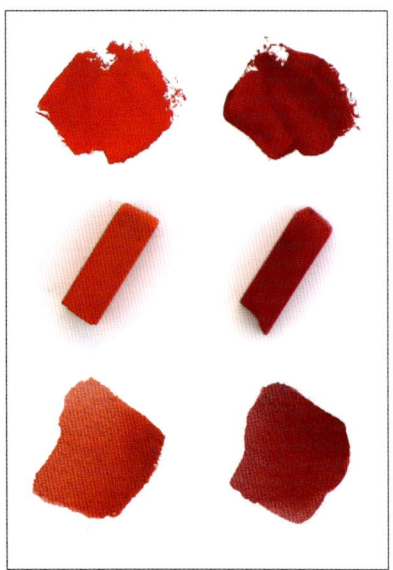 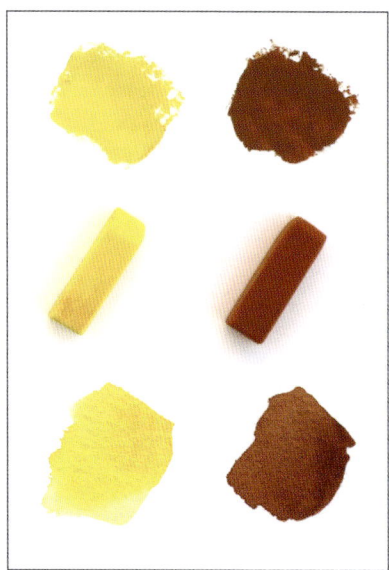 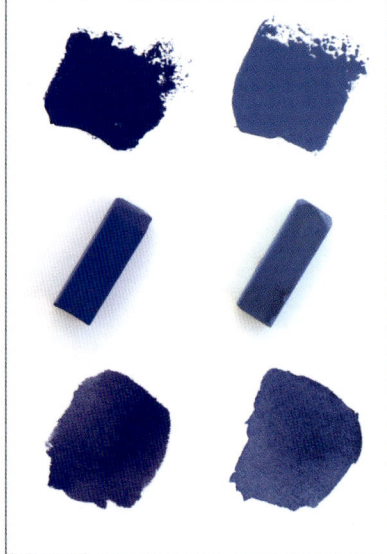

DIFFERENT VALUES AND TEMPERATURE

Two reds that differ in value and temperature: CADMIUM RED LIGHT (left) is lighter and warmer than CADMIUM RED DARK (right).

DIFFERENT VALUES AND SATURATION

Two yellows that differ in value and saturation levels: A lighter, more saturated HANSA YELLOW MEDIUM (left) and a darker neutral YELLOW OCHRE (right).

SAME VALUES, DIFFERENT TEMPERATURES

Two blues: ULTRAMARINE (left) and MANGANESE (right) are similar in value, but differ in temperature.

DEMONSTRATION: TARGETED PALETTE IN PASTEL

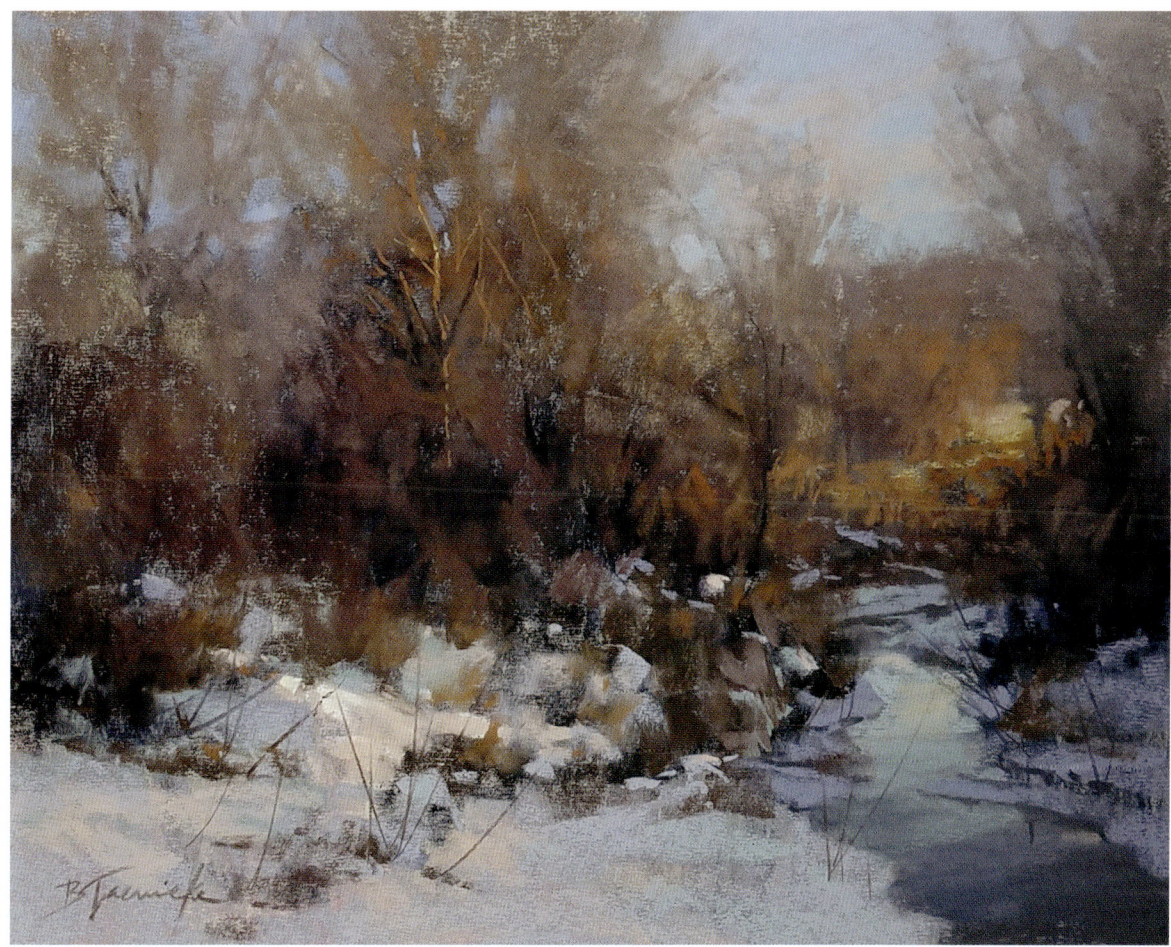

Barbara Jaenicke, *Golden Light of Winter Day's End*
Pastel on mounted paper, 11" × 14" | 28 × 35.5 cm

Every one of Jaenicke's paintings has a distinct color key. This is in large part because she builds a targeted palette based on a limited number of color groups. Jaenicke explains the relationship between individual colors and groups: "Once I establish the initial color groups, I build the rest of the palette using variations of value, temperature, and saturation of those initial colors, which facilitates the color harmony." (Also see Jaenicke's painting *Remembering Spring* on page 142.)

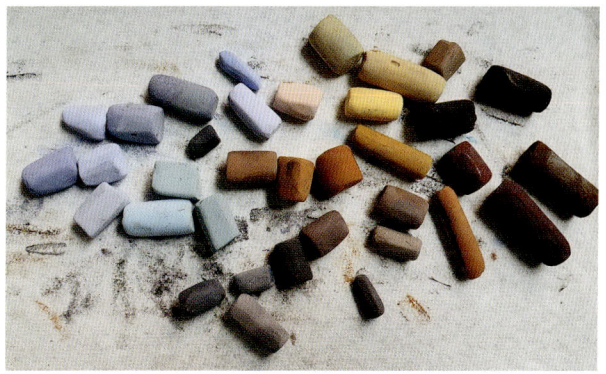

The thirty-five colors Jaenicke uses are all organized into two basic color groups: a cool-temperature group (formed by the blues and blue-violets) and a more dominant warm-temperature group (made up of neutral earth tones). Within each group there are variations of value, temperature, and saturation. There is no limit to the number of individual colors a painter may use in a painting as long as they are organized into a limited number of groups.

DEMONSTRATION: TARGETED PALETTE IN OIL

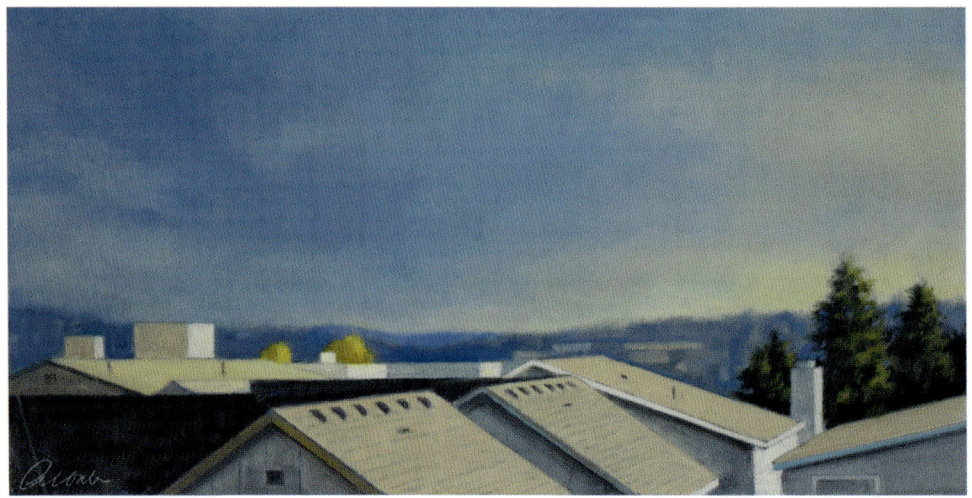

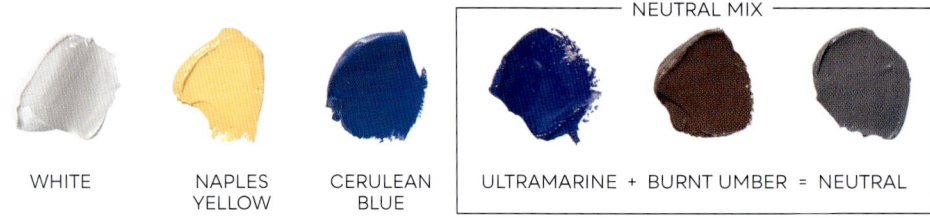

WHITE   NAPLES YELLOW   CERULEAN BLUE   NEUTRAL MIX — ULTRAMARINE + BURNT UMBER = NEUTRAL

Mitchell Albala, *Rooftops 59th Street, After the Rain*
Oil on paper, 7" × 14" | 18 × 35.5 cm

After the Rain is a painting with a fairly neutral harmony. Colors range from slightly neutral (in the sky) to very neutral (on the rooftops and fronts of the houses). This palette will allow me to more easily create the neutral mixes I need. Using a limited palette will also help keep my color mixtures more unified.

OBSERVE: To help create my neutral mixes, I make a gray color by combining the neutral pigment BURNT UMBER and ULTRAMARINE, as shown on the right side of the palette. This neutral mix will be added to nearly every color in the painting. When there is a little more ULTRAMARINE in the mix, the mixture leans cool, as in the sky. When there is less ULTRAMARINE, the mixture is not as cool, as in the dark rooftop in the lower left and the fronts of the houses.

KEY AREAS

SKY: Ordinarily, I prefer a single blue on the palette, but in this painting, the sky needs a hint of warmth that can only be achieved with a warm blue like CERULEAN. Thus, the sky is made with both ULTRAMARINE and CERULEAN, then desaturated with the NEUTRAL MIX, and finally hints of NAPLES.

LIGHT ROOFTOPS: WHITE and little bit of BURNT UMBER creates the warm buff color of the light rooftops.

GOLDEN TREES: Even the seemingly saturated yellow trees are made with NAPLES YELLOW, which is like an earth yellow and less saturated than yellows from the CADMIUM or HANSA families. The light sides of the trees are made with NAPLES, and a little BURNT UMBER is added to create the shadows.

GREEN TREES: The sunlit side of the trees are made with a mix of NAPLES and ULTRAMARINE, while the shadows are a combination of the NEUTRAL MIX and ULTRAMARINE.

LIGHT ON HORIZON: The strip of light on the horizon is made with NAPLES and WHITE, but also contains a hint of blue-gray sky color. The sky also contains a hint of the NAPLES. This helps unify the two color zones of the sky.

THE SPLIT PRIMARY PALETTE

A popular all-purpose palette used by many painters is the split primary palette. It is a compact palette with few enough pigments to keep color mixing manageable, but enough to allow one to mix nearly any color they want. It's also lightweight (fewer tubes for oil and acrylic painters to carry), making it a good option for travel and working outdoors.

The strength of the split primary palette is that it includes two of each primary: a cool and a warm. That temperature difference covers a wider portion of the spectrum, increasing the range of possible color mixtures.

WARM YELLOWS are closer to the orange-red side of the spectrum. Common varieties are the "medium" and "dark" varieties in the CADMIUM and HANSA families.

COOL YELLOWS lean away from the red-orange side of the spectrum, giving them a subtle hint of green. Common varieties are LEMON and NICKEL-TITANATE.

WARM REDS have none of the violet found in cool reds and instead pick up warmth from the orange-red side of the spectrum. Common varieties are CADMIUMS, NAPHTHOL, and CADMIUM ORANGE.

WARM BLUES lean toward the yellow side of the spectrum, picking up some green in the process. Common varieties are PHTHALO, PHTHALO TURQUOISE, MANGANESE, and PRUSSIAN.

COOL REDS lean toward the blue side of the spectrum, pushing them toward magenta or red-violet. Common varieties are ALIZARIN CRIMSON and QUINACRIDONE.

COOL BLUES lean toward the violet side of the spectrum, with none of the green hints found in the warm blues. The most common variety is ULTRAMARINE.

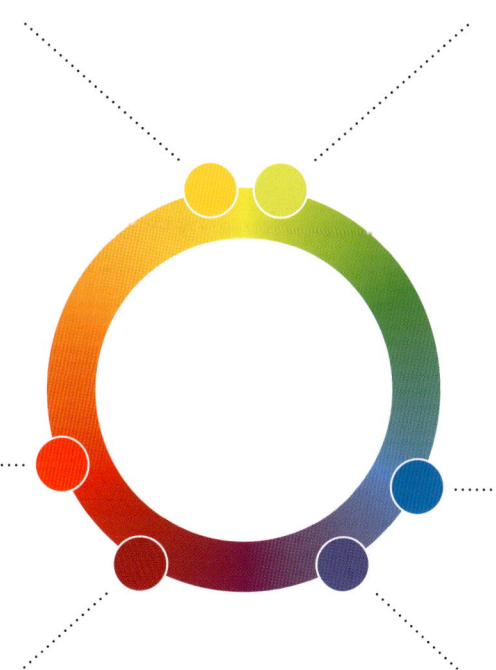

TAKING SIDES: COOL AND WARM PRIMARIES

The "cool" or "warm" labels we assign to pigments are based on which side of the spectrum they lean toward. For example, warm reds lean toward the orange side, while cool reds lean toward the violet side. Pastels are made from the same pigments as oil and water-based media and possess the same cool and warm attributes.

Colors in the split primary palette are usually saturated colors. However, those working with neutral harmonies (as a Tonalists do) can replace the saturated primaries with neutral pigments. For example, a CADMIUM or HANSA YELLOW might be replaced with YELLOW OCHRE or NAPLES YELLOW. (See "Two Roads to Neutrals" on page 162.)

SPLIT PRIMARY PALETTES AND PAINTINGS

As we see in the color wheel on the previous page, there are many different pigments that can fill the warm and cool slots on the split primary palette. The two split primary palettes shown here, from oil painter Scott Gellatly and watercolorist Bill Vrscak, each use a different set of primaries.

Note that the pigments in both split primary palettes are pure and saturated, yet the paintings have many colors that are neutralized to some degree. As with any palette, neutrals or grays will have to be mixed. (See "Two Roads to Neutrals" on page 162.)

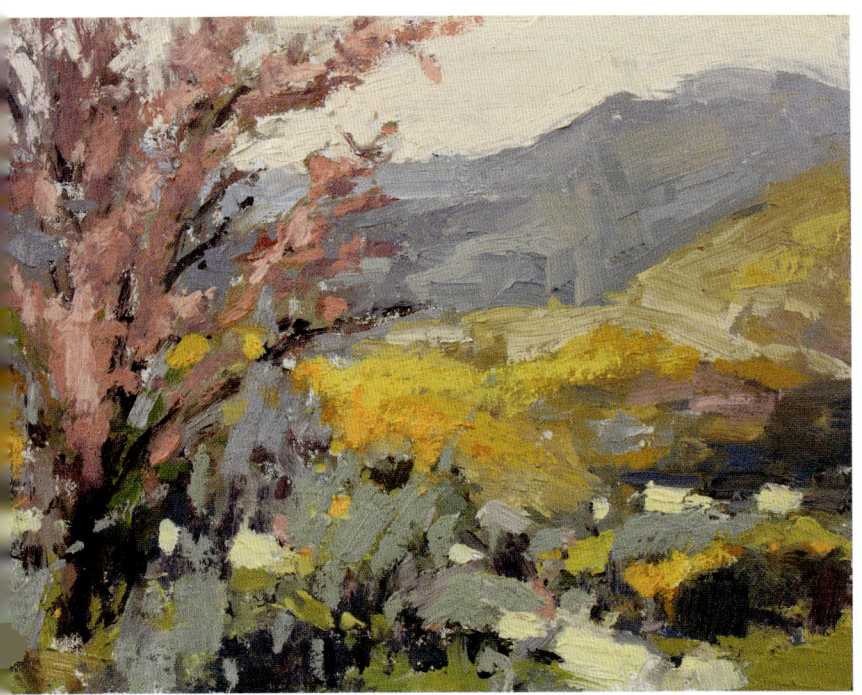

Scott Gellatly, *Desert Flora*
Oil on panel, 9" × 12" | 23 × 30.5 cm

 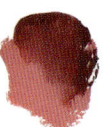

REDS

(WARM) CADMIUM ORANGE

(COOL) QUINACRIDONE RED

YELLOWS

(WARM) INDIAN YELLOW

(COOL) CADMIUM YELLOW LT.

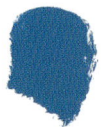 

BLUES

(WARM) COBALT TEAL

(COOL) ULTRAMARINE

When working outdoors, Gellatly uses a six-color-plus-white split primary palette. His choices maximize the temperature range within each primary. By using CADMIUM ORANGE instead of the more customary CADMIUM RED LIGHT, he gets an extra wide temperature range within the reds. (CADMIUM ORANGE is also richer than an orange produced by mixing red and yellow pigments together.) Straight from the tube, INDIAN YELLOW appears orange, but its tint is a distinctly warm, radiant yellow. COBALT TEAL has a stronger green bias than blues like PHTHALO or MANGANESE, so alongside ULTRAMARINE it allows for a wider temperature shift within the blues.

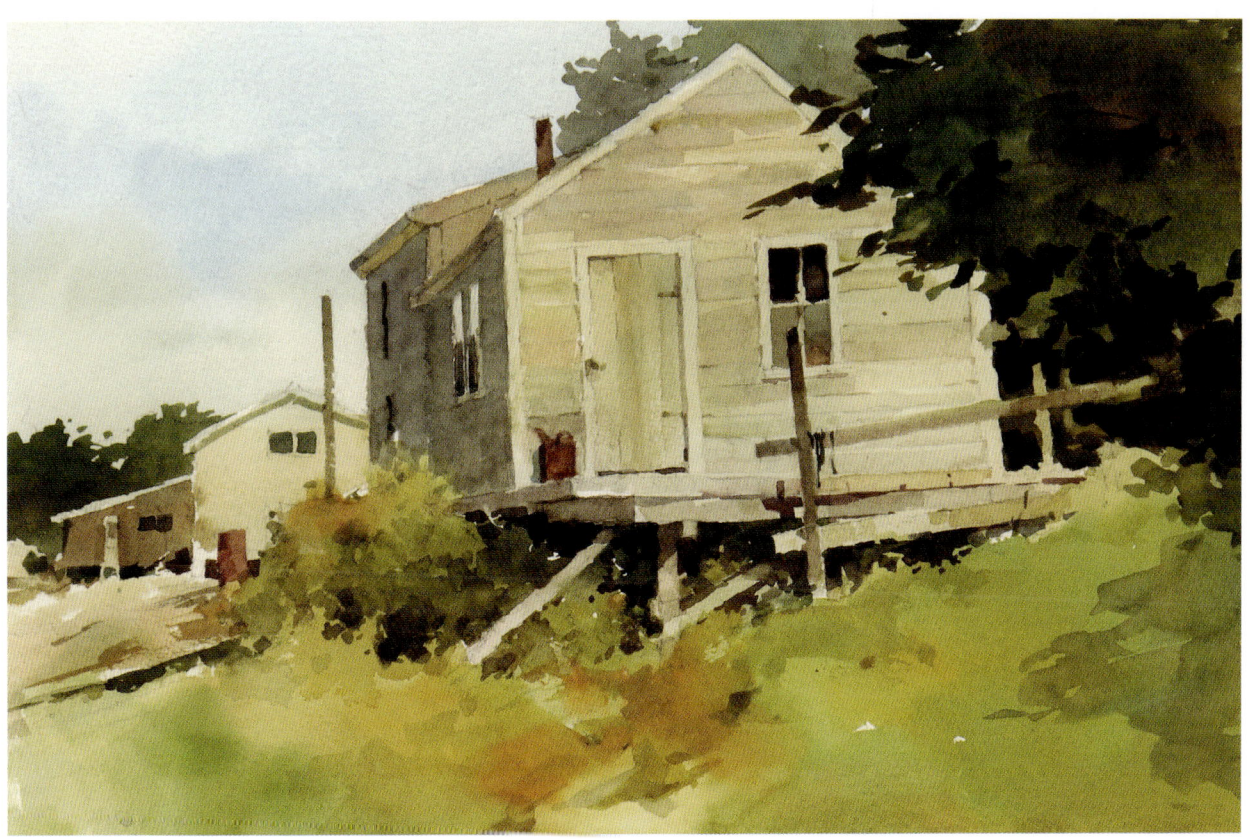

Bill Vrscak, *Cap'n Jim's Place*, watercolor, 12" × 18" | 30.5 × 46 cm

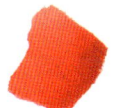 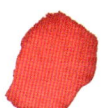 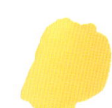  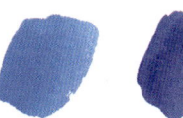

REDS	YELLOWS	BLUES
(WARM) CADMIUM RED	(WARM) CADMIUM YELLOW	(WARM) CERULEAN
(COOL) ALIZARIN	(COOL) AUREOLIN YELLOW	(COOL) COBALT

Vrscak uses an entirely different set of primaries than Gellatly. This isn't because watercolor is a transparent medium. Vrscak's colors are also available in oil or acrylic. (And Gellatly's colors are available in watercolor.) As with any palette, the artist chooses their colors according to how it meets their color intention and personal style. Vrscak says, "If the look of my blues and greens becomes too predictable, I will often change out some of the colors on my palette. For example, replacing AUREOLIN YELLOW with NAPLES or MANGANESE BLUE with CERULEAN."

TWO ROADS TO NEUTRALS

Every color that ends up in our painting has to be mixed, and neutral colors are no exception. Even painters who favor high saturation strategies rarely use *fully* saturated colors. This means that most colors need to be at least *partially* desaturated.

NEUTRALIZING WITH COMPLEMENTS

If you asked most painters how to desaturate or neutralize a color, they would tell you to add its complement. This is a tried-and-true method for creating neutrals. However, neutralizing complements rarely produce a "perfect" neutral without any color bias at all. They nearly always retain some of the hue identity of one of the complements. This color bias can be desirable, as it allows for more nuanced, color-based neutrals. But it also makes mixing complementary-based neutrals difficult to control. Often, we have to add a third color to achieve the neutral we want.

NEUTRALIZING WITH NEUTRAL COLORS

Alternatively, one can also create neutral mixes by using colors that are neutral to begin with. This approach is easier and more direct than mixing complements. Of course, you can also create neutrals with complements *and* neutral pigments.

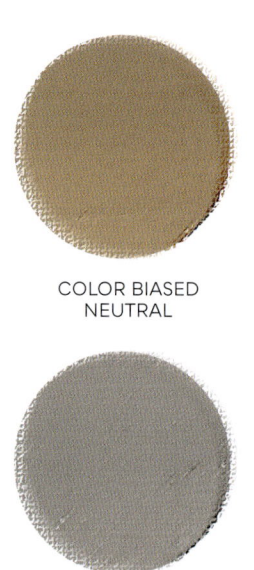

COLOR BIASED
NEUTRAL

UNBIASED GRAY

"NEUTRALS" VS. "GRAYS"

The terms "neutral" and "gray" are often used interchangeably, but they have subtle differences in meaning. A neutral is any color that is less than fully saturated. Neutrals will appear muted, dull, or "brown." Whether mixed or squeezed from a tube, most neutral colors have a color bias; that is, they still hold some hue identity.

The top swatch is a warm neutral with a bias toward orange. Neutrals are still colors, so the bias is important. It tells us which hue family the neutral belongs to and whether it is cool or warm. The bottom swatch is a "perfect" neutral that has no color bias at all, which means it appears neither cool or warm, or at least, it is hard to tell which hue family it belongs to. We call colors like this *grays*.

NEUTRALIZING WITH COMPLEMENTS

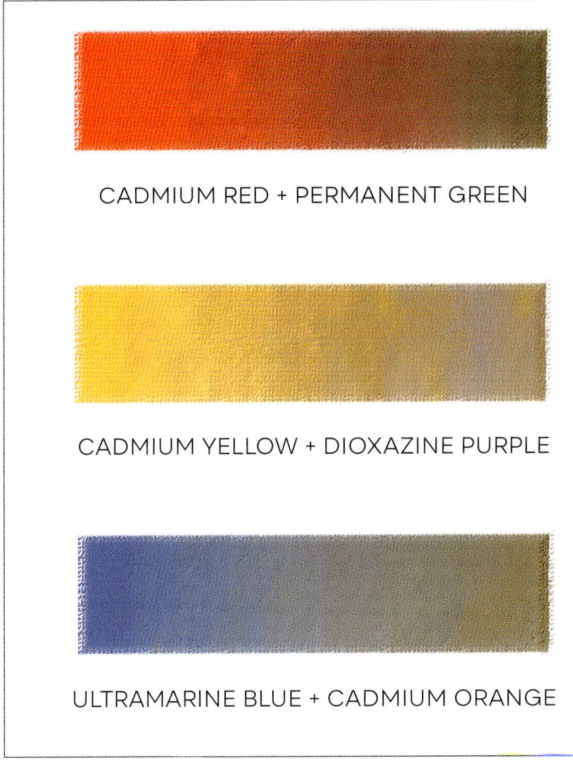

CADMIUM RED + PERMANENT GREEN

CADMIUM YELLOW + DIOXAZINE PURPLE

ULTRAMARINE BLUE + CADMIUM ORANGE

NEUTRALIZING WITH NEUTRAL COLORS

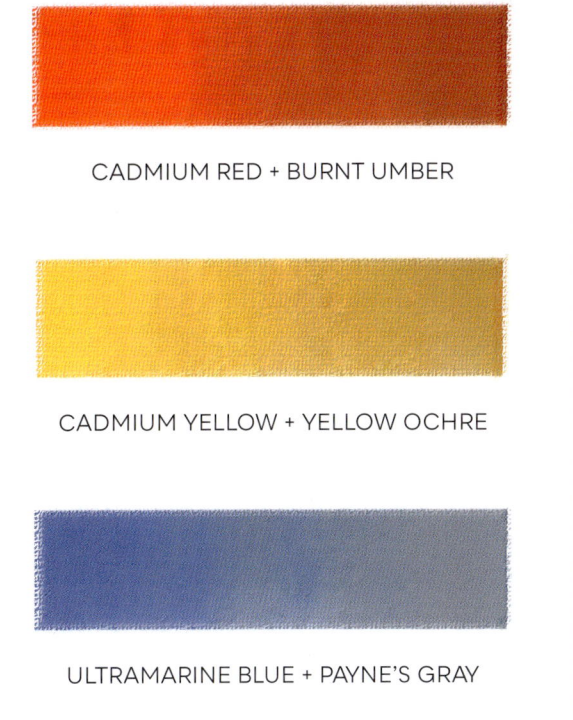

CADMIUM RED + BURNT UMBER

CADMIUM YELLOW + YELLOW OCHRE

ULTRAMARINE BLUE + PAYNE'S GRAY

In each string, the color on the left is fully saturated. As its complement is added, the mix becomes progressively more neutral. Note the color bias of the neutral mix on the right.

You can also desaturate pure colors by adding pigments that are neutral themselves, such as BURNT UMBER, YELLOW OCHRE, RAW SIENNA, BURNT SIENNA, VAN DYKE BROWN, or PAYNE'S GRAY, to name a few.

KEEP A COOL AND WARM NEUTRAL ON YOUR PALETTE

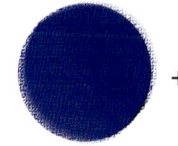 **+** 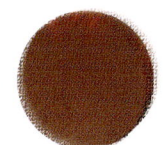 **+**  **=**

ULTRAMARINE BLUE   BURNT SIENNA   WHITE   UNBIASED NEUTRAL (GRAY)   BLUE BIAS (COOL)   ORANGE BIAS (WARM)

When including neutral pigments on your palette, consider having both a cool and a warm neutral. In combination, ULTRAMARINE BLUE and BURNT SIENNA can produce a wide range of both warm and cool neutrals.

Equal portions of ULTRAMARINE BLUE and BURNT SIENNA (plus white) produce a nearly perfect gray, with no color bias at all. When slightly more blue is added to the mix, the resulting neutral will have a cool blue bias. If there is more BURNT SIENNA in the mix, then it will have a warm bias.

PARTING THOUGHTS: THE NEVER-ENDING INQUIRY

"The noblest pleasure is the joy of understanding."

—LEONARDO DA VINCI

I've been painting for over forty years, and I've never stopped learning and striving for new and better ways to express the wondrous things I see in nature. One of the things that has allowed me to keep growing is an inquiry-based approach. I ask questions. I try new things. I seek out feedback from other painters. I even learned new things while writing this book, in consulting with so many of the contributing artists.

Painting can be a solitary endeavor, *but growing as an artist is not.* All good painters must, at least to some degree, remain students at heart. We tap into the wisdom of other creatives who may have the answers we seek, whether it's in the form of an instructor, a masterpiece hanging on the museum wall, or a book like this one.

As an instructor and artist, I work with principles and practices that can be *practically* implemented. This is what is reflected in these pages. Because these ideas and exercises have been so beneficial to my students (and to me), I'm confident that if you apply them, you too will see your work improve. I hope that what you have learned from this book will support you in the never-ending inquiry that is landscape painting.

Paint on!

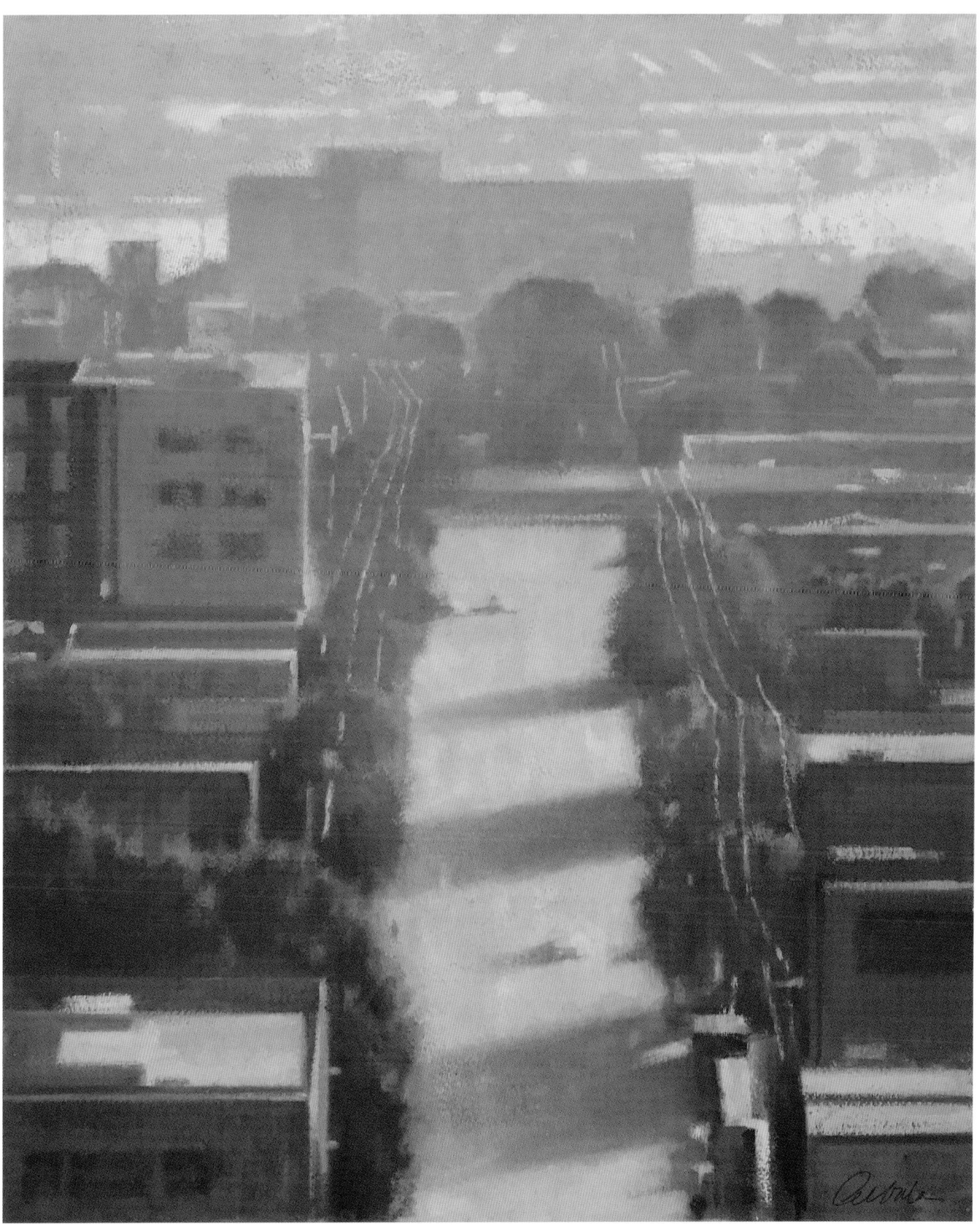

Mitchell Albala, *Toward a Western Light*, oil on panel, 15" × 12½" | 38 × 32 cm

RESOURCES

BOOKS

Albala, Mitchell. *Landscape Painting: Essential Concepts and Techniques for Plein Air and Studio Practice*. New York: Watson-Guptill Publications, 2009.
The "new classic" of landscape, with a comprehensive overview of landscape basics and techniques.

Gill, Catherine, with Beth Means. *Powerful Watercolor Landscapes*. Cincinnati, Ohio: North Light Books, 2011.
Not only for watercolor painters, this book presents well-illustrated lessons on composition, shapes, values, and subject selection.

Hoffmann, Tom. *Watercolor Painting: A Comprehensive Approach to Mastering the Medium*. New York: Watson-Guptill Publications, 2012.
Hoffmann not only covers watercolor technique but also offers valuable lessons on the art of simplification and massing.

Macpherson. Kevin. *Landscape Painting Inside & Out*. Cincinnati, Ohio: North Light Books, 2009.
A beautifully illustrated primer on indoor and outdoor landscape painting.

Roberts, Ian. *Mastering Composition: Techniques and Practices to Dramatically Improve Your Painting*. Cincinnati, Ohio: North Light Books, 2007.
An extremely practical guide to composition, with clear demonstrations and many landscape examples.

MAGAZINES

The Artist's Magazine
artistsnetwork.com

Pastel Journal
artistsnetwork.com

Plein Air Magazine
pleinairmagazine.com

Watercolor Artist
artistsnetwork.com

ONLINE RESOURCES

Acrylic University
acrylicuniversity.com
Virtual lessons geared specifically to acrylic painters.

The Artist's Network
artistsnetwork.com
A wealth of practical articles and video lessons for every medium and style.

Essential Concepts of Landscape Painting
mitchalbala.com/blog
The author's educational blog on landscape painting.

Mastering Composition
youtube.com/
IanRobertsMasteringComposition
Ian Roberts's YouTube channel, with video lessons on composition, color, and technique.

Painting Perceptions
paintingperceptions.com
In-depth interviews with contemporary painters.

VIDEOS

Creating Dynamic Landscapes with John MacDonald (Modern Masters Series). Boca Raton, Florida: Liliedahl Art Instruction Videos, 2017.

Paul Kratter: Mastering Trees (Landscape Masters Series). Boca Raton, Florida: Streamline Premium Art Video, 2019.

John MacDonald: Poetic Landscapes (Modern Masters Series). Boca Raton, Florida: Streamline Premium Art Video, 2020.

PODCASTS

The Artful Painter
theartfulpainter.com/artful-painter
Carl Olson, Jr.'s warm and lively interviews with many leading landscape painters.

Reasonably Fine Art Talk
youtube.com/CharlieHunterArt
Interviews, musings, and lessons from painter Charlie Hunter

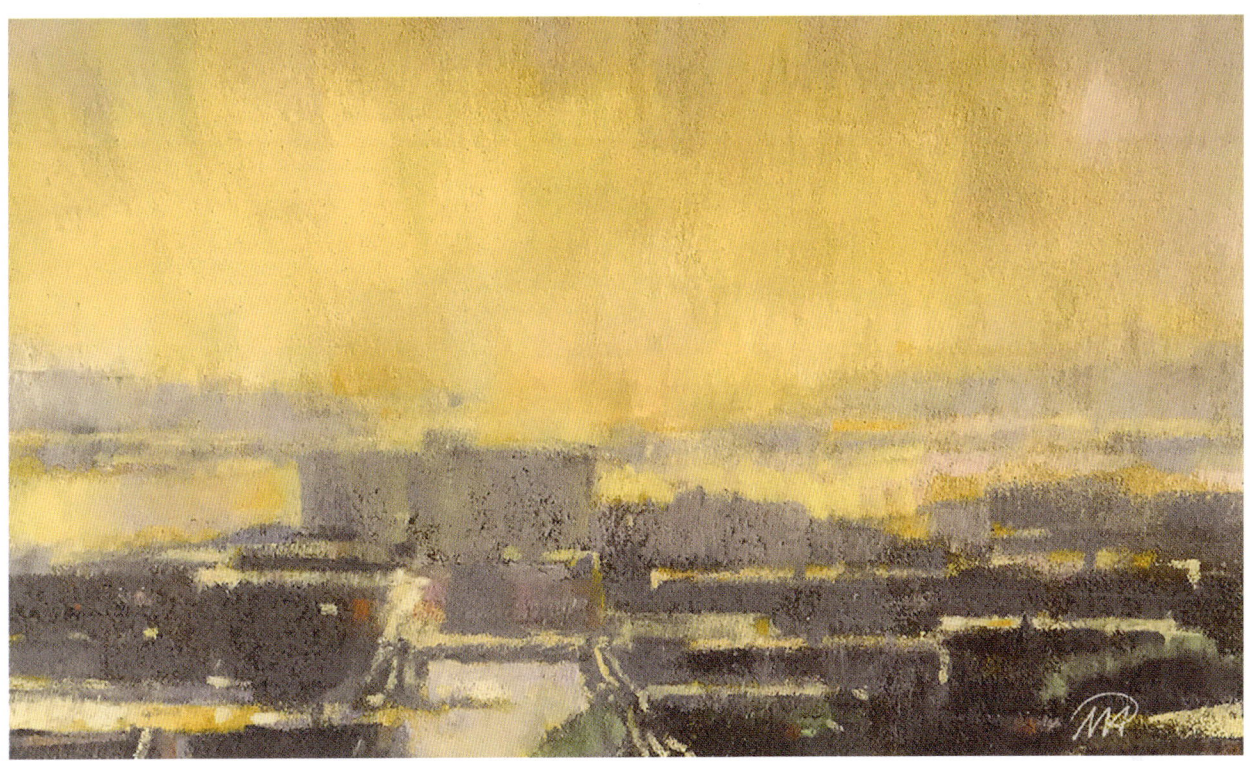

Mitchell Albala, *September Light, Salmon Bay*, pastel on paper, 5½" × 9" | 14 × 23 cm

ART MATERIALS

Ampersand
ampersandart.com
Makers of high-quality painting panels in all shapes and sizes. Ships worldwide.

Gamblin Artists Colors
gamblincolors.com
Quality oil paints made in the USA. Their website offers painters a wealth of color and technical information.

Golden Paints
goldenpaints.com
A wide range of quality acrylic paints and accessories (and the Williamsburg brand of oils), with practical resources and educational materials for artists.

Rosemary & Co.
rosemaryandco.com
Quality handmade brushes from England, shipping worldwide. Offers a wide selection of brushes of every type.

OUTDOOR EASELS

Artwork Essentials
artworkessentials.com
Plein air easels, pochade boxes, and wet-panel carriers.

New Wave U Go
newwaveart.com
Slim, lightweight, "anywhere" pochade boxes.

Open Box M
openboxm.com
Handcrafted plein air easels and equipment.

Sienna Easels by Jack Richeson & Co.
richesonart.com
Innovative plein air and studio easels.

CONTRIBUTING ARTISTS

Tony Allain
tonyallainfineart.com
pages 35, 147

Ray Balkwill
raybalkwill.co.uk
page 113

Cindy Baron
cindybaron.com
page 67

Rodger Bechtold
rodgerbechtold.com
page 120

Hester Berry
hesterberry.co.uk
pages 10, 122

Jill Carver
jillcarver.com
page 112

Alvaro Castagnet
alvarocastagnet.net
page 72

Sue Charles
suecharlesstudio.com
pages 14, 34

Bill Cone
instagram.com/bill_cone_art/
pages 56, 69, 78

Brent Cotton
cottonfinearts.com
pages 100, 119

Bill Cramer
billcramerstudio.com
pages 23, 148

David Curtis
djcurtis.co.uk
pages 128, 176

Oliver Akers Douglas
olliead.com
page 103

Kim English
page 134, 135

Scott Gellatly
scottgellatly.com
pages 107, 160

Catherine Gill
catherinegill.com
page 146

Mark Gould
markgouldart.com
page 109

Lisa Grossman
lisagrossmanart.com
page 169

David Grossmann
davidgrossmann.com
page 18

Marc Hanson
marchansonart.com
pages 26, 75, 108

Greg Hargreaves
page 60

Ray Hassard
rayhassard.com
page 49

Frank Hobbs
frank-hobbsart.com
pages 13, 36

Tom Hoffmann
hoffmannwatercolors.com
page 17

William Hook
wghook.com
page 27

Charlie Hunter
hunter-studio.com
page 117

Barbara Jaenicke
barbarajaenicke.com
pages 142, 157

Paul Kratter
paulkratter.com
page 7

Dale Laitinen
dalelaitinen.com
page 152

David Lidbetter
dlidbetter.com
pages 1, 45, 66

Carolyn Lord
carolynlord.com
pages 29, 104, 105

Karen Margulis
karenmargulis.com
page 145

David Mensing
davidmensingfineart.com
page 126

Renato Muccillo
renatomuccillo.com
page 129

Lisa Grossman, *Cadence*, oil on canvas, 40" × 60" | 101.5 × 152.5 cm

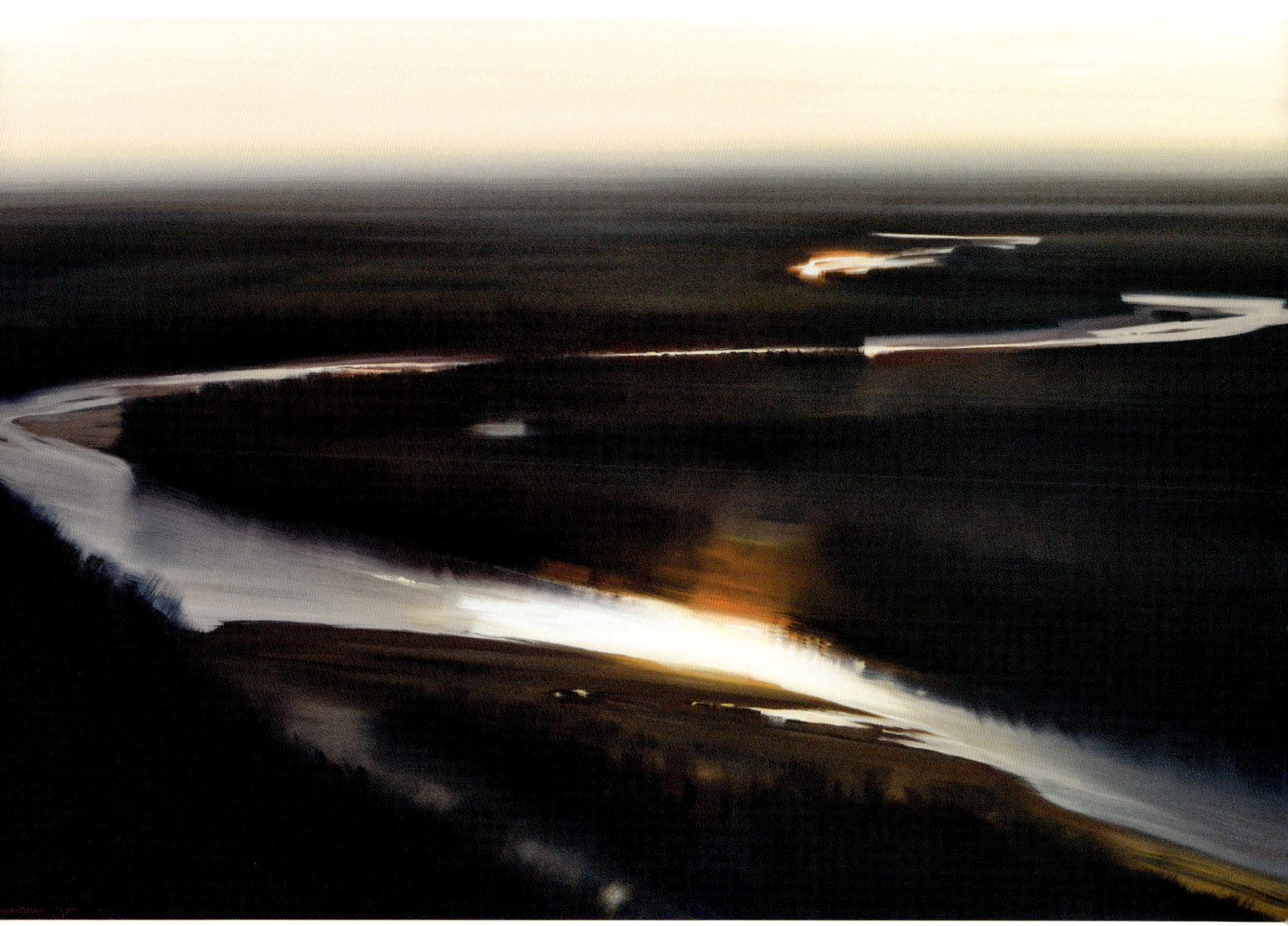

ACKNOWLEDGMENTS

The Landscape Painter's Workbook is, without a doubt, the largest, most time-consuming "painting" I have ever worked on. Although my name is on the cover, the development and production of a book like this is a team effort. It would not have been possible without the support of many other creatives.

The impact and reach of a book like this comes in large part through the diversity of the painters whose works fill its pages. I am indebted to the forty-six painters, from five continents, who graciously allowed their work to appear in the book. *Workbook* shines brightly because of them.

I was fortunate enough to have the support of several creatives who helped me thresh out many of the ideas in the book, offering keen insights and edits along the way. I am especially grateful to my two "before-Quarto" editors: artists Margaret Davidson and Joyce Prigot. Their encouragement and support, keen eyes, and insightful edits made a huge difference. Special thanks also to Donna Dumont, Scott Gellatly, Obadinah Heavner, Tom Hoffmann, and Patrick Howe.

Without students, there is no teacher. I want to thank all those who have participated in my workshops over the years. They were the first to try out many of the exercises, and many of the lessons we covered became the foundation of this book. Their questions and tenacity have kept me, and continue to keep me, on my toes.

And finally, I'd like to thank The Quarto Group for having the vision to see the potential for a second and different type of book on landscape painting. Special thanks to editorial director Joy Aquilino, whose patience in the earliest stages made all the rest possible.

ABOUT THE ARTIST

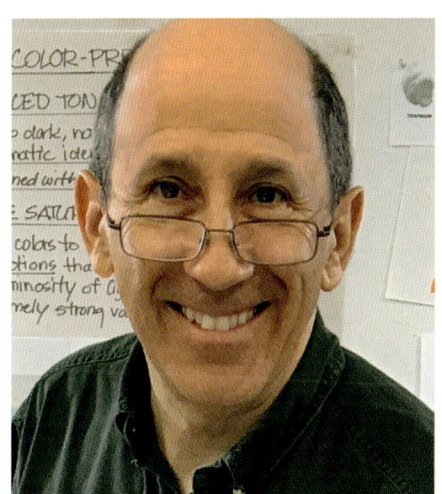

MITCHELL ALBALA is a highly respected painter, workshop instructor, and author. His semi-abstract and atmospheric landscapes have been exhibited nationally and are represented in corporate and private collections. He leads painting workshops in the United States and has offered plein air adventures in Italy. *The Landscape Painter's Workbook* is his second book; he is also the author of the best-selling *Landscape Painting: Essential Concepts and Techniques for Plein Air and Studio Practice* (Watson-Guptill, 2009). Mitchell has also lectured on Impressionism and landscape painting at the Seattle Art Museum and written for *International Artist* and *Artists & Illustrators* magazines. He hosts a popular painting blog, which can be found at his website: mitchalbala.com.

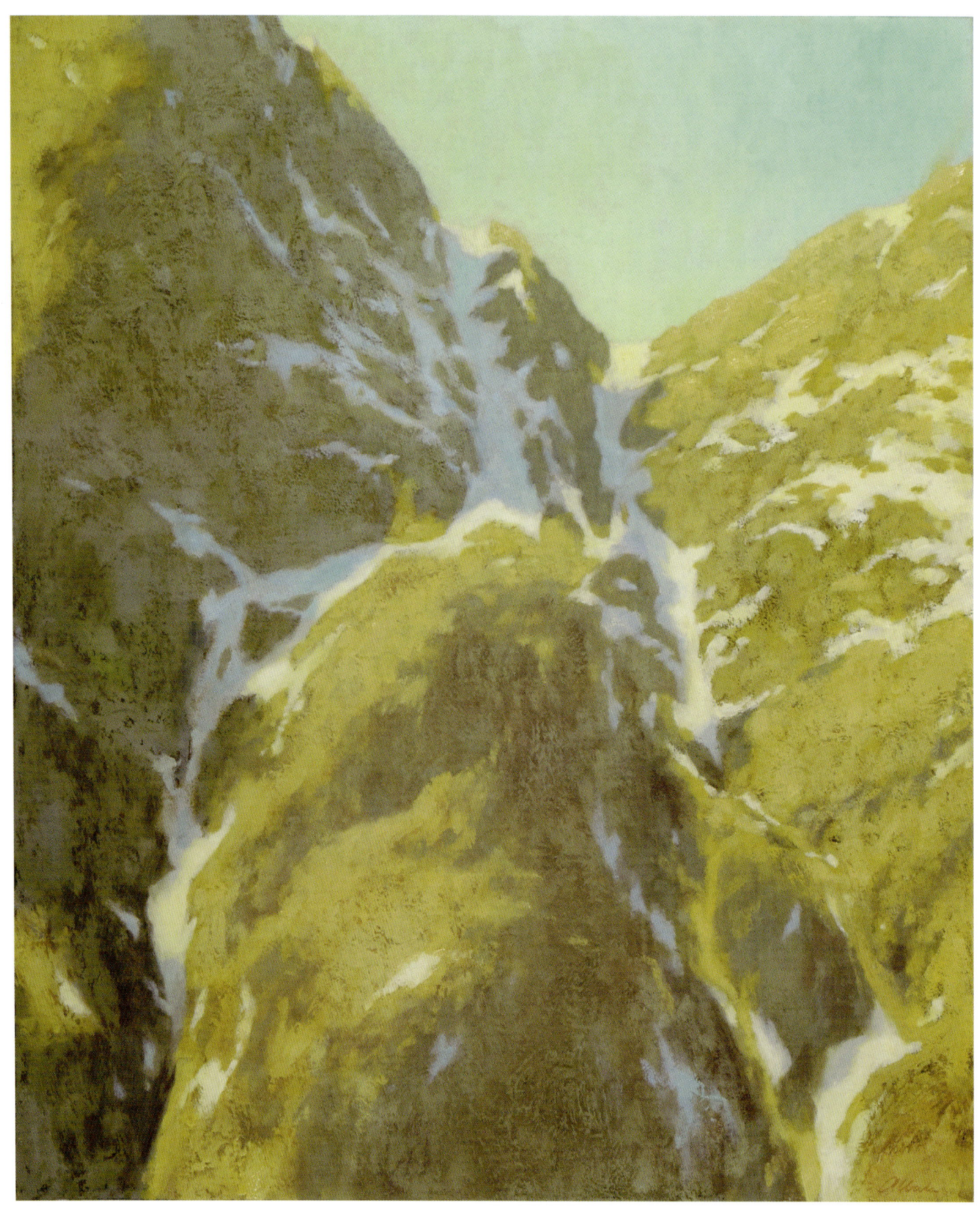

Mitchell Albala, *Snow Rivers in Half Light*, oil on panel, 18" × 15" | 46 × 38 cm

INDEX